CONTENTS

A MODERNISERS'
GUIDE TO
SCOTLAND

A different FUTURE

EDITED BY
GERRY HASSAN
AND
CHRIS WARHURST

Centre for Scottish Public Policy

The Big Issue in Scotland

Published jointly by
The Centre for Scottish Public Policy
and
The Big Issue in Scotland
1999

© 1999 The Big Issue in Scotland
and The Centre for Scottish Public Policy

The Big Issue in Scotland
29 College Street
Glasgow G1 1QH

ISBN 1 899419 04 7

The Centre for Scottish Public Policy
The Centre for Scottish Public Policy is an independent centre-left think-tank established in 1990 which aims to further public policy debate via a range of activities such as conferences, seminars, research and publications. It aims to develop Scottish based solutions to Scottish policy issues. In all its work, the Centre brings together people with a wide range of expertise to share and cross-fertilise ideas and experiences and improve the quality and range of public policy debate.

The Centre is Scotland's only membership based public policy institute, with both individual and corporate membership. For further details about the Centre, its work and membership please contact:

Centre for Scottish Public Policy
16 Forth Street
Edinburgh
EH1 3LH

Tel: 0131 477 8219
Tel/Fax: 0131 477 8220
email: mail@jwcentre.demon.co.uk

Designed by Artisan Graphics, Edinburgh
Printed by Dave Barr Print, Glasgow

ACKNOWLEDGEMENTS

This collection has been brought together through the contributions, advice and enthusiasm of numerous people and organisations.

Firstly and most importantly, a huge debt of gratitude and thanks is due to our wide array of contributors who gave freely of their time and expertise in often busy and hectic schedules. In numerous ways, the different writers in this volume shaped and structured this collection as it progressed, making new suggestions, recommending new ways to look at old subjects and challenging and changing our thinking on different policy areas. It has been a privilege to work on such an exciting and ambitious project with such a committed and engaged group of people. Of course, all contributors write here in a personal capacity, and their comments and opinions are not necessarily those of the organisations or political parties with which they are associated.

Secondly, a project as vast in scale as this has only been possible because of the long-term research work and priorities of the Centre for Scottish Public Policy. In the last few years, the Centre has made a significant and influential contribution to policy debates, particularly through the Governance of Scotland programme, and in the last year, we have built on this with a more specialist series of working parties and groups on Scottish governance. To these efforts, Pat Herd has provided excellent administrative support.

Many people gave freely of their time, advice and ideas on this project and it is impossible to mention them all individually, but in particular we would like to convey our thanks to the following for their encouragement and suggestions: Douglas Alexander, Alice Brown, Carol Craig, Beth Egan, Brian Fitzpatrick, Lex Gold, Gordon Guthrie, Matthew Haggis, Will Hutton, Iain MacWhirter, Agnes Samuel, Nigel Smith, Mike Watson and Allan Watt.

We would also like to thank the Barry Amiel and Norman Melburn Trust, Scotland the Brand and CWS Scottish Co-op for their generous financial support of this project. For supporting projects closely related to and sometimes feeding into this one, we thank Robert Whyte of Scottish Enterprise. We have also been very fortunate to have the support and encouragement of Neil Trotter of *The Big Issue in Scotland* and Colin McDiarmid of *The Herald*.

From the University of Strathclyde, we would like to thank Elaine Blaxter for offering her invaluable librarian skills. From the University of Glasgow we are indebted to Kirsteen Daly and Linda Maguire for their secretarial assistance. On a personal level, we would like to show our immense appreciation to our partners, Rosie Ilett and Lee Murray, who oversaw final proofs and edits of this collection and did so with humour, enthusiasm and professionalism.

We have enjoyed putting this ambitious collection together at this exciting time in Scotland's history. We hope readers will find it stimulating, provocative and a worthy contribution to the debate.

Gerry Hassan
*Centre for Scottish
Public Policy*

Chris Warhurst
*University of
Strathclyde*

FOREWORD

The Big Issue in Scotland is in the business of connecting people. Research done by London-based charity *Crisis* showed that it takes homeless people three weeks to disappear. Contrary to the stereotype of homeless people sleeping in shop doorways, most prefer to vanish from streets that are too dangerous to live on. Being public property often means being treated like trash. Homeless people are 30 times more likely than the rest of the population to take their own lives. The life expectancy of a homeless man is 47 compared with 72 for the housed population.

The Big Issue in Scotland makes homeless people visible. It provides a place where homeless people and the housed can talk on equal terms. It gives people back their names, people who are too often referred to as scroungers, wasters, junkies or just scum. And it gives people choice. In a society that values its citizens by what they can buy, The Big Issue in Scotland offers homeless people the opportunity to spend or save, to take back just a little bit of control and to regain the dignity that goes along with saying 'this is mine'.

The Big Issue in Scotland magazine is a way for some homeless people to make money. It offers economic activity as a means of addressing social problems. It's a business, not a charity. Our success depends on the success of the people who sell the magazine. If they can't do it then we all fail. We believe that if you give a man a fish he will eat for a day, teach a man to fish and he will eat for a lifetime.

At the turn of the century social reformer Sidney Webb used to tell a story about a well meaning lady of leisure who would spend her days visiting the poor of her parish, passing on tips to eke out their meagre incomes. She told one group of women that fishmongers would give away discarded fish heads and tails very cheaply and that these could be used to make a nutritious broth. She explained in detail how the soup was to be made and the women listened intently until she finished and asked if there were any questions. A woman at the back of the hall raised her hand and asked, 'Who ate the fish?'

At the turn of the Millennium we are still running our economies on the basis of passing down scraps.

The Big Issue in Scotland connects the social and the economic. There is no such thing as a successful economy where people are homeless and have no chance to participate. That isn't a healthy economy, it's a waste of our most precious resource. You can't get the economy right and then attend to the social problems because these problems are the consequence of an economy that is wrong.

Scotland has the chance to chart a different future, one that isn't structured on the basis of the powerful delivering to the powerless or the wealthy handing down to the poor. These essays frame some of the issues confronting the Parliament and the country from a range of perspectives. This is not a manifesto but the start of a debate. We cannot afford to wait for the politicians to find the solutions nor confine the discussion to Holyrood or the Mound. That responsibility has to be shared.

The Parliament does provide a chance to challenge the 'business as usual' culture, to modernise complacent public agencies grown comfortable in delivering the status quo and private business happy to see some do well at the expense of others. It provides opportunities to make new connections locally and globally with those who understand we all bear the cost. If we continue to pretend we can live in a disconnected world. Only by making those connections can we establish the trust needed to make Scotland a successful country for all its citizens.

Mel Young *Co-director, The Big Issue in Scotland*

GERRY HASSAN AND
CHRIS WARHURST

TOMORROW'S
SCOTLAND

As we approach the twenty first century, a new period of centre-left dominance has emerged across Western Europe. This situation confounds even recent assumptions. At the start of the 1980s, having lost most parliamentary elections and the battle of ideas, the centre-left was in crisis: the 'forward march' was not only halted but in full bedraggled retreat. This crisis was compounded at the end of the decade as the Berlin Wall fell, communist regimes collapsed and the triumph of neo-liberal capitalism was declared. Apocryphal tales were legion of the fate of the centre-left: this was the 'end of history'; social democracy's common heritage with communism consigned it to the dustbin of history. There were no U-turns to be made, no alternatives to look for on the horizon: we were all Thatcherites and Reaganites now (see Sassoon, 1996; 1999).

The late 1990s has been a period of resurgence for the centre-left and, in terms of government, on a much wider scale than those other left peaks in the immediate post-1945 era and 1960s. In four major European countries: the UK, Germany, France and Italy, centre-left administrations are in power. This is a centre-left different from its predecessors, and which some see as having made an uneasy accommodation with the neo-liberalism of Thatcher and Reagan. There are three possible centre-left modernising positions; an alternative to neo-liberalism that dismantles and replaces it, an accommodation with neo-liberalism that simply attends to its worst excesses; and an acquiesce to neo-liberalism whose only distinction is in the presentation. One reason for the unease is that whilst institutions have been won by the centre-left, the battles of ideas has still not, epitomised by the Third Way's struggle for clarity (White, 1998). So while on one level, the centre-left has returned to power across Western Europe, there is a widespread unease about what it means to be on the left and what social democracy means in a modern setting.

A modernising centre-left has had to come to terms with fundamental and far-reaching economic, social and geo-political change. It has had to reconsider some of its own assumptions and address some of the Thatcher-Reagan agenda. It has had to ditch the left's defensiveness and reactiveness. Such changes require the conveying of a modernising centre-left, different from previous generations.

This collection is rooted in that experience and addresses different concepts and visions of modernisation in Scottish centre-left politics. We believe that the new political environment in Scotland demands a new and revitalised centre-left politics. It requires a shift in emphasis away from a singular concern with institutions to a renewed engagement of ideas.

Despite the scale and ambitions of this collection, we cannot make claims to comprehensiveness. Arts and cultural policy are only touched upon, while issues of global politics, from the future of Russia to the debt crisis, are outwith our immediate focus. However, we hope that by trying to bring a holistic analysis into political debate and identify a new underpinning of values and vision to politics and policy, our overall approach will allow the reader to discern a position in areas not covered in the book.

A New Vision of Progress

Central to a new centre-left agenda is the politics of vision — of refinding the idea of progress and its agency in a world without the old certainties and easy distinctions of class politics and confrontation.

For most of this century, there has been a prevailing sense of progress dominated by the grand narrative of the Enlightenment, aspiring to a more rational and fairer society. Nowhere was this thought stronger than in Scotland, as David Hume, Adam Smith and Adam Ferguson contributed and shaped debates on political authority, civil society, rationalism and humankind's relationship with science, religion and nature (Brewer, 1989; Beveridge and Turnbull, 1989, 1997). This sense of progress was linked to a centre-left optimism: of social democratic parties slowly gaining their rightful inheritance as the champions of social reform within a maturing parliamentary democracy.

This idea of progress went beyond the confines of the centre-left and touched most elements of elite and public opinion. Each succeeding generation had the unquestioning assumption that it would be better off, and have more choices and more opportunities than the generation before it: better education and health, jobs, career advancement, quality of life and life expectancy. However, in the last twenty years the concept of progress has come under attack from a range of different sources.

First, there has been the neo-liberal critique. It argued that talk of progress was an outmoded and suspect ploy by self-seeking social democrats intent on defending their own sectarian values and interests. The evidence for this was social democracy's desire for state encroachment into business and peoples' lives. Neo-liberals denounced this intervention and its accompanying post-war settlement, and instead recast 'people' as 'consumers' who could exercise their sovereignty and choices through the market. Secondly, even the left began to question the value system underpinning progress. For some, the terror of progress was evident in the ecological problems of mass industrialisation. The green movement questioned a consumer society and economic growth based on identifying and satisfying new wants and needs. At best, rapid technological innovation creates new opportunities but also costs which are as yet unknown (Beck, 1992). Others on the intellectual left took a post-modern turn, re-appraising the universalist claims of the

Enlightenment. The grand narrative of progress was argued to be context-bound. Some of the criticisms are justified, particularly on the issue of partiality as it was recognised that imperialism and colonialism (Mazower, 1998) and patriarchy (Pateman, 1988; Johnston, 1993) underpinned notions of Enlightenment and European civilisation. Too often, however, the result has been to replace universalism with eclecticism. At worst this position has become manifest in irony, parody and the singular importance of critique; at best a relative radicalism has appeared in which all values are regarded as equally legitimate so that any analytical purchase on affecting social transformation is impossible (Newton, 1996).

Thus, for a variety of reasons the idea of progress has been attacked over the last few decades and its condition has mirrored the position of Western Europe's centre-left parties. When the idea of progress was central to Western Europe, the centre-left parties carried an air of confidence and purpose about their long-term direction. In the last twenty-five years, as the idea of progress has become more questioned, centre-left parties have lost their sense of place and purpose.

We believe that the idea of progress needs to be restated and reclaimed as pivotal to centre-left politics. We need to acknowledge the successes of social democratic parties this century. There has been an enormous increase in living standards in Western Europe, which has been combined with a substantial growth of education, health and other public services, while the rise of international and supra-national forums shows the potential for increased international co-operation and a politics of interdependency. Post-modernism too is now being critiqued itself as empirical examination reveals continuities and 'late' modernity (Giddens, 1990; Thompson, 1993). Many on the right, concerned about the consequences of Thatcherism's destabilisation of large parts of society, now accept the fallibilities of the market and the need for active, interventionist government (see Gray, 1998).

Developing a new idea of progress does not mean dismissing those progressive currents that are critical of the universalist claims of progress. A new kind of progress has to develop a relationship with environmental, feminist and cultural critiques of progress. We need a new, inclusive vision of progress. This means that whilst a set of shared values exists about the type of Scotland that we would eventually like to become, the means of its achievement, the type of contributions and the range of outcomes may be diverse. There are many variations in the forms of governance, for example — a point to be returned to below — even amongst the social democratic countries of Western Europe.

We have to recognise that societies with an outward-looking perspective, optimistic about themselves and the future, tend to be those that are happier, healthier, more cohesive, dynamic and successful. Societies without these characteristics tend to be marked by conservatism and cynicism, fear and failure. One crucial area that the centre-left currently shies away from is the economy, too easily reifying it, suggesting that the task of government is helping individuals participate in that economy or, again, band-aiding its worst excesses (Findlayson, 1999). We must be more confident about what government can do, even a Scottish government in which the major economic levers remain reserved matters, in terms of shaping the economy and not simply reading off political and social forms from it. Whilst there are constraints, there are also choices.

We believe that tomorrow's Scotland has to embrace the positive, and that doing so requires refounding the sense of progress as a core part of the centre-left. It must establish consensus amongst a range of agencies, interest groups and concerned individuals about the feasibility and desirability of progress and draw them into the agency of decision- and priority-making. This means developing a politics beyond the short-term horizons of politicians' immediate aim of winning the next election, to the longer-term and bigger picture: about developing a more outwardly focused, confident society which is prepared to take risks and support change.

From Government to Governance
The establishment of the Scottish Parliament had a symbolic

significance. Until its establishment and operation, the debate about the Parliament centred primarily on institutional concerns, presented as three key issues:

- strategies to achieve the Parliament;
- the new constitutional and political processes that would be encompassed by the Parliament;
- what the Parliament was not meant to be.

Thus, during the 18 years of Conservative government, home rule supporters focused on the most effective way of mobilising the majority support that existed for a Parliament in every major survey into a more active, engaged support, rather than on the ways a Parliament could affect economic, social and political change in Scotland.

This was an understandable approach based on the political realities of the Tory years. However, the other two factors are less easy to excuse. As for the second key issue indicated above, during the Tory years and even after the election of a Labour government, the centre of attention in terms of the Parliament has been nearly exclusively on the constitutional and political processes which shape it. In the Tory years, this focused on electoral reform and gender balance for the parliament, and under Labour, on the work of the Consultative Steering Group and McIntosh Commission (Scottish Constitutional Convention, 1995; Consultative Steering Group, 1999; Commission on Local Government and the Scottish Parliament, 1999). These debates while necessary were only of direct interest to a narrow section of the political classes. In relation to the third key issue, the Scottish Parliament has been envisioned as what it should not be, namely a 'Westminster of the North' (Crick and Millar, 1995) or an enlarged, better remunerated Strathclyde Regional Council full of parochial councillors drawn from a narrow demographic spectrum. This negative model has arisen against two powerful influences: firstly, the flawed 1970s devolution proposals for a Scottish Assembly which did not understand the deep seated fears held by the non-Labour majority in Scotland of being governed by a Scottish Labour minority after the experience of 18 years of minority Conservative rule (Hassan, 1998b). Secondly, a section of the Scottish political classes, through the cross-party Scottish Constitutional Convention wanted to create a new kind of politics which broke with Westminster and conventional Scottish traditions, but they have been less clear what kind of model they want to embrace. It is still unclear with the Parliament now established and operating, what, if any, vision our politicians and political classes have for it.

A much more philosophical point can be made about the Scottish Parliament debate. While this debate has emphatically rejected the Westminster model of government it has been located in a very traditional and narrow concept of institutional politics placing the Scottish Parliament at the centre of political activity and unashamedly at the top of the structure of political authority. However, this is a model of power which bears uncanny and unnerving resonance to Westminster's claims of complete political authority in the UK. This type of political organisation is one which is being increasingly questioned, as people become increasingly aware of the limitations of representative democracy and look for new forms of participative democracy to reconnect politics and policy to people.

Since 2 May 1997 and more so since 6 May 1999, the Scottish public has been looking in anticipation and expectation to the Parliament for political leadership and change. The Scottish experience in this respect has been out of sync with the times and is instead backward looking, focusing on an elite body made up of representative politicians, and as such has frozen energies and the right of others to speak with political authority in Scotland.

There have always been fears across home rule supporters that the Scottish Parliament could act as a model of centralisation, rather than decentralism. In other words, decentralisation from London would be replaced by a centralising Edinburgh, which sought to be exclusitory in its decision- and priority-making processes. It was to this end that many supporters put their energies into devising new constitutional and political processes to avoid the Westminster/ Strathclyde models. However, by focusing their energies on the

Parliament, rather than other agencies, the politicians have contributed to a situation in which the Parliament is seen to have sole legitimacy to speak for the Scottish people.

This situation has not helped the development of new ideas and modernisation. Instead, it has generated the sense of inertia, stasis and business as usual that has surrounded the Parliament. The difference between Scotland and the UK post-May 1997 could not be more pronounced here. The election of a Labour government in May 1997 after 18 years of Tory rule brought a release of energy and dynamism which seized the political agenda and imagination of the UK. Though we were all schooled to be realistic, things really did seem as if they could only get better. The establishment of a Scottish Parliament in May 1999 has yet to show much in the way of energy and vision and has certainly failed to capture the political imagination. In Scotland, the Parliament is the central focus of attention and political leadership is strangely old-fashioned, very familiar and even quaint. There is a sense in which the focus on the Scottish Parliament has revealed that it is invoking the wrong kind of politics, political environment and type of institution: this is the 1940s and 1950s Scotland of Tom Johnston — Churchill's wartime Secretary of State for Scotland — a world of comfort, centralism and government knows best.

What this emphasises is not that the Blair government is right and the politics of the Scottish Parliament wrong, but that the former has, for all the limitations of its agenda, grasped the new politics of governance, whereas the Scottish Parliament is still focused on a politics of government. We need to shift the Scottish debate from government to governance.

Focused on old-fashioned notions of government, Scottish debate has failed to appreciate the broader move to governance. This move recognises that in a complex and fast-changing, unpredictable world, government is only one amongst many different actors and agencies engaged in governance and policy. The role of government is changing from one that directly delivers services to one that is enabling and facilitative and where there is a general shift from representative to participative forms of democracy. The Scottish Parliament will have to recognise this move.

Everywhere, government will have to address processes, breaking the distinction between policy-making and policy-implementation and focus on outcomes, rather than outputs (Perri 6, 1997b). This involves new forms of accountability such as the UK Government's *Annual Report* and the Scottish Executive's *Making It Work Together* prospectus. These have a limited concept of accountability which shows the problems of taking business notions into politics, and also a sense of quantitative, rather than qualitative outcomes, but they are part of a wider process of reconnecting politics and people and rebuilding trust and confidence in government.

Beyond Holistic Government

We urgently need to devise a new system of Scottish governance and government. We need to establish new markers: holistic and smart government; government as an exemplar, facilitator and guarantor; an achievement-orientated, integrating and integrated Scottish governance; and a branding of Scottish governance (Stoker and Perri 6, 1997; Stoker, 1998; White, 1998; and see Alexander and Wilson separately in this volume).

This vision has to take us beyond current debates about joined-up and holistic government, and onto restating the case for public action and intervention and redefining the purpose of government. The integration of Scottish governance as a policy-design network must involve numerous external organisations, agencies, groups and individuals. It cannot be solely a top-down centre-led process, but must involve grassroot and community involvement from as many sources as possible.

Any process of change has to restate the importance of intellectuals, thinkers and ideas-orientated people in the sphere of public policy and politics. And it is here that we encounter a number of barriers: the relationship of intellectuals to centre-left politics, and the long-term decline of 'public' intellectuals — people within and outside academia who combine analytical and practical expertise, with a commitment to social change.

Historically, centre-left intellectuals in the UK have had a distant and often dismissive view of mainstream centre-left politics and of the pragmatism and compromises of post-war Labour governments. The high point of centre-left thinkers and the Labour Party establishing a synergy — the 1940s and 1950s — the highpoint of Fabian socialism — is the exception which proves the rule (Marquand, 1999). Since the 1960s, left thinkers have been much more influenced by new left, feminist, green, and of late, post-modern currents, and contemptuous of the compromises of labourism (Kenny, 1995).

Other factors have reduced the pool of intellectual resources from which the centre-left is able to draw. For example, with Thatcherism's assault on the higher education sector, academics have become increasingly specialised, over-stretched and disconnected from an inclusive idea of politics. Wider socio-economic and cultural trends have reduced the potential of the public intellectual. This was raised in the special issue of *Marxism Today* assessing 'the Blair project' in a debate between Stuart Hall and Eric Hobsbawn who dismissed it as neo-Thatcherite and Geoff Mulgan, Head of the No. 10 Downing Street Policy Unit who disagreed:

> *Surprisingly few intellectuals are now actively involved in society, as councillors, activists or school governors. Instead, the world is viewed as second hand, through books, or books about books… an individualised culture has taken shape in which it is easier to be cynical, detached and opposed, rather than to run the risks, the emotional exposure, of being committed and engaged (Mulgan, 1998: 16)*

This is an historic moment in Scotland, the UK and across Western Europe, and to seize this opportunity we need to reconnect centre-left thinkers with real politics and policy, and to do that we need to have an inclusive vision of a centre-left politics and a comprehensible idea of the kind of society we want to bring about.

To affect this change means addressing one of the central contradictions of the modern age: why people feel simultaneously free and at the same times powerless to change the world. The influential thinker Zygmunt Bauman (1999: 1) has summed up this predicament:

> *If freedom has won, how does it come about that human ability to imagine a better world and to do something about that human ability to imagine a better world and to do something to make it better was not among the trophies of victory? And what sort of freedom is it that discourages imagination and tolerates the impotence of free people in matters that concern them?*

This book is the first substantial, and cross-party, attempt to look to the future and ask difficult and searching questions, not just in four years time at the next elections for the Scottish Parliament but beyond that time frame into the next millennium.

The various contributions to this book are not soley focused on the powers of the Scottish Parliament. They are not addressing a Scotland which is a one parliament model of authority as the SNP propose, or a two parliament system as Labour and others propose, or even, a three parliament model, as pro-Europeans advocate. This book is about a Scotland that is much more than that — examining wider concepts of policy design and governance, to devise a new system of Scottish governance relevant to the twenty first century. It is about restating the relevance of politics to everyday life in this age of apoliticalness and making politics relevant and engaging. It is about a Scotland and a future that works — tomorrow's Scotland.

SECTION ONE:
THE DEBATE OVER IDEAS

CHAPTER 1

MODERNISING SCOTLAND:

GERRY HASSAN

NEW NARRATIVES,
NEW POSSIBILITIES

'The Scottish Parliament adjourned on 25 March 1707 is hereby reconvened' said Winnie Ewing, mother of the house on 12 May 1999. The first words of the new Scottish Parliament and entirely the wrong words and sentiments. The Parliament born in the last year of the twentieth century has nothing in common with the Parliament of 300 years ago. The names used might be the same, but the meanings, nations, and values are entirely different.

The campaign for a Scottish Parliament lasted approximately one hundred years from Gladstone's attempts to address Irish home rule with Home Rule All Round (Mitchell, 1996). In a contemporary sense, the debate about Scotland's place in the United Kingdom as we currently understand it is a mere thirty years old dating back to Winnie Ewing's famous by-election victory at Hamilton in 1967.

The contemporary debate about a Parliament has lasted for the last thirty years, not three hundred, which has important consequences. First, the rise of the SNP in the 1960s was a response to the crisis of the British state not delivering economic and social goods. This in turn manifested itself as a crisis of British social democracy: Hamilton happened at the same time as Wilson's devaluation of the currency and his reputation (one recovered, the other did not).

Second, Scottish identity and nationhood today has nothing in common with the feudalistic and pre-modern concepts of Scottishness that existed at the Act of Union. Scots identity and nationhood today is not rooted in pre or post-1707 concepts, but in what modern Scots feel about Scotland today, defined by our economic, social and cultural values.

This is where Ewing's comments strike entirely the wrong note. She sees Scotland 1707–1999 as some kind of inter-parliamentary spasm, before 'normal' service was resumed. Her case is based on restoring what was wrongly taken or 'stolen' from Scotland: its ancient, independent Parliament — an essentialist and outdated nationalist viewpoint, for which modern nationalists should have no time.

The Meanings of Modernisation

There are a plurality of modernisations on offer in Scottish and UK centre-left politics. Within the Labour government, the Blair-Mandelson version of modernisation has become enmeshed in a limited top-down concept of politics (Gould, 1998). This version of 'the project' has creative elements within it, addressing the limitations and conservatism of labourism, while acknowledging the failure of progressive ideas to challenge 'the conservative century' (Blair, 1996; Mandelson and Liddle, 1996).

This dominant view of modernisation is less radical than other modernisations. Another version, drawing from new left currents within and outwith Labour has been influenced by a progressive critique of labourism, and by feminism and green politics. At a UK level in the late 1980s and early 1990s this group coalesced around the Labour Co-ordinating Committee and the journal *Renewal* (Thompson and Lucas, 1998), while at a Scottish level, Scottish Labour Action developed a modernising agenda around the national question (Hassan, 1998a).

Modernisation is about ensuring that economic, social and political institutions adapt and are relevant to changing realities of work and society. It involves championing innovation from whatever source: the private, public or voluntary sectors, civic or social entrepreneurs. In the political realm it means moving beyond the narrow confines of constitutional reform as Charles Leadbetter wrote:

> *Most of the institutions we rely upon to protect and guide us*
> *through this tumult — governments, trade unions, companies —*
> *seem paralysed. We are on the verge of the global twenty-first*
> *century knowledge economy, yet we rely on national institutions*
> *inherited from the nineteenth-century industrial economy.*
> *(1999: viii)*

Modernising Nationalism: A CAse Study of Donald Dewar

Donald Dewar's speech as First Minister at the formal opening of the Parliament on July 1st 1999 was marked by his sense of public service when he commented: 'We are fallible. We will make mistakes. But we will never lose sight of what brought us here' (Dewar, 1999: 2). What surprised many observers was the audacity of Dewar invoking the classic symbols of Scottish nationalism: Wallace and Bruce, alongside other images of traditional Scotland: the Enlightenment and the Clydeside shipyards:

> *In the quiet moments today, we might hear echoes from the past:*
> *the shout of the welder in the din of the great Clyde shipyards; the*
> *speak of the Mearns, with its soul in the land; the discourse of the*
> *Enlightenment when Edinburgh and Glasgow were a light held to*
> *the intellectual life of Europe; the wild cry of the Great Pipes; and*
> *back to the distant cries of the battles of Bruce and Wallace. (p.1)*

His speech on that historic day touched an emotional nerve, encapsulating many of the paradoxes of being Scots: of defining ourselves by the past, not the future. Any modernising nationalism has to identify its own icons and symbols. These have to be relevant to a Scotland of the twenty first century, and while Wallace and Bruce have a part in the imagined community of Scots identity, it should not be a defining part. Dewar's invoking of their symbolic and iconic status, without any countervailing modern examples, gives support to an unreflective, romanticising nationalism irrelevant to modern Scotland.

The speech also captured the wrong vision of Scotland with its emphasis on the great Clyde shipyards. The metaphors and meaning of Red Clydeside and the West of Scotland male, manufacturing tradition are many, but it is enough to observe they have located Scotland in a straightjacket of fetishing and privileging such identities to the exclusion of others, as Kerevan wrote: 'Scottish intelligentsia has been busy inventing a proletarian myth about the nation's 20th century history' (Kerevan, 1999b). This has linked into a culture of victimhood, rather than celebrating success and risk which can be seen in the 1980s lament for a lost Scotland in the Proclaimers *Letter from America* with its cry, 'Bathgate no more, Linwood no more.'

The Three Types of Scottish Nationalism

Academics and analysts have located Scottish nationalism within neo-nationalism, which McCrone outlines:

- Neo-nationalism occurs in coherent civil societies which are not independent states, but have a degree of political autonomy.
- There is a complex relationship between cultural and political nationalism which emphasises 'civic' rather than 'ethnic' nationalism.
- Multiple national identities, rather than mono-cultural identities are the norm: Scots and British, Catalans and Spanish, Québécois and Canadian.
- The self-government movement is not aligned with support for one party — the nationalist movement is defined as bigger than the major nationalist party.
- There is an ambiguity about the aims of the nationalist party and whether it supports full-scale independence seen in phrases such as 'home rule', 'autonomisme', 'Souverainete-Association' or 'Consociation'.
- A variable geometry of power exists with political debates taking place on three levels: the nation, the state and supra-state such as the European Union (McCrone, 1998: 128–9).

A problem with this analysis is that McCrone overstates the degree to which Scottish nationalism is neo-nationalist, posing a remarkably essentialist and romanticised view. Neo-nationalism has been an influential force in recent Scottish politics, associated with a civic, inclusive, cosmopolitan view of the world. It is championed by the SNP leadership, most of the Labour and Liberal democrat parties, and much of Scots civil society and institutional opinion.

However, other less attractive strands of Scots nationalism exist. Another, enjoying a new sense of strength in recent years is the unreflective, romanticising politics associated with *Braveheart*. This often apolitical glorifying of the past carries consequences for the present and can be seen in the campaigns: 'Rise Now and Be A Nation Again' of the *Scottish Sun* and 'I am a Real Scot' of the *Daily Record*.

A third kind of Scottish nationalism promotes an atavistic, ethnic based sense of identity and an exclusive sense of Scottishness. It is wary of a pluralist, multi-cultural, multi-racial Scotland, and in particular, English 'white settlers'. This view has been associated with micro-groups such as Settler Watch, but its influence creeps into wider Scottish society through such dubious phrase as 'the Englishing of Scotland' which gained currency in the late 1980s.

These three Scots nationalisms over-lap and influence each other, and are not an exclusive list. How people react to the catch-all term 'Scottish nationalism' defines much of Scottish politics. The pre-1979 left still worries about the dark side of nationalism and equates it with fascism and racism; it still considers the politics of class over nation. The post-1979 left have reclaimed nationalism as their own, refinding earlier traditions and intertwining the politics of self-government and solidarity.

Tom Nairn, the most influential left writer on Scots nationalism in the last 25 years, explains the differing nationalisms:

Politics in Scotland has turned into an orthographic battle between the Upper and lower cases. Almost everyone is some sort of nationalist...there is full upper-case Nationalism which does indeed yearn for the 1707 Parliament to be recalled...many but not all Nationalists are in the Scottish National Party, or sometimes may vote for it. However, there seem to be plenty of both upper-case and small-cap Nationalists in the Scottish Labour Party, and also among the Liberal Democrats, while an unknown number of small — or tiny — 'n' nationalists support the SNP less for its ideology than because it registers the most effective protest against Them. (Nairn, 1997: 196–7)

This contesting of differing nationalisms causes problems. The maximalist 'we are all nationalists' view offends upper-case Nationalists who see their pedigree being diluted and with it less chance of coalescing nationalist opinion around the SNP and gaining full-blown independence. From the other side of the spectrum, Labour Unionism — a long and respected tradition — wants to brand all Nationalists upper-case for the opposite reason — to minimise the size of Nationalist opinion and equate the SNP with separatism and a minority cause. Thus, these two opposing perspectives — upper-case Nationalists and Labour Unionists want for very different reasons to resist the 'we are all nationalists' argument — one to keep exclusive ownership of it and protect its dogmas, and the other, to brand it an ethnic, backward politics. Both these perspectives are out of touch with the realities of modern Scotland.

Beyond the Old Certainties

The new Scotland necessitates rethinking the old concepts of unionism and nationalism. These two traditions have more in common with each other than they have differences. Unionism — 'a form of state nationalism — ideological allegiance to the existing state' (Mitchell, 1998: 117) prioritises the importance of British identity in Scotland and the centrality of the Union with England. Scottish nationalism has stressed the importance of Scottish identity, culture and history. Both have had ever-changing relationships with each other and a Scottish Parliament. Only in contemporary times has Scottish nationalism become synonymous with support for a Parliament, whereas earlier versions emphasised cultural or literary, rather than political identities. Pre-Thatcherism, many Unionists saw a Scottish Parliament as the best way to secure the Union, and embraced Scottish autonomy in the form of administrative devolution. Both tended to define themselves first and foremost as 'Scottish' and wanted to preserve and expand Scottish distinctiveness within the Union.

The difference between unionism and nationalism, particular of a lower case 'u' or 'n', is often more style, language and values, than substance, with a substantial degree of overlap between the two. A revealing way of viewing Scottish politics is not to think of unionism and nationalism as two opposing camps facing each other as in Northern Ireland, entirely separate from each other and with no common ground. Instead, these two large entities intersect and overlap each other to a marked degree.

This interweaving of unionism and nationalism shapes the unique terrain of Scottish politics and identity with three areas:

- a Unionism of exclusive British identity;
- a mixture of unionism and nationalism, of Scots and British dual identities;
- a Scottish Nationalism of exclusive Scottish identity.

The balance between these three areas has shifted dramatically in post-war times towards the Scottish end of the spectrum. One can add Scots-British dual identities and exclusive Scots to get 70–80 percent ratings of people with a predominantly Scots identity. This can be counterbalanced by adding Scots-British dual identities to exclusive Britishness, resulting in 60 percent seeing themselves as British. This wrongly poses the debate as an either/or. Most Scots feel comfortable about being Scots and British at the same time (and possibly, European, world citizens, Irish or Asian as well), and see little future in exclusive, mono-cultural identities. A 'little Scotlander' mentality is just as unattractive in the modern world as a 'little Englander'.

Different Nationalisms: The SNP and Neo-nationalism

The SNP is not currently a party of neo-nationalism, although this seems the leadership's ultimate aim. Neo-nationalism embraces multiple national identities, such as Scots and European, which the SNP supports, but also Scots and British, with which the SNP has problems. The party's answer until recently was a Council of the Isles along the lines of the Nordic Council but, this addressed political representations of Britishness, not social and cultural British identities.

Andrew Wilson MSP recently attempted to do this in a controversial *Sunday Times* lecture stating: 'Many aspects of what we understand as Britain and British institutions will remain with independence...' (Wilson, 1999: 10). He went on: 'A UK market in goods, labour and services will remain, but as part of a wider European market. We will still share many cultural institutions...' (p.11-2). The SNP has trouble acknowledging British identity in Scotland and its role in post-independence, while it has operated as a traditional nationalist movement restricting itself to political identities, ill at ease with Scots, let alone British cultural identities (see Hassan, 1996: 181–3).

Neo-nationalism invokes a sense of ambiguity about ultimate political aims and the final destination of self-government. For all the SNP's much vaunted gradualism under Alex Salmond, it has remained committed to independence, even though it was last in its list of ten SNP priorities in the Scottish Parliament elections. Independence has a special place in the hearts of SNP activists: it is their Clause Four totem that allows activists to think the SNP is special and unlike other parties. Political activists need these symbols, but two wider points stand out. First, the SNP leadership's room for manoeuvre and revisionism to develop a neo-nationalist perspective is restricted by grass roots opinion. Second, SNP activist opinion is shaped by a very narrow, excluding sense of identity and politics: 'Scots not Brits', 'Scotland Free or a Desert' which is neither practical or progressive.

This inflexible politics finds common ground with Labour Unionists who wish to brand the SNP as separatists, rather than social democrats. According to Brown and Alexander: 'There is and always has been more to Scottish politics than identity politics...' (Brown and Alexander, 1999a: 47). After the Scottish parliament elections, they argued 'the politics of idealism will triumph over the politics of identity' (Brown and Alexander: 1999b).

The Left and the National Question: The Red Paper Twenty Five Years On

This collection aims to develop a radical centre-left agenda, grounded in an understanding of the national question and Scottish nationalism. One source of inspiration was *The Red Paper on Scotland* edited by Gordon Brown in 1975 (Brown, 1975b). It was impatient, questioning and drew on a broad range of contributors from the centre-left, from Labour, SNP and no party (although, in typical left style all 29 essays were by men). It attempted to address the historic construction of Scottish nationalism and the post-1967 electoral rise of the SNP (Nairn, 1975).

Brown's introductory essay 25 years on makes fascinating reading, much still pertinent. The *Red Paper*'s aim was 'to transcend that false and sterile antithesis which has been manufactured between the nationalism of the SNP and the anti-nationalism of the Unionist parties...' (Brown, 1975a: 8). Twenty five years later, Brown was trying to maximise that 'false and sterile antithesis' with the politics of idealism *vs* identity.

More importantly, Brown saw constitutional change as meaningless unless linked to economic and social change. The same was true of Scotland's status in the UK: devolution *vs* independence was a sterile choice in isolation:

Scottish socialists cannot support a strategy for independence which postpones the question of meeting urgent social and economic needs until the day after independence — but nor can they give unconditional support to maintaining the integrity of the United Kingdom — and all that that entails — without any guarantee of radical social change (p.8–9).

This is as relevant today as it was then, although, perhaps the Gordon Brown of 1999 would not agree with the Gordon Brown of 1975. The debate about Scotland's constitutional future, between devolution and independence, is often more about Labour and SNP positioning, than an understanding of these issues. There is an unholy alliance between upper-case Nationalists and Labour Unionists exaggerating the difference between the two traditional choices which has to be resisted by those who want the best constitutional and political future.

A neo-nationalist perspective would acknowledge the constraints of the globalising economy, and recognise the need for multi-layered governance and shared sovereignty. A radical centre-left politics would aspire to move the debate from devolution to the wider terrain of self-government, as Gordon Brown argued all those years ago: empowering people, opening up institutions and processes, creating opportunity and choice and redistributing power.

Caledonian Dreaming: The Vision Thing and Scottish Politics

The future of Scottish politics remains uncertain, but various elements can be sketched. We are currently in a transitional period where new rules, processes and attitudes are being established. The first Scottish Parliament elections were fought in a very British manner, with Labour depending on resources and ideas from British Labour, fighting primarily on its Westminster record. A Scottish political system is slowly evolving, and the next Scottish Parliament elections will be very different.

Second, we now live in an age of multi-layered politics from which several consequences flow. Political parties will have to get used to acting differently at different levels of government, from Scottish Labour with its 'turf wars' between First Minister Donald Dewar and Scottish Secretary John Reid, to the Scottish Liberal Democrats, who leaving aside their Scottish Parliamentary Group position, were criticised at the Hamilton South Westminster by-election for attacking tuition fees, while being in power at Holyrood.

Multi-layered politics necessitates different political strategies at different levels, something that requires a learning curve for the parties and media.

Multi-layered politics means multi-layered governance. Scottish politics is not just about the Scottish Parliament. Scotland is about more than a one or two or even three parliament (counting Brussels) model. It is about different layers of politics, institutions and identities.

Third, we are witnessing the slow death of Labour one-party dominance in Scotland with a new electoral system for the Parliament and eventually local government reflecting the four, and sometimes five or six (counting the Scottish Socialist Party and Scottish Greens) party realities of Scotland. This change from a Labour one-party state to a more pluralist order was always going to be slow and evolutionary, rather than a big bang, but it offers opportunities for all the parties. For Labour, it offers a non-institutionised politics, for the SNP and others, real influence and the prospect of power, while for Scotland, a more open, transparent politics.

Fourth, in the longer-term, a SNP-led administration, as a minority government or coalition is likely. This will be a defining point: offering the prospect of a realignment of Scottish politics whereby the non-Labour vote increasingly coalesces around the SNP as happened at points in opinion polls in 1998. The experience of government will be as defining for the SNP as everyone else, giving them influence and power, but not necessarily bringing Scottish independence any nearer.

Finally, processes of Labour and SNP modernisation have so far been partial, top down and party leadership driven. Scottish Labour has failed to outline a positive agenda for changing Scotland, and the Scottish Executive's first legislative programme shows a failure of imagination and ideas. This is about more than the Millbanking of Scottish Labour and allegations of control politics (see Taylor, 1999), and is about Labour's institutional and political dominance of Scotland. This has made it the political establishment, shaping much of Scottish civic life, with similarities to one-party dominant systems across the world. It has distorted Scottish politics and democracy to the ultimate cost of Scottish Labour.

The SNP in the last year has swung from the Laffer Curve and flirting with Reaganomics to 'A Penny for Scotland' and traditional 'tax and spend' social democracy. This is the SNP at its worst: an opportunist catch-all political party travelling the breadth of the political spectrum in less than one year. The SNP's post-election analysis admitted the 'Penny for Scotland' was tactically wrong, (Russell, 1999) but it was the SNP's equivalent of John Smith's 1992 Shadow Budget: in principle defensible, but, politically disastrous and wrong. The SNP should learn the lesson in the same way that Labour used Smith's Shadow Budget, to distance themselves from 'tax and spend' politics.

The SNP are an old-fashioned social democratic party. At every opportunity they support public sector demands for more funding and resources; they uncritically support every wage demand from teachers, nurses and doctors in an attempt to outflank Labour; and try to cuddle up to institutional Scotland to capture intact the old Labour order, rather than critique and campaign against it. A new SNP would be more than just neo-nationalist, it would seek to dismantle the old Labour order and devise a new centre-left Scottish politics.

There is a vast array of possibilities and opportunities here. We need to think anew, be radical and daring and challenge conventional wisdoms to prevent Scottish devolution ending up as some latter day Stanley Baldwin safety-first politics. There are many conservatives in all Scotland's political parties who would settle for that, because they like the certainties and order of the way things currently work.

Scotland can do better, and radicals of all political parties and none, must make sure that we shift the debate, challenging the Scottish political establishment, corporate Scotland and institutional elites in their old, cosy, closed ways, and demand a new, open, transparent order. This will require new visions for Scotland developing, as Churchill put it 'a lighthouse not a shop window' (Willetts and Forsdyke, 1999: 104): about how government works and best serves the people, new models of governance, and new ways of working in the public sector which tackle some of our worst inequalities in education and health. It is about an inclusive Scotland, with new models of partnership and mutualism, opportunity and choice expanded, and creativity and innovation championed in the 'old' establishment and 'new' sunrise industries.

The dream of Scottish home rule was always about more than a Parliament on the Mound — our Camelot on the hill. The early labour movement pioneers and idealists who set up and maintained the nationalist movement through difficult times were inspired by more than that. Their vision was of a Scotland which challenged the old vested interests of clubland and corporate Scotland and established a self-government beyond the political realm in the economic, social and cultural. That is a genuine clarion call for modernisers in any or no political party to unite behind today. We have achieved the constitutional change our predecessors could only dream of; it is time to bring the political change and the new Scotland into being.

CHAPTER 2

JAMES MITCHELL

CONSENSUS: WHOSE CONSENSUS?

In their study of post-war consensus, Dennis Kavanagh and Peter Morris define consensus as 'a set of parameters which bounded the set of policy options regarded by senior politicians and civil servants as administratively practicable, economically affordable and politically acceptable' (Kavanagh and Morris, 1994: 13). There are a number of problems with the notion of a Scottish political consensus using this or any other definition. First, we should guard against claims that a consensus exists as it may simply be an attempt to lend legitimacy to a particular point of view and question the legitimacy of alternative viewpoints. Consensus can all too often be a form of conservatism dressed up in more alluring garb. Second, the Kavanagh-Morris definition is elitist in the extreme. Even if there is broad agreement amongst senior politicians and civil servants, that should not remove the legitimacy of other points of view. If an elite consensus exists, should that be a cause for concern, because it is likely to stifle innovation and new ideas.

Third, can we talk about a democratic consensus? Does it make sense to use such crude measurements as polls and surveys to identify a public consensus? How many people must agree to create a consensus? There are some other problems associated with the notion of consensus. The term 'parameters' is imprecise and it is not quite clear where these lie. Consensus allows for disagreement but the point at which disagreement results in a break with consensus is unclear. All of these points are relevant and should be borne in mind whenever we hear references to consensus and the other legitimising terms — new, modern, civic society — current in contemporary Scottish politics.

The Anti-Status Quo Consensus

Each political party wishes to be able to speak for a majority and each claims to do so on some issue. This lends it legitimacy and authority. The language of consensus is as much about a search for legitimacy as it is about democracy. Throughout the years of Conservative rule it was typical of supporters of a Scottish Parliament, blurring the various distinctions from independence, federalism and devolution (and ignoring the varieties within each of these types) to refer to the consensus in favour of a Parliament.

In truth, there was only a consensus amongst these parties against the then status quo. Added to this was a consensus that broadly supported a left of centre, progressive socio-economic agenda. Again, this ignored the varieties within this consensus. Indeed, lumping together supporters of SNP, Labour and Liberal Democrats was never credible. While there has been broad agreement amongst most Labour and SNP voters on a range of socio-economic issues, Liberal Democrat support has been far from homogeneous and as often as not had more in common with Tory voters.

When the multi-party nature of Scottish politics is recognised it becomes possible to see consensus as a very outdated notion, associated with a time when two big parties dominated the political scene. A consensus could be said to exist when they broadly agreed on things. The notion of a positive consensus — in favour of something — simply did not and does not exist. The multi-party politics of Scotland reflects the minority status of all parties. Scottish politics is neither the two-party conflict model that used to exist in Britain but neither is it a consensual model. Scottish politics is all about a plurality of minorities with shifting coalitions creating majorities on individual issues.

It is significant that the anti-Tory coalition pre-1997 was just that — a negative coalition. It was united in opposition rather than in support of something. But was there nothing positive to the old left alliance against the Tories? Indeed there was. Scots voted overwhelmingly for a Parliament and convincingly for it to have tax-raising powers (and that is exactly how it was seen by the electorate) not because they wanted some symbol of their nationhood but because they saw it as a means to a more progressive socio-economic end. The evidence from the largest study of its kind ever undertaken shows that Scots voted Yes/Yes for a more progressive Scotland and to avoid Thatcherism, whether full-blown or watered down (Denver *et al.*, 2000). However, the broad consensus that existed was under-developed. It amounted to little more than slogans. Whether it was laziness or timidity, the broad basis of a potentially positive consensus was never developed. It was far easier to build around an anti-Tory message than around new ideas and policies.

Even proposals for the Parliament were under-developed and ill designed. The new Labour Government paid lip service to the Convention's work but careful analysis shows that apart from the voting system (working out their own representation was more important than how the Parliament would work for Scotland) the Convention had a very limited impact on the final product. In important respects, the Government ignored the Convention — and the Scotland Act 1998 was a better piece of legislation as a consequence.

It is remarkable how little effort went into working out the powers of the proposed Scottish Parliament amongst the Scottish consensus that supported change. The SNP did not even participate. Constitutional Conventionists will protest that they spent countless hours on this. At one level this is true but it was significantly ill informed. How else do we explain the absurdity of the 'tax-varying power'? During the referendum, supporters of the 'tax-varying power' sounded like hard-line nationalists who argued for a Yes/Yes vote — they asked us to vote for it not for the measure itself but for what it might lead to. Against the expectations of many and despite the most half-hearted and confused campaign by supporters of the measure,

Scots still voted convincingly for tax raising powers for their Parliament. A meaningful tax-raising Parliament has yet to be delivered but no-one seems to have noticed.

New Alliances Post 1997

The battle lines have been redrawn since the referendum — Labour, the Tories, the Liberal Democrats and the Scottish media are allied against the SNP but nobody would claim that this grand coalition is in favour of devolution. And this is certainly not a positive consensus. Scottish Tories have probably come to terms with devolution but that is far from true amongst their English colleagues. The beat of an anti-Scottish (devolution) drum may be faint in Scotland but in England it is becoming ever louder. Every opposition in modern times has played the Scottish card against the governing party at Westminster but for the first time an opposition is playing an English card (see Mitchell, 1996).

Even the Liberal Democrats have to be questioned when it is claimed that they are part of a positive consensus. It is difficult to make much sense of the Liberal Democrats. On paper they remain supporters of federalism but federalism appears to be little more than a slogan or, at best, a handy response to suggestions that unilateral devolution is unstable. The federalist party of the UK has not yet produced a credible or coherent policy explaining how federalism would work. Ask a Liberal Democrat how many units of the federation are envisaged for a start. The Liberal Democrats may be in coalition with Labour though more in the style of John Major, memorably described by Norman Lamont as being 'in government but not in power'. No-one seems to have told the Liberal Democrats that they were supposed to demand support for policies that they supported but Labour opposed in negotiations on forming a coalition, and not demand support for policies they both support. New Labour's team probably could not believe their luck; but then again they had experienced the Liberal Democrats in the Convention. No wonder Labour was willing to move to an alternative voting system. The Liberal Democrats, that quintessentially consensual party, reflects many of the problems associated with consensus — it is very confused and still in search of a purpose.

It is striking how quickly the home rule movement has been hijacked after devolution. Throughout the twentieth century, the Scottish self-government movement was a radical democratic movement. The old system, of 'senior politicians and political elites of civil servants', was indeed based on the kind of political consensus of Kavanagh and Morris. It was this that Scottish voters rejected in September 1997.

Those interests, who liked the cosy and politically corrupt old consensus, have not been replaced. In addition, there was always more agreement in the broad left consensus against the Tories on socio-economic matters than there ever was on Scotland's constitutional status. Differences were greater within the parties than between Labour and the SNP on socio-economic issues. Support for serious efforts to tackle the mal-distribution of wealth and power in Scotland existed within these two parties and was reflected in Scottish society. That consensus was not natural. It had nothing to do with some innate decency amongst Scots, as romantic nationalists and dreamy socialists imagine. It was created as a consequence of a socio-economic structure that has been one of the most shameful aspects of Scotland in the twentieth century combined with the dynamics of party politics. There is no evidence that the socio-economic structure of Scotland is about to change dramatically and there are grounds for fearing that party political dynamics will conspire to maintain the socio-economic status quo. Expressed another way, the new negative 'consensus' which is emerging will work to ensure that though devolution has been won, little else may change.

It is a tragedy of contemporary Scottish politics that the National Question allowed for the creation of a temporary consensus to emerge that created the Scottish Parliament but that an existing consensus on socio-economic issues is being drowned. Having once joked that the Scottish Parliament should erect a statue of Margaret Thatcher to commemorate the individual who had done most to bring it about, I now see real danger in doing so. My fear is that some will come to think that Scots unite behind her policies not against them. The Conservatives may have lost the battle on Scotland's constitutional status but they have been amazingly victorious on socio-economic issues. Even as that party has declined, its agenda has remained firmly that which dictates the course of Scottish politics and society. Scotland looks set to be marked by Conservatism without Conservatives. The Tories are quite literally redundant in Scotland.

Business, that section of Scotland consistently least supportive of devolution, now holds sway. Michael Forsyth's former assistant, now working for the CBI, lectures elected Scottish politicians on their need to know more about business without anyone laughing in his face. Business leaders are feted by Labour and SNP leaders as Mandela-like saviours of the nation rather than business leaders seeking to reconcile themselves before the nation. A stranger to Scotland could be excused if she thought that business leaders had been at the vanguard of the home rule movement and that the trade unions, unemployed and the poor had been its most vehement opponents.

In her memoirs, Margaret Thatcher wrote that: 'The balance sheet of Thatcherism in Scotland is a lop-sided one: economically positive but politically negative' (Thatcher, 1993: 623). Thatcher was not noted for her ability to understand Scotland, but these words accurately sum up the Scottish predicament today. A broad, but negative consensus ensured the defeat of Conservative politicians but failed to build on the agreement to create new, distinctively progressive policies. No doubt this was partly because the time, energies and emotions poured into opposition left little left to think about anything else. The challenge today is to ensure that while a coalition of majorities is formed against independence, that does not become an entrenched coalition on other matters. Consensus is probably an unhelpful term as it tends to lump too much together. It would be well to recognise that Scottish politics involves shifting coalitions of minorities.

CHAPTER 3

WHY SHOULD WE RESPECT CIVIC SCOTLAND?

LINDSAY PATERSON

A Civic Parliament

This, we are told, will be a civic Parliament, an emanation of the institutional life which Scotland kept intact throughout three centuries of parliamentary union. It is therefore civic also in a moral sense. It will eschew the nastiness of ethnic nationalism because it will be embedded in the civic decency of the civic institutions. And it is civic in a structural sense. Its every action will be monitored by committees with roots in civic life, it will seek civic views through the Civic Forum, and will be surrounded by a penumbra of civic lobbyists.

The question is, will it? What if civic Scotland does not like parliamentary scrutiny? What if the Parliament finds that new nice politics simply balks at reform? What if the Scotland which has yielded the Parliament finds politics close to home just too awkward for comfort? Maybe the discomforting responses to these questions, and not consensus, will be the real story of the next decade.

A Civic Union

Civic society matters for more than being a potential brake on the Parliament's radicalism (or spur to its endeavours). It is important ultimately because it has run Scotland in the Union. If we believe that there are Scottish social achievements worth cherishing, or Scottish values worth defending, they are due to the successful activities of civic institutions. Scotland has a civil society in the normal, descriptive meaning of the term — the many ways in which citizens associate with each other free of direct state interference. But its civil society is also supremely civic — a non-state sphere that is imbued with all the authority but also all the pomposity that are the legacies of three centuries of successful national leadership. Scottish identity is not the survival of some pre-Union golden age, nor the outcome of Westminster beneficence. It is the legacy of repeated renovations of that identity by civil society in the intervening period. The Scotland which the Parliament inherits is a firmly non-parliamentary creation.

The reasons for that are well-known. The Union was partial — an amalgamation of parliaments but of little else. It safeguarded the autonomy of law, local government, education and presbyterian religion. In the early eighteenth century, these features were far more important than the distant, corrupt and rather weak old Scottish Parliament. So Scotland developed in that century in much the same way as it would have done had there been no Union at all. The lawyers — especially the sheriff — regulated, the church moralised, and education socialised; and none of these institutions were subject to significant interference from the British state. Even the very few high profile instances of state involvement show how exceptional that interference was. The military suppression of the Jacobite rebellion was as popular with these Scottish civic institutions — and with the overwhelmingly Protestant majority — as in most of England. The apparent threat to the integrity of the legal system by allowing appeals in civil cases to the House of Lords had little direct impact in practice. And the permitting of landowners' interference in the election of ministers of the church had the effect only of altering the balance of religious and political forces within Scotland, not of undermining the kirk itself: it secured the ascendancy of the moderates, even when the radical presbyterians were in a slight majority and so, incidentally, permitted the Scottish universities to flourish largely free of religious interference.

All this circumstance was then reformed in the nineteenth

century in response to social and economic change. The burghs and county councils were strengthened. The regulation of the poor law, the parish schools, and much else was transferred from the church to local and national boards of middle class notables. The churches split but only into various versions of presbyterian Protestantism which thus gained an even tighter hold. And the lawyers continued to give it all coherence, co-ordinating proposals for legislation which could then be presented to Westminster by the always large Liberal majority among Scottish MPs. Whenever a clear Scottish consensus existed for any direction of reform, Westminster concurred.

The governing system was reformed again as mass democracy and the welfare state grew in the twentieth century, and this development provides the immediate background to the last 30 years of debate about home rule. Powers were indeed removed from local agencies, and also nationalised where previously they had been the province of voluntary bodies. But they were by and large not taken out of Scottish hands altogether, despite claims to the contrary by Scottish Tories and Scottish nationalists in the 1940s. The reason was the Scottish Office; which was in no sense merely a field office of Whitehall. It planned, it made policy, it lobbied for Scottish interests, and it therefore also provided a focus for civic Scotland more generally.

The network of quangos and advisory bodies which it sponsored may have been dominated by white, middle class, middle-aged men, but not because of any unionist conspiracy against Scottish democracy: such people dominated policy-making throughout the Western democracies. It was, to the contrary, because these stalwarts were then the very embodiment of Scottish civic life. What the Scottish Office was doing by means of its consultative mechanisms in the 1950s was no different in principle from what the new Parliament proposes to do now. The difference is that the bodies with which the Parliament will consult are more democratic internally and far more socially open than their predecessors half a century ago.

A Civic Campaign

From the 1960s onwards, of course, the campaign for home

rule became inextricably entwined with a campaign to open up this system of consultation. That was the dominant concern of social democrats and Liberals — thoughtful and eventually influential politicians such as John P. Mackintosh, John Smith, Donald Dewar, David Steel and Jo Grimond. Their argument was that, far from Scotland not having a state, the problem was that the state was just too powerful, and had to be democratised. In principle, democratisation need not be tied to the setting up of a Scottish Parliament. In practice, that seemed the most available route, especially since there already existed in Scotland all the other national branches of government — bureaucracy, legal system, government agencies and so on.

That line of argument was one influence on the devolution debate in the 1970s, but lacked the political potency which it later acquired. What gave it urgency was the coming to power of Margaret Thatcher, when suddenly the character of the relationship between the Scottish Office and Scottish civil society was subjected to unprecedented strain. Discrete and elite consultation may have been enough in the 1950s when all major political factions agreed on the broad ends of politics — mild redistribution through public welfare and through a mixed economy dependent on regional development grants. It could not last when there appeared to be a deep ideological fault-line at its core. The allegation that Scottish government paid inadequate attention to civic Scotland was much more cogent when that government was increasingly at odds with the social democratic ethos of civic life.

The democratising argument also became infused with a vague nationalism. The inadequately democratic Scottish Office was not only hostile to social democracy; it was now felt to be hostile to Scotland itself precisely because, during the three centuries of Union, Scotland had become equated with the civic institutions. All nationalist movements are at least to that extent democratic: they insist on governments being responsible to the civic life of the nation. Scottish nationalism has been much more democratic than most, first of all because the SNP came to be dominated by the ideological soul-mates of Mackintosh, Dewar and like-minded thinkers such as Neil MacCormick, Stephen Maxwell and Isobel Lindsay — but also because there has never really been a stark divide in civic Scotland between nationalist and social democrat anyway. So far as ideology is concerned (as opposed to personal biography) MacCormick might have as easily been in the Labour Party as his old friend John Smith, both could have been with Menzies Campbell in the Liberals, and in principle all three could have been in an executive led by Donald Dewar. And all four have shared a passionate and erudite attachment to Scottish civic culture.

So the argument which won in the 1997 referendum was about making Scottish government responsive to civic Scotland — essentially returning to what worked quite well until the 1960s. That is ultimately from where all the talk of new politics emanates. It has been modified and made richer by other currents of thought, most notably by feminism and the green movement. As in many other countries, these groups have campaigned in Scotland for a new style of government; unlike elsewhere, by the 1990s they had attached most of that programme to home rule. But, novel and important though these renovating ideas have been, they share the same structural analysis as the old social democratic reformers: Scottish government had to be opened up to civic Scotland. Indeed, it is because these various currents could coalesce that they have been so politically successful.

That success now appears to compel the Parliament to work with civic Scotland. There is to be consultation on draft legislation and even on whether there should be legislation. The parliamentary committees are to be the conduit for inserting civic ideas into the legislative debates. The Civic Forum is to help articulate civic ideas into a coherent national form. The parliamentarians will rely on advice from civic organisations for the very practical reason that these organisations are well-informed, and provide a counter-weight to the civil service. People in general will expect there to be such consultation because civic Scotland is trusted — far more so than any kind of politician (or journalist). And people outside the Central

Belt will want consultation because there is still a residual mistrust of the Parliament's right to do anything at all. What was once a reason to oppose home rule altogether has been transformed by the clarity of the referendum result into a reason for insisting that a Parliament should consult.

A Non-Civic Future

However, it cannot all be like that. There has always been a line of argument in the case for home rule which says that the whole point is to challenge civic Scotland. Here is how Tom Nairn (1997: 205) characterises the history of civic autonomy:

> *Institutional identity seems to me broadly the same as managerial identity or, less flatteringly, 'bureaucratic identity'. The self-management of civil society historically found in Scotland implied a class which administers and regulates rather than 'rules' in the more ordinary sense of political government or direction.*

Avoiding politics — according to Nairn — has distorted the whole of Scottish culture, and it is from that condition that home rule can rescue us. Nairn's analysis has never commanded more than minority support in any party — even the SNP — but is widely popular among intellectuals. Although a position firmly on the non-social-democratic left, it has notable similarities with emerging thinking on the Scottish right, which itself draws on two decades of writing on these themes by Michael Fry:

> *Partisan spirit and alternation in power do foster constant critical scrutiny, diversity of opinion and efforts at reform. In Scotland, by contrast, government is conducted behind closed doors. Debates are predictable and lifeless. The consensus, however well-meaning, inevitably turns inert, inflexible and hostile to novelty. (1987: 255)*

This line of thinking invites the Parliament to challenge the civic elites by encouraging popular participation against them. It says that the whole problem has been a complacent civic establishment which has used the rhetoric of social justice to fend off more fundamental reform. It says, too, that the only nationalism worthy of the name is one which challenges the civic institutions which have depended for their very existence on the Union itself. The SNP is then castigated as insufferably cautious, in thrall to vested civic interests which it endlessly courts because it knows how trusted they are. A nationalist party with this philosophy at its core could never be enough: if the Union is so heinous, then why are the civic institutions created by the Union apparently beyond nationalist challenge? (See here Paterson, 1998c.)

The forces working for consensus are so powerful at the moment that this alternative critique will remain muted for the first few years of the new Parliament. Maybe it will, in fact, never surface at all, except as in the animus towards the governing parties which comes from the nationalist fringe, the Tory rump, and the anarchist populism of Tommy Sheridan. In that case, all the Parliament will do is indeed renew Scottish pluralism. That would be no small achievement after 18 years of acute tension at the heart of Scottish government, and after 30 years of declining consensus on how Scotland should be run. Such a democratised pluralism would continue to yield the kinds of cautious social democratic reforms which underpinned the Scottish welfare state. I suspect it is Donald Dewar's prime ambition. The history of what civic Scotland achieved when the Union was working properly cautions against holding that ambition in contempt. And at least Dewar has a coherent philosophy, unlike almost all his party political opponents.

But the Parliament — far less the Scottish Government — is not in control in this respect. If the main parties do not challenge the civic elites, then other parts of civic Scotland will. Part of the myth of consensus has been that consultation will reach agreement. In fact, the gulf between the dominant civic groups and the dissidents is now much wider than the party-political divisions that consensual consultations are supposed to overcome. In education, for example, the frustration with what Walter Humes has called 'the leadership class' is widespread among radical teachers and community educators, determined to hang on to a vision of education as liberation even while acknowledging that Scottish comprehensive schools have achieved a lot (Bryce and Humes, 1999; Humes, 1996).

In the politics of land, the radical proponents of community ownership would go far further than the cautious proposals emanating from Jim Wallace's department (proposals which seem to have forgotten that some of the most effective campaigning for compulsory public ownership of land came from the old Highland Liberal Party). In urban regeneration, the gentle public nudges to private consortia which the Scottish Government inherits from new Labour will be at odds not only with the radicalism that is represented in different ways by Sheridan and the Scottish Green Party, but also with the tradition of architectural renewal which numerous Scottish writers have culled from the work of Patrick Geddes. And — from a quite different political direction — the Scottish Labour Party's distrust of anything voluntary will allow the Scottish Tories to remind us that public action need not be state action. Refounding themselves as the voice of voluntary social action could, in the long run, be the Tories new dawn.

I doubt, then, that the Parliament will get away with being cautious. The consultations and committees will provide platforms for radical dissent that have never before received national sponsorship in Scotland. That will be chaotic at first, but effective dissent does not have to be coherent. It will be a long time before any of this dissent is articulated systematically as a political programme — as long as it takes either for the Scottish Labour Party to become truly autonomous, or for the SNP to discover that radical nationalism cannot be in awe of civic institutions. But the main point will be that the changes will be popularly driven, and will have their impact through a change in popular attitudes and political culture. It would be a more serious challenge to unionism than any of the SNP's campaigning has been hitherto, because it would be a popular undermining of the civic institutions which have autonomously attached Scotland to the Union. The emergence of this radical questioning of civic Scotland would be as fundamental a shift as the emergence of anti-Tory Scotland in the last half century. In the end, its consequences for Scottish government and culture will be as profound.

Endnote

1 Scotland's civic life in the Union has been covered by numerous books, such as Fry (1987), McCrone (1992), Morton (1999) and Paterson (1994). Further information can be found in them and their extensive bibliographies. The history of campaigning for home rule is covered by Mitchell (1996) and in documents collected by Paterson (1998a). Nairn has developed his critique in Nairn (1997). Challenging educational elites is the subject of Humes (1986) and Bryce and Humes (1999). Radical land reform is dealt with by Wightman (1996). New ideas on urban regeneration come from Glendinning and Page (1999). The importance of the voluntary sector was shown by SCVO (1997).

CHAPTER 4

A NEW SONG FOR SCOTLAND:

THE MAKING OF THE SCOTTISH CONSTITUTION

TOM NAIRN

The reappearance of the Scottish Parliament in May 1999 unleashed nothing less than a tidal wave of criticism and downright recrimination. In this brief period, the Scottish art of ingratitude was to attain new heights. One pundit outdid the next in homicidally faint praise, stabbing put-down and angry condemnation. Two hundred and ninety-two years on, and with what was our nation served? With a dismal, self-centred assembly of self-interested incompetents playing at being a Parliament. The parcel of rogues had returned. But now the 'bastards' are no longer 'selling the nation out' to England — rather, they seem to be getting her back again on some kind of deplorable post-hire-purchase deal, and handling the business rather badly.

There is no need to go into details here, or of its results when the Parliament reassembled on 1 September, 1999. Presiding Officer David Steel felt obliged to deliver a stately official rebuke to the media as a whole. He asked that the Scottish Parliament be 'given a chance', and attacked the *Daily Record* for 'bitch journalism'. More thoughtful commentators such as Iain MacWhirter were driven to ask why it had happened at all:

The assault on the Parliament probably has something to do with latent philistinism and cretinism in the Scottish character. There is a chronic lack of self-confidence... thinly disguised by bluster and hyperbolic criticism... In demeaning the Parliament they are demeaning themselves. (1999: 7)

I am sure MacWhirter is right. It always seemed likely that a Scottish Parliament would have to justify strongly its existence. Now we know from bitter initial experience that this is indeed so. However popular in London, being properly devolved good boys and girls is useless on the home terrain where the stakes are so much higher. Behind the disenchantment there lay in truth a great expectation, which it was all too easy for malignant dim-wits to exploit with the techniques of UK tabloidism.

Between May and October 1999 press scurrility was paralleled by a political offensive aimed at the 'normalisation' of the new Parliament. That is, aimed at establishing it as just another subordinate part of the British state. Here, the Old Constitution reasserted itself by building up its traditional instrument, the Scottish Office, and arguing for 'partnership' between the latter and the incoming government.

As usual, 'sensible policies' was the refrain of the stabilisation song. In relation to the popular wish for more significant change, this normalisation actually meant down-grading — confining the novel polity to playing its due part within new Labour's scheme of things. Since the advent of Blair, 'sensible' has come to signify conformity with 'the project'. Political folk-gardening, as it were, allowed — nay, encouraged — to contribute a distinctive border here, or an admirable shrubbery there, but only as elements in the overall grand design of British modernity. The trouble is, it was just this sort of political small beer which was arousing all the popular unease, all the press mockery and carping.

By September, in fact, it had dawned on many Scottish parliamentarians that it was possible to be damned for cowering beneath the parapet as well as for charging rashly over the top. And also, that the former fate might be worse. After all, being terribly responsible and tame for Scotland was already incurring derision, with no compensating gains. As for the opposite, going over the top

— well, this may go against the whole grain of philistinism and the inferiority complex, but there is the chance that it just might come off.

The Twilight of the British State?

The resolute opponents of 'identity politics' (led by Gordon Brown) have all along been assuming that the Parliaments in Cardiff and Edinburgh could settle down into the soberly reliable machinery of Great British constitutional order (Brown and Alexander, 1999a). I suspect this position was already an illusion back in 1997. By the time of the next Westminster elections, it may be little more than an embarrassing memory. It is really time that the absence of the Emperor's new clothes was more frankly registered. There is no such order.

It perished some time between Black Wednesday and May 1997. Burn-out seems to have taken place during this period of dingy twilight, even although the cadaver has continued mechanically walking, or perhaps stumbling, onwards. Thatcher had suffered from a delusion: the vision of a radical social and economic revolution which would leave the UK state totally unchanged. Blair followed this up with a vision which was at least less contradictory: the vision of some things being changed in the state — but just those bits of archaic statehood which suited his purposes; for example, devolution, control of interest rates, the arrangements in Northern Ireland or the House of Lords. The assumption still endured, however, that most of the underlying historic framework would go on as usual. This was modernisation - not reconstruction. It was 'radicalism' (a term the Tories had made part of the climate), and not revolution. With appropriate dosages of coolness and think-tank edification, the hope was simply that this revised old order might work better than ever. It did not occur to Blair that the ancien régime really hung together. Vital parts of such an organic body cannot be altered without affecting, or at least threatening all the rest. The modern UK may never have cohered logically (as generations of apologists have said) but that was partly because it used other sorts of glue, such as emotional solidarity, Protestantism, symbolic observances, an imperialist superiority complex and a strong élite culture.

'Blairism' believes in rejuvenants. Indeed it is itself a self-consciously rejuvenant force. But the administration of modernising doses also has limits imposed by nature. What was possible in 1832 and 1910-11 may be impossible in 1998–99. Written constitutions can be amended or reformed or even be replaced when they stop working or get out-dated, but not a constitution made up of sacral observances, tacit assumptions and emotive rituals.

The Charter 88 constitutional reform campaign had argued that the UK state should be re-constituted, as the necessary condition for modernisation (including devolved powers). This argument was put again by one of the campaign's founders, Anthony Barnett, a few months after Blair's government took office (Barnett, 1997). But it was too late. The 'time' had already passed. Empiricism, convention and the rule of custom had all re-established themselves by the end of 1997.

Project-implosion

By 1997, the Scottish and Welsh Parliaments were on the way to realisation and the peace process was advancing in Ulster. In essence, the periphery had been dealt with, and was now confidently expected to settle down. But in a moribund order, 'settling down' is another term for quiet suicide.

The House of Commons may never again be more than the present pantomime relic of its former self. The Lords may subside into a kind of placeman's endorsement of 'elective dictatorship', and the two-party system be transformed into an increasingly nationalist contest — ostensibly 'British' but in reality more and more English — for long-term control of a rump UK state. The peace process may fail completely. Even the Ulster Protestants, the most faithful of the old British tribal units, may end up losing their faith. And of course, all the tribes may end up falling out hopelessly over Europe.

None the less, things were expected to settle down. It is no use saying that a new Parliament should not be obstreperous, gratuitously nationalistic and different just for the hell of it. The problem is what it should be, positively speaking, and here there are of course no rules of guidance. This is because of the way British devolution has been carried out. Had it been part of an overall reform of the central constitution, then there would certainly have been guiding rules and principles — templates about which the lawyers and parties could have disagreed. However, Britishness was never like that. Actually it was historically founded on the avoidance of 'all that'.

The protagonists of home rule are all naturally very glad that the act of coition took place after 1997. On the other hand, only a year or so on — an extremely short time by UK constitutional standards — they cannot fail to be aware how coitus has become interruptus. The moment of liberation has indeed been followed by increasingly blatant withdrawal symptoms. For example, at this moment, no-one seems to have the slightest idea whether or not new Labour will reform the electoral system. Yet this was always perceived as the core of constitutional modernisation. There are, however, persistent rumours of acute displeasure with the effects of proportional representation in Wales and Scotland. With regard to Europe, no-one knows when, or if, the government will hold a referendum on joining the European common currency.

The fact is that the Blair Government has reformed the ancient order just sufficiently to ensure its collapse. It has rendered it irretrievably unstable. There is now no chance whatever of returning to the old, unthinking modes of UK statehood. Instability — the 'slippery slope' of late twentieth century legend — is now lodged at the British or multinational level, not on the terrain of the new governments and assemblies themselves. What new Labour has done is to foster a climate of radical expectation and change - without having either the agenda or the will to push through such large, central shifts. Above all it has no firm constitutional agenda for living up to its own rhetoric — presumably because it also feels that, at bottom, the English majority electorate is not interested in these more radical ideas.

The Missing Constitution

Because no Great British agenda is now likely to prosecute central reform, it appears to me that the Scottish Parliament will have to make up and pursue its own. It will have no option but to continue framing a constitution for itself. I say 'continue' because this was what all the campaigns and conventions which led to the recall of a Scottish Parliament were doing in any case from 1980 to 1997. This is what the 17 years, the Claim of Right and the Constitutional Convention were really about — the affirmation of popular sovereignty as a right. That is, a right and not just an ethical protest against certain policies or attitudes of one London government. It was asserting Scottish democracy, not simply as a one-off vote or an anti-Tory majority of the moment but as a system, a settled entitlement. If that means anything at all, surely, it means a constitution, or the wish for one.

Obviously, this desire was never one for the old Scottish constitution of 1706. Hence it meant (or implied) a successor to that, a contemporary equivalent (of which home rule was the approximate or initial form). Everyone remembers the two main recipes for forward movement. On the one hand, SNP Nationalists thought the people should just vote to do it on our own, regardless of what was happening or not happening elsewhere in Britain. On the other, Unionists such as the Labour Party and the Liberal Democrats thought that it both would and should come about as part of some general, all-encompassing change — a democratisation or revolution of British statehood. This was perceived at different moments as socialism, or else as sagely-planned federalism and all-round home rule. I think it is safe to say that nobody imagined a version of Scottish self-determination might arise without either of these preconditions. But this is exactly what has happened.

None of the grand plans were realised. Nor are they now ever likely to be realised. Scottish and Welsh self-rule have emerged in blatant contravention of the old blueprints. They have fallen into irretrievable existence — as it were — through a pragmatic half-revolution. UK statehood has been deprived of its former axis —

Sovereignty with the capital 'S' — but not given any new one. Rhetoric is now being made to stand in for the recasting of the state. We are informed every other day that Sovereign authority is henceforth to be 'shared', or dispensed outwards and downwards; but no laws have been provided for this process other than the ancestral ones — that is, the shamanic guidelines of 1688 and 1832 about fairness, compromise, the advantages of bigness over smallness and not rocking the boat still farther.

Thus has a kind of constitution-less semi-statehood been born in Scotland. The problem now is what to do with it, and about it. As UK Sovereignty and all its accoutrements go on collapsing, the question cannot avoid becoming more acute. The sliding terrain of UK deterioration is carrying politics towards a rediscovery of English rights and responsibilities.

Even in 1979 a Scottish polity might have re-entered into much quieter waters of 'decline' — a multinational order on the wane certainly, yet still possessing some residual stability and instinctive authority. Twenty years later, what it encounters is a UK held together by personal charisma, one-party public relations, and a nostalgia for Sterling.

Apocalyptic Politics

The party politics of the new Parliament remains dominated by apocalyptic or 'black hole' ideas deriving from pre-home rule times. This time was the era of phased re-birth that extended from the 1970s up to the 1997 referendum — one-stop Independence versus all-Brit Transformation. No-one at the time knew whether Scottish autonomy would be realisable at all, or how it would work.

It is true that there were foreign experiences for comparison. The trouble was they were all so drastically different, and involved histories and constitutional systems having little in common with the UK (Nairn, 2000). Within the archipelago the available examples were Irish — concrete enough, but hardly inspiring confidence. Most of the comparisons with Ireland were conducted, we should remember, well before the days of either the Republican economic miracle in the South, or the peace process in the North.

As a result, the poles of Scottish political debate were fixed in a curious time-warp. There were but two sides. In one corner stood one-leap Independence, the vision of an ethnic jail-break founded upon the 'conversion' of enough Scottish voters to place the SNP into a stance of moral authority. 'Scotland Free by '93!' remains one of the best-remembered moments of this version of nationalism (Nairn, 1989). On the other hand stood a British Union conceived as immutable. Immaculate Britannitude brandished an ideology of 'flexibility'. Everyone in between these two choices was just confused.

Confusion decisively won this debate and deposited us in the present. Unfortunately, many of the old-time attitudes have been deposited alongside it. Political parties are among the most conservative of human institutions, and such rigid and carefully-nurtured ideological faiths are not easily discarded. For example, anyone who thinks that the Scottish Parliament might become a state like the others in today's UN world can still be presented as no better than the kind of demented slob who would smash up a family heirloom picture with a sledge-hammer — in the mind of Labour opponents of 'identity politics' (Jones, 1999). On the other hand, anyone still thinking, or hoping, that the UK still has life and good-will in it, or that British society has some redeemable features, is just a dupe helping to imprison the Scots forever in a 'pretend parliament' — new Labour's insulting version of local government.

Futures Uncertain

As far as relationships with England and the new English are concerned, only one rule is any good: 'With them, if we can. Without them, if we can't!' That is, we can quite well do without the UK state — or certainly, with a lot less of it. But this does not imply the black coal-hole of separatist fantasy, exile to an undead realm in which the southern cousins all become aliens. British-Irish society has proved a lot stronger than that, and it would be strange indeed if British-Scottish and British-Welsh society were not the same. No-one has ever thought that English society could not survive without

'Great Britain', and stay pretty well as it is at present. British civil society can survive, and will now have to survive, the development of many new political or even state control-systems within itself.

What this change implies is that such developments will have in future to be negotiated. A New Britain can no longer be prescribed from the Thameside heights on the basis of 'consultations' alone. That was how local government was re-organised over the period from the 1960s to the 1990s (including the Poll Tax). Scottish, Welsh and (if it ever happens) Northern-Irish self-government is not 'local government' in that sense. It is not 'regional government' either, since this would imply a centre-region constitutional order, the very thing that British Sovereignty has always avoided, and indeed despised. The only thing Scots can realistically think about Blair's New Britain is that it will have to be founded on equality. Holyrood may not head an independent state, but in such a context it will have no option but to try and behave like one — that is, to go on seeking the equal, federal-style partnership which eluded it throughout the long era of Union.

The only way that Scotland can now negotiate democratically to renovate the UK is through its own input, by stating its national case for Britain, or for the Britain it wants. What range of institutions and policies would the Scots like to see remain British (rather than, for example, become European, or be transferred to Holyrood)? Would the English agree? And how can they decide, without distancing themselves from Westminster, and looking separately at the matter? This stance is difficult to define, since there are really no precedents for it. It is a kind of 'de facto independence', with the implication that the Scottish Parliament is (in a serious sense) 'neither one thing nor the other' — and therefore has to try and carve out its own status (Nairn, 2000). The constitution-building I described before appears the only way of carving out this status. We need, so to speak, to enact the Claim of Right and show by juridical means that it was not merely an historical document of protest or complaint.

Redness Lives!

Every question which has so far been decisive and emotive in the return of Scottish government has indeed touched upon inequality: the 50-50 campaign for women's representation, the scandal of minority non-representation after the first election, the on-going battle over student tuition fees, the moves to reform the Scottish local government franchise, land-ownership and the abolition of feudalism, James Macmillan's protests over residual anti-Catholic discrimination — Scottish society is disfigured by inequality which demands action at the same time as England-Britain is getting more unequal under Blair.

This brings us back to the 'red' conclusion of many years ago. It is not the socialism foreseen by most contributors to Gordon Brown's *The Red Paper on Scotland* in 1975. Yet turning back to that remarkable document today, there still seems a strong thread of continuity. 'The irresistible march of recent events places Scotland today at a turning point — not of our own choosing but where a choice must sooner or later be made', wrote Brown (1975a: 7). Nationalism had fostered 'a revolution of rising expectations', he went on, which could not be met by political independence alone (p.7). It demanded an accompanying social and economic transformation aimed above all at inequality; and a measure of self-government in Scotland was a necessary part of tackling this blight. The main responsibility still lay with British socialism, however. All the positions in the 'Introduction' and many of those in the rest of *The Red Paper* led back to this prediction. Devolution had to be 'real', he maintained, and to involve both 'genuine economic control in devolved areas' and 'taxation powers in relation to democratically decided levels of public service provision' (p.19).

History was to play the cruellest of tricks upon this *Red Paper* perspective — and upon its editor. Twenty-two years later Labour was indeed to return to office, and set about transforming the UK, and the Scots were, as Brown had foreseen in 1975, very much in the vanguard of that upheaval. But everything else in the world in the meantime had changed, sometimes beyond recognition. 'Red' had lost its old meaning. New Labour had shed most of what had been taken for granted in 1975. A neo-liberal economic order had conquered the globe and by the end of the century seemed the kind of absolute horizon which Empire and the Cold War had previously been. Blair's post-socialism was now upon the metalled road laid down by Thatcherite Conservatism, and implacably devoted to further 'modernisation' along similar lines. The ascendancy of the finance-capital castigated in *The Red Paper* had, paradoxically, come to pass under a Labour government — and in the very person of the old manifesto's inspirer and most powerful voice. It was this socialist visionary who ended by transferring control of interest rates — and hence of much economic activity — to a Bank of England committee.

The Scots have now obtained a good deal of what Brown's 1975 book asked for — but in a context which no-one dreamt of, and which has either nullified or transformed the sense of all its policies. The 'irresistible march of events' has brought another 'turning point'; but not one where Scots will invent socialism for Britain or the rest of a startled world. 'Genuine economic control' and democratic powers including the tax powers voted for in the 1997 referendum are still in the Scottish Parliament package. At least today's Chancellor of the Exchequer has not, as far as I know, repealed his old verdict on these matters. So what are the powers now for?

Socialism may have evacuated the scene. Inequality has not. On the contrary, the gross human and societal contrasts depicted in much of that 1975 *Red Paper* 'Introduction' are more offensive and menacing than ever. The difference is that they now tend to be viewed as inseparable from a 'global capitalism' to which no general alternative exists — and which, indeed, UK government concentrates its efforts to promote. The Scots got 'what they asked for' in the 1970s — and are now asked (by the same voice, disconcertingly) to do nothing with it which might risk offending Westminster's grand-capitalist strategy, with all its panoply of 'continuity and tradition'.

The young, radical editor of *The Red Paper* would certainly have given a firm 'no' in answer to this request. Nobody thought then that in a not-so-distant Scotland nationalists and a re-constituted Scottish labour movement would join together — however uncertainly at first — in opposition to a London Labour government (and clearly, though for the moment quite hypothetically, to any other strain of government likely to be asserted there). But so it is. Through a more egalitarian, and more European, constitutional approach, Scottish government will have to work its way forward to as much 'genuine economic power' and as much native democracy as it finds that it needs for the realisation of such enduring Red aims. That's the new song, and the one Sheena Wellington was singing on 1 July.

CHAPTER 5

FROM 'OLD' TO 'NEW' SNP

GEORGE KEREVAN

Scotland is not modern. The sudden public disappointment with the new Scottish Parliament is a first indication that neither the Scottish Executive nor the opposition parties are ready to be revolutionaries and rebuild a modern nation.

The original Union with England involved a pact with a swathe of Establishment institutions who were allowed to survive as long as they accepted and buttressed the retention of political power in London - Church, education, the legal profession. In the twentieth century, this concordat has expressed itself more and more in the extension of a vast quangocracy of appointed executive bodies run by the great and the good: the Scottish Council, the Scottish Development Agency and Scottish Enterprise, the Scottish Arts Council and hundreds of others.

This corporatist state now lies at the centre of Scotland's lack of modernity. Under the Union status quo, we are run by an appointed Establishment without the accountability or competition that makes for efficiency or entrepreneurship. Promotion is by an almost Masonic passage through the right schools, the right clubs and the right political connections.

When this quangocracy was threatened by Thatcherite free market reforms in the 1980s, it opted to join the popular forces in favour of a devolved Scottish Parliament in the hope that devolution would protect the quangocracy's interests from London.

A Scottish Parliament that sends out the grant cheques to the same old quangos run in secret by the same old faces, will merely reinforce the traditional status quo. A status quo which drains discipline, enterprise, fraternity and personal responsibility from Scottish civic and economic life. A framework which rests on appointment by patronage and not democratic merit and on the moral hazard of seeking London subsidies rather than local entrepreneurship. The dismantling of this quangocracy and the democratisation of Scotland represents the heart of the modernising agenda. What gives the quangocracy its cultural strength?

Twentieth century Scotland's quest for political and economic modernisation is the direct result of the moral and entrepreneurial suicide of the Glasgow bourgeoisie after the First World War. After the 1921 Crash, the great Clydeside businesses, family owned and under-capitalised, lost their entrepreneurial spirit. Rather than develop new markets, the conservative Glasgow Tory business community sought Imperial tariffs to protect themselves from foreign competition. They formed a New Unionist Consensus with an aspirant Catholic Labour leadership understandably anxious for integration as well as state help from London to protect jobs. London subsidy replaced traditional Scottish enterprise and the major urban classes found common ground in ceding a degree of autonomous power to a growing Scottish Office and its bureaucracy. This New Unionist Consensus was delivered complete with an new bureaucratic ideology: 'state planning' and the subsequent rise of the Establishment quangocracy to enforce it (see Kerevan, 1981, 1999a).

Modernism, Nationalism and the First SNP

Twentieth century Scottish nationalism is nothing more than the attempt by Scottish civil society to modernise itself from within. Modernise in the sense of breaking with this conservative New Unionist Consensus, the resulting quangocracy and its entropic cultural dynamic, totally at odds with that required to run a modern industrial, market economy in a global setting.

The modernisation debate goes to the heart of why the SNP

was born when it was, in 1934. Contrary to later mythology, the early SNP — while ideologically eclectic — was never just an eccentric fringe or a 'Whisky Galore' cultural movement. The party emerged from a current of the most prominent Scottish intellectuals who were directly under the influence of international Modernism in literature, architecture and philosophy — the opposite of tartan exceptionalism (Findlay, 1994).

Cultural Modernism was an intellectual break with the Victorian veneration of tradition. It came from the social ferment, resulting from the rise of genuine industrial societies in America and Germany. The new small nations of Europe born out of the Great War - Czechoslovakia and Finland for instance — were already highly influential in the Modernist movements in literature and architecture. Scots intellectuals saw them as powerful examples of what an independent Scotland could achieve in the world in sharp contrast to the collapse of the Scottish economy after 1921. Here was an alternative to the New Unionist Consensus and social decay.

Scottish intellectuals between the two wars were far from traditionalists or ivory towered academics. Writers such as Muir and Greive were leading international lights in the fashionable and influential Modernist movement in Western literature. Muir was a friend of Kafka, and T.S. Eliot believed that Grieve should be the Yeats of Scotland. Indeed, 1934 — the same year that saw the founding of the SNP — also saw Scotland hosting PEN, the international writers' conference which was the driving intellectual centre of literary modernism.

The result was a powerful cultural movement — the Scottish Renaissance — and the crystallisation of political nationalism into the SNP. It was far from marginal, receiving prominent backing from Lord Beaverbrook and the *Scottish Daily Express*. Glasgow Chamber of Commerce, spiritual home of the New Unionist Consensus, was forced to issue an anti-nationalist manifesto, two months before the official launch of the SNP, signed by 456 business and Establishment figures (Brand, 1978).

But the new nationalist movement was limited in four ways.

Firstly, unlike Finland or Czechoslovakia, the old ruling class had not been swept away by war or revolution. In fact, though dealt a body blow by economic crisis and labour unrest, it had survived by co-opting the Labour Party into joining the New Unionist Consensus. Without a major split in the Scottish bourgeoisie, the SNP could not become a mass force.

Secondly, this stability of the Scottish middle class Establishment divided the early SNP over tactics. Should it try to win over the Scottish Establishment to independence? A move which might result in surrendering independence for devolution in a forlorn attempt not to challenge the Establishment vested interests guaranteed by the Union. Or should it try and be more radical? This devolutionist-home rule divide would physically split the SNP in 1942 and not for the last time (Finlay, 1994).

Thirdly, much of the modernist wing of the national movement were easily seduced by the lure of state centralist planning which the New Unionist Consensus had evoked as its ideology. But state planning merely tied Scotland to London's financial coat tails for another fifty years.

Finally, to the SNP's left lay a competitor. The Independent Labour Party (ILP) split from the Labour Party in 1932 taking much working class home rule sentiment with it, despite the SNP's strong espousal of a populist, anti-capitalist Social Credit philosophy. Only with the post-war eclipse of the ILP would left wing nationalism find a home in the SNP.

The Second SNP: Nationalism as Wilsonian Social Democracy

World War Two and the early 1950s were the great hiatus in twentieth century Scottish history. The forces of modernisation, nationalist or otherwise, were confounded when prosperity seemed to return with the wartime command economy. This aberration confirmed the Glasgow bourgeoisie in their retreat towards protection and the New Unionist Consensus and away from industrial modernisation. Working class patriotism kindled a new British identity for a whole generation.

But all this concealed the failure of the Clydeside bourgeoisie to modernise. The banking cartel were even able to hide from public view a near melt-down of the Scottish banking system in the early 1950s. Economic nemesis arrived with the 1957 recession as American and newly-modernised European businesses destroyed obsolescent Scottish heavy industry. By the early 1960s, the Clyde shipyards were collapsing in the middle of the century's biggest ship-building boom and 30,000 Scots were being forced to emigrate every year (Saville, 1996).

At this point, as whole sections of industrial household names were eliminated, the Unionist state stepped in with a vengeance. An inward investment strategy, coupled with the mass migration of Glasgow's population to new towns, seemed to imply economic regeneration, though it would prove no more sustainable than Stalinist central planning in Eastern Europe.

But it did begin to break up the stasis of Scottish society. The Tory majority melted as the young workers in the new towns and the rapidly expanding ranks of public sector employees, voted first Labour and then SNP. Their left wing radicalism quickly turned against the incoherence of the Wilson government after 1964.

As inflation and unemployment took off — because Wilson, Heath and Callaghan were no more capable of modernising UK Plc than they were Scotland — the fortunes of the SNP began to rise. But this was a new, second generation SNP staffed by trades unionists, CND supporters and many activists and supporters of the labour movement disillusioned with Wilson. Henceforth, independence would be about economics and how best to use the windfall of North Sea oil to rebuild the Scottish economy.

The ideology of the SNP in this period turned into a mixture of socialist corporatism and moderate Scandinavian social democracy. This was no Poujadist movement, certainly not after the early 1960s. It was a left-wing, modernising movement trying to take up where Harold Wilson had failed. This current was found not only in the SNP.

The weaknesses in this second SNP were inherent in its approach to the problem of Scottish modernisation. Wilsonism had saved the dying bourgeoisie through nationalisation and by co-opting them into the proliferation of quangos that his and later administrations invented throughout the 1960s and 1970s. Scottish society became resolutely corporatist which merely refroze it back into the stasis that the 1960s had begun to melt. The SNP's political programme of the period, though increasingly left wing, did not challenge this situation. It merely tried to out left the Labour Party in the hope that the mass of Labour voters in the Central Belt would vote SNP.

The SNP failed to see that Wilsonite-Callaghan corporatism was a fundamentally conservative force trying to plaster over the remaining declining elements of the British imperial trading economy. Aping it in Scotland was no solution to Scotland's modernisation project. Nor was chasing the Labour vote per se. The Labour Party vote in Scotland was a conservative vote, hiding from change in a harsh world economy after the 1974 oil crisis.

SNP mythology blames the party's decline after 1979 on internal feuding and the popular confusions resulting from Labour's botched first devolution bill. While some of this is true, it misses out the deep conservative tide in Scottish society that gathered pace in the 1970s — a corporatist, statist tide that the SNP itself helped to promote. Little wonder then the electorate voted for the real conservatives — the Labour Party.

Alex Salmond is the final, if more sophisticated, embodiment of the second SNP's social democratic vision. His case — intellectually more coherent than the ever-changing neologisms of new Labour — goes as follows: Wilsonite state socialism is out but a milder Scandinavian social democracy is in. An independent Scottish social democracy will be able to combine an efficient economy (stimulated by low business taxes like Ireland) with high social spending (paid for by higher personal taxes). Salmond believes the middle classes will vote for this programme because they have always accepted a high degree of social responsibility (Kerevan and Marr, 1998).

The Third SNP and the Y Generation

The test of this Social Democracy with a Scottish face came on 6 May 1999. New Labour triumphed, the SNP polled only 29 percent. What went wrong? The impersonal calculus of the first ever Scottish general election suggests that the old voting blocks are already breaking up — that a new generation is at hand with a different world view from traditional tax-and-spend social democracy. The SNP's approach — symbolised by the projected 'Penny for Scotland' tax differential with England — proved a gamble too far.

The SNP leadership believe that their internal polling revealed a broad middle-class sympathy with the 'Penny for Scotland'. But it also revealed working-class unease in traditional Labour areas, where the SNP did not win — putting a serious question mark over the SNP's thirty year old strategy of capturing the Central Belt Labour vote intact.

Twenty five percent of employees are self-interested public sector workers — perhaps enough to garner support for tax-fed, bigger public expenditure but not enough to support an independence majority. Even if Salmond wins a majority at Holyrood, it is likely to be based on a voting block too conservative to support outright independence, merely a Catalan-style autonomy.

Besides, the 'Penny for Scotland' went a long way to alienating the Scottish business community. Post-Thatcherite Scotland is a new country and not one frozen in aspic at the time of the 1979 referendum. Privatisation and deregulation have created new Scottish entrepreneurs and new Scottish multinationals outside the social orbit of the quangocracy. Their attitude is anti-London, anti-bureaucratic, internationalist, often pro-SNP, but not corporatist or traditionally social democratic.

One of the glaring contradictions in Salmond's project is his use of fast growing Ireland as a model for an independent Scotland. No one could call Ireland social democratic. If anything, it is an Anglo-Saxon style, free booting economy driven by the energy and re-branding of a younger generation who have broken free of the shibboleths of the Irish Civil War. To make its own political breakthrough, the SNP will have to enthuse just this generation of young people now growing to maturity in the years after the fall of the Berlin Wall. Americans call them Generation Y.

Contemporary, quango Scotland is still largely run by the post-war Baby Boomer generation of forty- and fifty-somethings. They have a naive belief that the bureaucratic state born of war will solve all problems like a guardian angel. They were followed by the intermediate Generation X, born in the still ideological 1960s and 1970s. These thirty-somethings, who form the cadres of the present SNP, are a frustrated generation. They share their parent's corporatism mixed with the deep frustrations of not having enjoyed the socially liberating 1960s. They hated Thatcher, partly for her Little Englander attitudes, and because her radicalism exposed their own social conservatism.

The voters in the Holyrood elections after 2003 will be from Generation Y, for whom Thatcher is a name in a history book. Without a Cold War, their world is not ideological. Their social world is bonded by friends and the Internet, not political institutions, so unlike previous generations, they feel no tension between a strong community and individual identity. The Y generation is not social democratic because it has little time for traditional bureaucratic politics or politicians. But that does not mean it lacks a social conscience, merely that it will exercise it in a non-bureaucratic way.

London and Britishness have no more special significance to the Ys than Los Angeles and Hollywood. They will be the generation that prizes Scottish independence because their cultural references are already effortlessly international, yet their Scottish identity is unquestioned. But only if a third SNP emerges which engages with the enthusiasms of the Y generation. This requires a new political language of personal liberation, and a new concept of what independence would look like, based on radically democratising and de-constructing corporatist Scotland.

What does modernisation mean for the Y generation? Institutionally, it means the abolition of the quango state including Scottish Enterprise, the Arts Council and the rest. It means replacing it with a new, more fluid civil society and putting an end to Central Belt hegemony as towns such as Inverness and Perth rapidly grow. Politically, it means the wide-ranging development of democracy into every nook and cranny of our society — from judges to provosts to health boards — to bring in fresh thinking, youth, talent and openness.

Culturally, for the Y generation modernisation means replacing the fixation with cynicism, workerism and parochialism born of the corporatist era with an internationalist, erotic, populist, confident cultural practice — in short, re-branding Scotland as modern not Braveheart.

Economically, for the Ys are a generation of entrepreneurs, it means taking risks, being weaned off subsidies, concentrating on local entrepreneurship for world markets rather than foreign direct investment, growing customer-oriented service industries, making jobs rather than saving them, being Hong Kong to Europe's Asia.

Already a large number of the cadres of the SNP are entrepreneurs, young bankers and high tech engineers — a far cry from Central Belt shop stewards or social workers. They are hardly traditional socialists even if they have a Y generation, neo-Victorian personal morality about community involvement. In this context, Salmond's ideological references to social democracy can be seen as obfuscating the difference between Y generation social activism and Central Belt statism. But it is a confusion that will have to be resolved if a twenty first century nationalism is to be shaped.

Conclusions: A New Scottish Nationalism

What will this third Scottish nationalism look like? Nationalism and modernism are synonymous because only the modern vehicle of the democratic nation state frees us — no matter how imperfectly — from the intellectually and economically restrictive bonds of tradition, ethnicity, hierarchy, caste, gender, and religion.

Globalism will not eliminate this civic national identity, but instead will give it a new content. The twenty first century will be one where world cities — such as Los Angeles or London — and compact, vibrant small country regions — such as Scotland or

Catalonia — directly service the global republic. Small nations, like small companies, are the wave of the future because they mean shorter lines of communication and faster reaction times. Globalism itself is stripping the large collective states of an earlier era back to core cultures and core economic regions, which can now navigate unaided in the global society of the twenty first century (Ohmae, 1995). National downsizing, if you will.

The new role of government will be to manage ever-faster change, primarily at a cultural level. This will mean an emphasis on educational experiment, intellectual copyright legislation, and open communications in all media. An SNP based on the Y generation and its cultural entrepreneurs will fit more easily within these trends than Unionist political movements attempting to invent a new, parochial Britishness.

New Labour cannot modernise Scotland despite its rhetoric because Scottish new Labour's very power base is the quangocracy itself. The first Scottish Executive is led not by Blairite radicals but by conservative Scottish lawyers plus assorted ex-local government leaders linked to the quangocracy. It has merely filled the quangos with its own placemen.

None of the foregoing is to be taken as a plea for the rejection of the community solidarity that underlines the SNP's social democracy. Managing change is a collective task, very different from the individualist fantasies of Ayn Rand. Paradoxically, from the shards of twentieth century Scotland's conservative corporatism could be born a partnership culture very much adapted to the twenty first century. For managing permanent change well — indeed leading change globally — requires the unity, cooperation, shared goals, global language, and international links that has defined Scotland over the past three centuries.

Before such a future can be realised, we must first complete the modernist revolution. We have a new Parliament. It must take back civil power from the quangocracy or become its tame creature.

MODERNISING THE MODERNISERS

JACK MCCONNELL

Modern day Scotland is full of contradictions and inconsistencies. While one in four children is born into poverty, 22 per cent of families own a personal computer. A child has a greater chance than ever before of growing up in a household with just one adult, and there are more people in retirement than in full time permanent work. A job is no longer for life and women are exercising more financial independence than at any point in history.

In the face of enormous social and political change, successful parties have re-invented themselves to appeal to an ever more discriminating electorate. The most visible re-invention is of the Labour Party, significantly since 1994, but with the seeds of change sown in the 1980s. Shaken by the success of a popular but extreme right-wing government, grass root members and a new generation of leaders on the left have recognised the need for change. Losing every battle at every turn — organisational, political and intellectual — forced the left to evolve or face extinction.

In Scotland, we faced particular defining moments. The very different fortunes of the Conservative Party in Scotland, compared to their national performance, gave the evolutionary process in Scotland a different focus. The constitutional implications of the governing UK party having just 10 out of 72 MPs in Scotland fanned the glowing embers of the campaign for constitutional reform after 1987, both within the party and among the wider population. With another defeat in 1992, however, the message hit home that the need for constitutional reform went hand in hand with a need for policy reform. The prospect of a Scottish Parliament ruled by a Labour Party with a policy programme rooted in the 1970s and 1980s was going to neither inspire confidence nor, crucially, win votes to get us there. And now in a different environment, following the undisputed success of the 1997 and 1999 election campaigns, the left in Scotland must meet the challenges of the new decade, including those that result from the proportional electoral system in the Scottish Parliament.

The Success of Modernisation

By 1997, Labour's re-invention was so complete that political dominance stretched way beyond an electoral landslide. The battle of ideas had been won and the opposition was marginalised. Key to this success was not just that policy had been refined and modernised but the party had been too.

The key reforms during this period were the introduction of 'One Member One Vote' for decision-making, the commitment to a mechanism for equalising gender representation and a new party constitution in the form of the revised Clause Four. These changes were backed by a modern and professional approach to campaigning and a membership that remained vigorously loyal to the party's fundamental principles and values.

Who are the Modernisers?

Those arguing for change in Scottish Labour over the 1980s and 1990s are difficult to categorise. The reality is that there have never been exclusive 'modern' and 'traditional' clubs and factions. Even the left and right badges of the 1970s and 1980s have become largely redundant (Hassan, 1998a). Some members, who were at the forefront of the equal representation campaign, clearly a modernising movement, have opposed new Labour's economic management. Many unions, who were the catalyst for policy development relating to defence diversification and family friendly employment practices, were diametrically opposed to 'One Member

One Vote'. Some of those traditionally hostile to devolution have been the biggest supporters of the new Labour approach that finally delivered it. Those most keen to see involvement and participation improved and modernised nationally have at times been the culprits in terms of exclusive politics locally. The crucial point, however, is that the virtual transformation of the party has been supported by both members and voters, illustrating both the necessity and the rewards of what was, at times, a painful process.

The Future Direction of Modernisation

In 1999, where do those from all wings of the party who have supported all or part of the modernisation agenda now go? What is next for women's representation? Can we stop the traditional selection system rolling back the progress made in 1997 and 1999? What is to be the identity of Labour in Scotland? How do we repeat the feat of 1997, which gave us 56 seats and 46 per cent of the vote? Can we rejuvenate the party with membership increasing again — a lively youth section, members involved and developing into community advocates for what we do? Most importantly of all, how do we prepare Scotland for the next century; keeping apace with change, creating wealth and sharing it out more equally, improving life chances and aspirations all round.

Our new Parliament presents challenges for those across Scotland who spent so many years battling to create a new form of democratic politics within the UK. Realising the potential of the new politics, and the new Parliament, looked at times an impossible dream, but devolution will have a political momentum. In time this momentum will fulfil the promise of a more mature, less simplistic approach to Scottish political debate which will challenge us all to rethink our attitudes.

Modernisation for Social Change

The future involves further modernisation of the party and our policies — guided by the values that gave birth to the party and steered us through good and bad times. These values should underpin our plans for the years ahead and the targets we set ourselves. We need solutions based on the realities of the 1990s which will make a difference to those most excluded from our political processes and society.

Modernisation is not a retreat from the politics of the left; on the contrary, it is the lifeblood that will keep the left relevant and dominant in an increasingly challenging world, but we must learn to articulate and communicate our values and vision effectively in that world.

The demand for devolution and a new politics in Scotland was itself the great modernising clamour of the 1980s. Modernising the party to deliver and reconnecting with the people was the real change of the 1990s. In the new century, modernisers must renew and rebuild to make the new Parliament succeed and stabilise the UK. But we must also fulfil our historic destiny. Modern policies, modern approaches, and open government focussed on the priorities of the majority, not the age-old Scottish establishment — will transform the lives of ordinary Scots. In moving from defining a modernisation strategy in opposition to winning power at first UK, then Scottish level, we need to move into a new stage of modernisation of delivery, policy-making and policy-implementation which is capable of developing and renewing itself while in power.

Modernisation is not an end in itself. Modernisation of the party and its policies must have a clear political goal. Only by modernising the approach to public services, attitudes towards equality, relationships with the private sector, democratic systems and the sustainability of development, can Scotland become a fairer and more successful country for all her citizens. This approach is the genuine modernisers' agenda — not some secret plot to implement Tory policies by the back door, or some effort to keep Scotland from exercising autonomy in the devolved areas, but a genuine and real effort to transform life chances in communities across Scotland.

The truth about life in Scotland today is that existing public services fail too many working class communities for reasons of quality as well as quantity. Our education system fails children from poorer backgrounds, our health service is skewed in favour of the more prosperous households, and the environment is best where those who have most live. These are the realities and the challenges, that modernisation has to address.

Even the word 'modernising' may spark fear and suggest treachery to many. But we must be clear: there is no question about the need to modernise. The real questions are what, when and by how much. As in most of life, it is the issue of relationships that needs more discussion — between people and their governments, the electorate and the elected, leaders and those they lead, the private and the public sectors. These concepts are much harder to grasp than the idea that we need a modern NHS reflecting lifestyles of today. What is it that we are looking for from these relationships? As society has changed, so have our expectations and thus, our political expectations and processes.

Modernisation, we have to be clear, is a process that never ends. We cannot adapt the left's values to the 1990s and then sit on our laurels, because the economic, social and political environment will soon move on and leave us addressing an agenda of a past age — as has happened before. We have not put ourselves in this unprecedented position — of dominating the UK political scene at the end of the century after nearly 20 years in opposition — only to throw it away.

We have to move onto the next stage of modernisation, what has been called 'modernising the modernisation' (Latour, 1999), re-appraising the left's message in light of the complexities and uncertainties of the modern world. We must also acknowledge that while we cannot promise a future that is more simple and unchanging than today, as previous lefts attempted to do, we can look at new ways of creating a more safe, secure world. Modernising the modernisation means we have to be honest about the difficult choices in the modern world, recognising that we cannot go back to a world pre-1979 or a less dynamic, changing world; instead, we need to embrace those forces of change and harness them to the goal of a more inclusive society.

Modernising the Party

Modern Scottish Labour politics can be characterised by a number of strands:

- Less oppositionalism and more discipline. Real internal party democracy, recognising the role of the regular activist but acknowledging a role for the passive member as well.
- Improving women's representation, the participation of ethnic minority communities and links with civic Scotland.
- Recognising the link with the UK but developing our Scottish programme within that.
- Remembering our history with pride but knowing that the future is a very different environment in which to realise a vision of democratic socialism that is valid and effective.

None of this though is possible if we return to a small unrepresentative membership, disenchanted and disenfranchised, or a public image of men and women interested in power for power's sake, ignoring public opinion or the validity of democratic choice. We have moved on from that, but the party as a whole does not yet feel ownership over the new environment and structures. Indeed there is a romantic vision of the past as if life in Labour was more democratic and radical when the party was in perpetual opposition.

The modernisation policies of the 1980s and 1990s will not continue into the next decade unless we keep developing and creating new ideas and drawing on new resources, skills and inputs. We need to modernise the modernisers — recruiting, enthusing and developing generations of party members who will challenge the status quo, demand more and make the party adapt to the circumstances in society around us.

What kind of Labour Party will exist in Scotland in 2010? Will it still have the ideas and dynamic to create the policies and organisational momentum to deliver change? Who will be the modernisers in the next decade and will Labour be capable of motivating and involving them? If the modernisers are to be modernised, the next generation of party activists needs the encouragement and space to develop the ideas that will bring about that constant renewal so vital for any governing party of the left.

The key element of renewal in the new century is communication between the party and its members, between government and people. The 'what did the Romans ever do for us?' syndrome continues to stick with the Labour Government even in the face of a genuinely radical agenda. Major shifts in public policy such as the Working Families Tax Credit have gone unacknowledged, even by many party members. So we have to face the fact that we are not communicating the success of our economic and social reforms generally. New forms of meaningful engagement are as important inside political parties as they are within society as a whole. Educating, involving and listening to party members are vital for continued success and delivering in government.

Modernising Participation

One of the first speeches that Tony Blair gave to a local government audience after the 1997 general election suggested that if councils did not have a consultation strategy, they needed to get one quickly. Participative democracy and taking government closer to the people are key principles for Labour. We must understand that people are not jumping up and down to participate or to respond to consultations, but that does not mean that we should not try.

In the same way that local government is creating innovative ways of finding answers to the question 'what is it that people want?', Scottish Labour could employ equivalent tactics. Citizens' juries and focus groups (albeit with a new name!) are clever tools to reach and engage people who have perhaps not participated in the past. The danger, as always with these strategies, is that they tend to be seen as mechanisms for giving the leadership what they want. We must break out of the 'us and them', 'old and new' mentality. We have got too much to do to let these perceived divisions drag us down.

Modernising Policy

Policy-making in Labour has undergone a revolution. Out are the motions, composites and drama on conference floor, and in is detailed policy discussion on a rolling programme of debate and deliberation. As with all structures, new or old, there is always room for improvement. Big controversial debates on conference floor at least gave people a sense of ownership of the resulting policy, albeit limited. We have to convince people that policy forums can give them ownership too — real ownership — which only comes from grassroots involvement at the outset, and a better standard of local party organisation.

The challenge for those of us in positions of public responsibility is to trust in the ability and motivation of the membership. The reforms of the policy-making structures are a great step forward, but we are only in the first phase of policy commissions and forums in Scotland. Their effectiveness as a way of delivering change and ensuring widespread ownership of policies has yet to be proven. A way of showing branches, CLPs, trade unions and ordinary members that their submissions are part of the final outcome must be found. Otherwise we are in danger of creating a 'black hole' where good ideas vanish without any structured consideration.

Modernising the Movement

The trade unions in Scotland are coming to a swift realisation that the new political settlement is having a profound affect on the way they operate. There is no doubt that the very existence of the Parliament is due to the persistence of the home rule movement in which the trade unions have played a significant part. In the murky days of the early 1980s, it was the commitment of unions such as the NUM and TGWU that ensured devolution remained on the political agenda, as trade unions had done in previous times (Keating and Bleiman, 1979; McLean, 1990, 1991).

However, in all the effort to create the Parliament, the unions have not had the chance to adapt their own structures. The creation of the Scottish Trade Union Research Network is a good example of the sort of collaboration that is now taking place. Linking university researchers with the unions will enable them to participate in policy development at a much higher level than before. There are also moves for greater devolution within the UK unions themselves, recognising that union members in Scotland, in order to be represented effectively, need the opportunity to develop their own 'Scottish solutions'.

All of this bodes well for the future of the Scottish Labour Party as the whole movement adapts from the long years out of power to the years in power that are ahead. Greater involvement of trade union members and increased direct communication between the union hierarchy and lay members will have benefits for union policy and subsequently Scottish Labour policies.

But we cannot be complacent. Imagining a Scottish Labour Party in 2010 with a large, active and participative membership, in touch with communities, you quickly realise that the interaction between the Labour Party and the trade unions has to be more than just top-level discussion between the two sets of hierarchies.

Modernising Communications

A lot has been written about the technological revolution and the rate of change is breathtaking. But only now, as we begin to realise the impact of the revolution, do we comprehend the implications for those who are excluded. We must ensure that we do not become a nation of the connected and the disconnected because the revolution is happening all around us and has consequences for all society.

We must, however, ensure that we make the new technology work for us. In a world of seemingly endless acronyms — FTP, ISP, RAM, http — it is easy to forget the important issue, which is not how it works, but how it works for us. Purely informative websites such as those of the Scottish Executive and the Scottish Parliament are great and an exciting development in our democratic culture, but the potential of Information Communication Technology (ICT) goes far beyond simply providing information.

Scottish Labour must seize the opportunity of what the technology offers. Discussion forums on policy at local, national and even international level; e-mail updates of news and developments, events and activities; networks of activists in health, environmental or transport sharing ideas and information; the opportunity to question key party figures. The possibilities are endless, and limited only by our imaginations and attachment to traditional methods and can herald a revolution in how we organise government, public services and society (Byrne, 1997).

Modernising the Modernisers: A Conclusion

In Scotland we have our work cut out for us. We are shaping and building a new democracy, with no predecessors with whom to compare ourselves. High expectations and problems associated with a new emerging democracy are all challenging the energy, enthusiasm and good intentions of the fledgling Parliament.

The focus of our energy so far has been to make the Parliament a reality; now that it is, our focus must be on what the Parliament can deliver. If the Parliament is truly a sign of a renaissance in Scotland, then it is not just the process of democracy that has been reborn, but the whole purpose of that democracy. Changing the constitutional landscape was a means, not an end and we now have to consider the new political landscape in which we are operating. This is a landscape with no map, no footpaths, not even a rough track to guide us, but we have to be bold and raise our eyes to look beyond the next step.

Following the political change which has taken place in England and reflected most in the Labour landslide of 1997, Labour in Scotland must convert the constitutional change of 1997 into political change here too. Change which can deliver for our people and which can make devolution relevant and stable for all.

Modernisers in Labour politics have for some time argued that they are about finding new solutions to old problems, accepting that traditional answers do not always get it right. Government in the twenty first century is about being creative, innovative and pushing traditional boundaries. It is, ultimately, about taking risks. And perhaps the biggest risk is to fail to capture the imagination of the public at large. We have to engage them, inspire them and persuade them of what we can achieve.

SECTION TWO: AN ECONOMIC AGENDA

| BEYOND
ALF YOUNG | KVAERNER:
| THE SCOTTISH ECONOMY
| IN A GLOBALISING AGE

Saving 1200 manufacturing jobs at Kvaerner's Govan shipyard on the Upper Clyde became the defining economic act of the Labour government during Scotland's constitutional transition. The troubled Norwegian conglomerate's decision to exit shipbuilding globally was the kind of challenge generations of post-war Labour politicians in the industrial north knew only too well. Their crisis response — complete with a high profile task force led by former engineering union general secretary Sir Gavin Laird and a world-wide search for alternative buyers — had been honed by past Labour and Tory governments alike on the tombstones of countless other traditional industries. From Singer at Clydebank and British Aluminium at Invergordon to British Leyland at Bathgate, Scott-Lithgow in Greenock and a whole string of steel mills culminating in Ravenscraig, the script had been serially refined over more than two decades. The only thing missing this time was the designation of Govan as an enterprise zone. That initiative was not needed. For Kvaerner found its buyer, in the shape of GEC: the British engineering conglomerate Lord Weinstock created from relentless acquisition already owned the Yarrow naval yard, just across the Clyde.

However the post-Weinstock GEC had no more interest than Kvaerner in remaining in shipbuilding. It already wanted government approval for the sale of its Marconi defence interests, including its Yarrow and Barrow shipyards, to BAe. Offering to buy Kvaerner Govan would get the government off a painful political hook and, given the way these things usually work, might persuade Whitehall to smile more kindly on a major act of consolidation in the UK defence sector. Future British governments might pay a heavy price in sharply reduced defence procurement choice. But this would be one industrial site where the gates would stay open. At least for now.

Leading the political charge to save Govan was not the newly elected Labour-dominated Executive at Holyrood, but John Reid and one-time Fairfield apprentice Lord Gus Macdonald at the transitional Scottish Office. No midnight pizza was left uneaten as the British Labour presence in Scotland brokered the deal. Many other Scottish jobs were under threat — in the knitwear and electronics sectors, in tyre production and jeans manufacture, for instance — but saving Govan became, for a brief period, the entire raison d'être of industrial and economic policy making north of the border.

But, as edgy transition gives way to the new established constitutional order, a bigger question remains unanswered. Beyond the Kvaerner rescue, what kind of economy do we want Scotland to become in this era of globalisation, the Internet and post-industrial angst? And what part, if any, can government play in bringing that kind of economy about?

Continuity and Change in the Scottish Economy

In some ways, Scotland's economy in 1999 is already radically different from the 1979 model, when Labour was last in power. But in other ways, familiar economic anxieties still persist. Our historic preoccupation with unemployment rates substantially and consistently much higher than Great Britain as a whole — at times sixty or even seventy per cent higher — has largely gone. Not only has claimant count unemployment fallen for most of the last decade, there was even a brief period in 1994/95 when Scottish registered unemployment fell below UK levels. Full-time jobs for men are becoming more scarce. The numbers for women have been largely static. In the past 20 years the main growth in employment has been part-time work for women (Peat and Boyle, 1999). But while unemployment is no longer the political obsession it once was, we have grown complacent about residual levels of joblessness which, in the era up until the mid-1970s would have been considered intolerable.

We have become a service-dominated economy. Glasgow is now a retail, leisure and education hub rather than a great manufacturing city (see, for example, Warhurst *et al.*, 2001). Call centres employ far more Glaswegians than the remaining shipyards (Glasgow Development Agency, 1999). Only a quarter of Scotland's GDP and less than a fifth of all our jobs are now in manufacturing. Our remaining industrial output which, since 1995, has markedly outstripped the UK as a whole, has one largely foreign-owned sector — electronics — to thank for almost all that out-performance (Peat and Boyle, 1999).

Scotland escaped the post-Lawson-boom recession at the start of the 1990s. And since then overall Scottish economic growth — which, for most of the 1980s, trailed far behind the UK as a whole — now matches and at times exceeds the UK trend. But that heavy manufacturing and export dependence on computer assembly and silicon chip fabrication and our more recent enthusiasm for call centres both carry strong resonances of our earlier heavy dependency on metal bashing. As margins are further squeezed in the hardware end of electronics and e-commerce increasingly bypasses the human interface that a call centre still represents, Scotland may once more find itself over-exposed in some of the new twilight industries.

In the late 1970s Scotland's wealth was relatively evenly spread across the country. The advent of oil off Aberdeen and the rise of Edinburgh as a financial and now a government centre have ensured widening disparities in regional per capita GDP. Scotland's south-east is actually our north-east, with prosperity levels in the old Grampian region fully 50 per cent higher than the region around Glasgow. That said, Scotland has become a more attractive place to live and work. Our historic propensity to export large numbers of our citizens has abated from the massive net out-flows recorded in the 1950s and 1960s. There are signs, in the present decade, that the trend in out-migration has finally been reversed (Peat and Boyle, 1999).

At the start of the 1980s, the corporate cause celebre in Scotland was the prospect of the Royal Bank being taken over by the Hong Kong and Shanghai Banking Corporation, a move decisively blocked by the new Thatcher government. Today's prospect is of Bank of Scotland succeeding in its aggressively hostile bid to acquire NatWest, an ailing English clearing bank nearly three times its size. And if the Bank of Scotland fails to land its prey, the Royal is hotly tipped as a rival bidder. Between these two contrasting bids, many Scottish companies, most notably the Distillers and Arthur Bell whisky groups and a number of once mutually owned life offices, have lost their independence. By way of contrast brewer Scottish & Newcastle survived a hostile bid from Courage only to swallow its would-be predator at a later date.

With major Scottish companies making acquisitions as far away as the western seaboard of the United States, no one talks about erecting a protective tartan ring fence these days. But significant numbers of Scottish quoted companies continue to surrender their independence. Stakis, Kwik-Fit and Scottish Highland Hotels are only three recent examples. Others — Cala and Clyde Blowers for example — have quit their listings and gone into private ownership. And a third group, notably the John Wood Group and Motherwell Bridge, never quite seem to make it to the flotation stage. There have been significant new Scottish entrants to stock market listings, companies such as ScottishPower and Stagecoach. But most of them — in the utility, milk and bus and rail sectors for example — are enterprises born of government deregulation and privatisation.

The total stock of Scottish quoted companies is little changed in the past two decades. Despite the discovery of North Sea oil and the phenomenon of Silicon Glen, Scotland has produced very few world-class companies of its own in either of these technology-enriched sectors. There is no Scottish Nokia, let alone a Scottish Microsoft. Since its formation in 1990, Scottish Enterprise has worried away at the relatively poor levels of new business formation in general in this part of the British Isles and at our inability to commercialise more of our academic research base. The agency claims progress in making entrepreneurship and wealth creation respectable activities once more in modern Scotland. But that progress can seem painfully slow.

Taking Globalisation Seriously

When that snail's pace is set against the technological roller-coaster we are all living through in this globalising age, it is easy to take fright at what might happen to Scotland's economy if we do not take some of these imperatives a lot more seriously. I am writing these words on a personal computer on a desk at home which, in terms of sheer processing power, is more than a match for the air-conditioned roomful of whirring tape and main frames which number crunched everything the entire physics department could throw at it when I was a student in the mid-1960s. I have had three discrete careers since then and fully expect my two sons to have even more. Today, when I write a column for *The Herald*, it is translated onto newsprint by processes that barely existed fifteen years ago. My words are also accessible to a growing army of Internet browsers all around the globe.

With an airline ticket I can criss-cross that same globe at will and find a Big Mac or a Coke wherever I go. Not to mention a Body Shop or a Benetton store. If I stay at home, I can fax and e-mail to my heart's content and buy goods from almost anywhere with delivery guaranteed in days. When trouble erupts somewhere, within hours it will be on our television screens, thanks to mobile satellite links and Kate Adie. What we eat now borrows liberally from all the world's cuisines. What sport we watch now knows no national boundaries.

None of this was possible when I was a lad, watching transatlantic liners sail from the Clyde twice a week, laden with economic migrants seeking a better life in North America. Yes, they used to send us back parcels of American comics. But they took weeks to arrive. And the idea of phoning those relatives, let alone visiting them, was for the privileged few. It is the sheer pace of all the changes we have faced in less than a lifetime that shocks. And there's no obvious reason to believe that that relentless pace will slacken in the future. As Stan Davis, one of the most renowned American gurus has put it, the industrial economy, which turned Scotland into a proud metal basher to the world, lasted 190 years. The information economy, based on the remarkable power of engineered silicon, is barely four decades old and already approaching its maturity. Beyond 2020, say, what Davis calls the bio-economy, one based on what we know today as genetic engineering, will truly come into its own. 'You can't ride on tracks you haven't laid down', Davis concedes (Davis and Davidson, 1991: 145). But, in a world of such profound change, any country, big or small, which aspires to be better than it was yesterday and to grow more prosperous than it is today, needs to be so clear sighted about what it is there for, so flexible in its organisation, strategy and skills that it can stay competitively on the rails, whatever lies round the bends ahead.

Embracing the Future

Too often the change message comes across as something to do with only the new technologies, the business only of those who understand Java or gene therapy. But the kind of change we are talking about here is no respecter of national boundaries or business sectors. In an age when supermarket chains are turning themselves into banks, filling stations are turning themselves into convenience stores, and football clubs are emerging as massive leisure brand names, no one in government and no one in business can afford to be complacent about the competition tomorrow will bring.

As I have already noted above, some of the biggest business success stories in Scotland in recent years have been about companies redefining and squeezing fresh competitive advantage out of the most mundane of market sectors, from running buses and selling milk to fitting tyres and selling insurance. Companies which see change not just as a competitive threat but as a huge new opportunity — a chance to play a role in shaping and profiting from that change — will, increasingly, dominate every business sector in the decades ahead. You do not have to subscribe 100 per cent to Andy Grove's dictum - 'Only the paranoid survive' - to see that as president and CEO of Intel, the US multinational whose chips or microprocessors dominate the world computer market, Grove came to believe in the value of paranoia because he was convinced that the crisis points in every company's evolution, the really challenging episodes in every individual career, are not events to fear or loathe, but opportunities to refocus, regroup and change for the better (Grove, 1997).

This is not an easy message to embrace. It does not sit easily with the Scottish psyche. If we are honest with ourselves, it is not a message to which too many Scottish homes, too many Scottish schools, colleges and universities or too many Scottish businesses instinctively warm. But it is one that every one of us ignores at his or her peril. Each of us, as individuals, has to recognise that the world where a job was for life has gone forever. More and more of us need to reskill ourselves at regular intervals to survive as actors on the economic stage. More and more of us, like Charles Handy's (1994) portfolio worker, also need to embrace flexible new ways of deploying these skills.

Employers too need to think long and hard about which of the many fast-changing ways of organising a workforce will deliver the strongest commitment and the highest quality output from those they employ. And, when they have got their head round that issue, they need to look again at their business, what it is for and where it is going. In a world where the control button seems permanently pressed in fast-forward mode, every business has to assess and reassess its strategy, its organisation, its product or service range and its investment plans. Can we do what we do better by doing it differently? Are there things that we do that we should not be doing? Are there things that we are not doing that we should be getting into? What would we do if the train hit the buffers tomorrow?

To survive and profit from Andy Grove's paranoia demands a lot more from everyone. But the prizes are significant. Many Scottish businesses have the potential to be bigger and more successful than they are today. If enough of them become bigger and more successful, the Scottish economy will prosper too. One of the main barriers is a failure of corporate self-belief and the comparative security of the comfort zones we already inhabit. But the kinds of changes we have discussed are progressively eating into that comfort zone. The big challenge now is for us all to make those step-changes in how we operate before we round that bend and find that the world's changed anyway and we have just run out of track.

CHAPTER 8

KNOWLEDGE, SKILLS AND WORK IN THE SCOTTISH ECONOMY

CHRIS WARHURST AND
PAUL THOMPSON

Introduction

This chapter aims to highlight the misconceptions and misunderstandings about knowledge, skills and work in contemporary advanced economies, drawing out the implications for Scotland. However the task is not merely to problematise current strategies for the economic development for the country, but rather to offer a more comprehensive and empirically sensitive account of knowledge, skills and work that signals possible ways for Scotland to develop its economy and human capital, and so improve the country's preparedness for the twenty first century.

There is a remarkable consensus among the advanced economies' policy-makers, business writers and serious academics about current economic trends and consequent changes in work and each country's skill base. In a re-labelling of the big picture, it is said that we are now living in a post-industrial, information or knowledge economy. On both sides of the Atlantic, governments are pursuing this approach with considerable vigour, as Robert Reich (1993), Tony Blair (1998) and Stephen Byers (1999) exemplify.

In Holyrood too, the previous identification with Silicon Glen has broadened out to the embracing of 'smart Scotland', as knowledge becomes the leitmotif of economic development right across the political divide (see Scottish Office, 1999c). Our argument in this chapter does not dispute the importance of supporting 'real' knowledge work, such as that associated with high tech clusters in biotechnology or electronics, given the capacity of that sector to develop the skill base and export orientation of the country. What we do question is the extent to which the experiences of that part of the economy can be generalised and used as a model to drive public policy. High skill, high wage, knowledge-led work is being outstripped by the growth of other types of employment, notably at the low end of the service sector. It is not all gloom, however. If knowledge in work is more broadly conceived it is possible that Scotland's policy-makers can develop a more inclusive conceptualisation of knowledge and development of human capital.

The Coming of the Knowledge Economy: Retracing the Steps

The promotion of the knowledge economy can be located within debates about broader shifts common to the advanced economies: notably the rise of the service sector and the decline of manufacturing. These shifts are associated with a technological dynamism announced as the end of the 'machine age' and the emergence of an 'information age'. The key asset for national economies and firms is knowledge. As one recent study put it; 'Future prosperity is likely to hinge on the use of scientific and technical knowledge, the management of information and the provision of services. The future will depend more on brains than on brawn' (Barley, 1996: xvii). It can be seen that the implicit model of the traditional knowledge worker is someone who has access to, learns and is qualified to practice, a body of knowledge that is formal, complex and abstract. Competitive advantage for firms is said to lie in developing this abstract knowledge — hence, technical and professional employees are promoted as the archetypal modern worker.

In such circumstances, networks are said to replace hierarchies, both within and across firms, with old-style command and control management replaced by co-ordination based on managing ideas and information (Castells, 1996). This change is driven by the complex nature of knowledge work itself, which is essentially concerned with problem-solving, problem-identifying and strategic brokering between the two processes. The key employees of the information age are what Reich (1993) calls 'symbolic analysts' — for example engineers, consultants and advertising executives — who trade globally in the manipulation of symbols and ideas.

Not only does management as an activity change, much of middle management can be eliminated because they were co-ordinating functions which have disappeared, or processing information which can be directly accessed through IT by senior colleagues.

This horizontal co-ordination is replicated at lower levels within firms through the increased use of team-working to involve workers in problem-solving and continuous improvement. Empowered production and service employees should be 'working smarter not harder', with their workplaces offering new possibilities for creative expression, greater satisfaction, more security and enhanced personal growth.

Given the widespread acceptance of such arguments amongst academics and business writers, it is not surprising that there has been a policy impact. The priority for governments must now be 'facilitating the diffusion and application of knowledge', according to Graham Vickery of the Directorate of Science, Technology and Industry at the OECD (Vickery, 1999: 10). Scotland's development agency has based its current strategy on 'the emerging "knowledge" economy, where economic value is found more in the intangibles, like new ideas, software, services and relationships, and less in the tangibles like physical products, tonnes of steel or acres of land' (Scottish Enterprise, 1998: 3). This requires an accommodation in Scotland's economic structure in terms of its employment base and skills development.

The new skills to be developed in Scotland are the 'thinking' skills used by those working in research, sales, marketing, management and information technology (Scottish Enterprise, 1998; Scottish Enterprise Network, 1999). Knowledge work has thus become a mantra for the country's future economic development, offering

Scotland a rationale for the development of human capital in the workplace, a blueprint for the creation and expansion of competitive 'world class' Scottish firms, the attraction and continued presence of foreign firms in Scotland, and so a way for preventing Scotland becoming a peripheral low skill, low wage national economy within the intensely competitive global economy.

Interrogating the Hype

Knowledge and work needs to be disentangled conceptually as well as empirically. Limited space here does not allow a full critique of this mainstream account of the emergent knowledge economy (see instead Warhurst and Thompson, 1998; Thompson and Warhurst, 1999). The main points can, however, be summarised.

Firstly, proponents exaggerate the scope of the knowledge economy. Occupations requiring 'thinking' skills will expand, but that expansion will be limited in scope and potential for employment growth. Only seven per cent of the fastest growing occupations in the US — the imputed model of economic transformation — could be classified as knowledge workers who manipulate symbols and ideas, and for the most part these occupations are middle level engineers, computer professionals and associated technicians (Henwood, 1996).

Secondly, proponents wrongly conflate the expansion of service sector employment and the rise of knowledge work. This fails to appreciate that most tertiary sector growth has occurred not in knowledge work, but in the low-paid interactive service work of serving, guarding, cleaning, waiting and helping in the private health and care services, as well as retail and hospitality industries — both in the US and UK.

Thirdly, much of the content of service work remains highly routinised and stringently monitored, for example in call centres (Taylor, 1998), and at the lower end often low paid. While there a is huge variety of service sector work, the 'McJob' not the 'iMacJob' is more likely to characterise new employment.

Fourth, while companies are trying to lever more tacit knowledge from employees through participation in micro-level problem-solving, evidence from the UK (Edwards et al, 1996; Ingersoll Engineers, 1996) and the US (Milkman, 1998) demonstrates that most companies remain traditionally managed, and wedded to a low-trust, low skill, authoritarian route to competitiveness.

Fifth, if we look more explicitly at the character of 'knowledge work', we often find that little manipulation of knowledge is taking place. Financial services, for example, frequently require little more of workers than information transfer - the inputting of customer details on to pre-programmed screens and software (Leidner, 1993). It is important to note that being more highly educated does not necessarily indicate a higher level of knowledge inherent in the jobs in which people are employed. The rise in credentialism results in a misleading appearance of the growth of more knowledgeable workers. The OECD *Jobs Study* (1994) notes that there are now many workers and managers who are vastly over-qualified for their jobs.

Finally, even 'real' knowledge work is changing. Technical and professional employees have expanded massively as an occupational group in the recent period (OECD Jobs Study, 1994). Suggestions that such employees represent the new model worker, however, rest on a gross over-simplification of their current working experience and organisational status. Although still relatively highly paid, many of these workers are now experiencing increasing bureaucratic and managerial control in their work, are losing professional autonomy and are increasingly exposed to market pressures that constrain their time for creative experimentation (Warhurst and Thompson, 1998). Moreover, while increased regulation and quasi-market competition also affects public service employees, that much-maligned sector, is nevertheless, the source of much of the growth of high skill occupations (Crouch, 1999).

These points are consistent with trends in the Scottish economy. Data on employment growth, actual and forecast, indicates a very different employment profile (Scottish Enterprise, 1997). Rising from 68 per cent in 1986, the service sector now provides 74.5 per cent of jobs in the Scottish economy, with manufacturing contributing only

15.6 per cent of jobs and agriculture 1.5 per cent. Nevertheless, within this aggregate data, and a point seemingly over-looked by Scottish Enterprise in its strategic development plans, about one third are service jobs mainly in the public sector and over one fifth in distribution, hotels and catering. The next biggest increase will be in personal and protective service jobs, again mostly within the public sector (Scottish Enterprise, 1998). Significantly, most of these jobs are expected to be filled by female, part-time workers. There will be some growth in the numbers employed as 'knowledge workers', if that term is loosely applied to a range of old and newer professional and technical occupations, although caution is again required here for this will occur mainly in the public rather than the private sector.[1]

From Knowledge to Knowledgeability

Powerful forces are reshaping the world of work, but we should not get carried away with all the rhetoric of an emergent knowledge economy. Whilst knowledge might be vital to the securing of firm and national competitive advantage, it would be inappropriate to build an economic development strategy based on mainstream accounts of a knowledge economy and its associated work. It is not just the archetypal 'real' knowledge work of 'symbolic analysts' that has importance for the securing of competitive advantage but also the knowledgeability of more routine workers, both in manufacturing and interactive service work. To facilitate this shift in emphasis from knowledge to knowledgeability, the traditional hierarchy in which knowledge work has been premised on that which is abstract, technical and explicit must be modified. In contrast knowledge which is contextual, social and tacit has been taken to be of lesser value, significance or centrality to work (see Thompson, Warhurst and Callaghan, forthcoming, for further discussion). Abstract knowledge is not the only type that is required in the modern workplace. Even in traditionally lower skill occupations, there is increasing pressure upon employers to deliver quality product (whether service or good), requiring employees to develop and mobilise other forms of skills and knowledge in the workplace. In many contexts, it is not 'thinking' skills which are of increasing importance to most employers, but 'person to person' social competencies.

In interactive service work, for example call centres, societal or social knowledge derived from broader shared understandings, values and beliefs is most utilised by employees in their transactions with customers. Management are keen to recruit and select employees with 'communication skills' involving listening ability for example, or what they refer to as appropriate 'life experience', enabling potential employees to be able to work under pressure. Such skills are more difficult to identify and quantify than technical knowledge but are crucial to interactive service work.

Such social competencies and tacit knowledge are also central to enabling workers to become involved in what Milkman (1998) refers to as the 'micro-management of production'. Until recently, management has tended only to tolerate or accommodate the informal working practices that arise from this tacit knowledge. But such knowledge began to come out of the shadows in the 1980s in the form of quality circles and is now being extended through team-working. Firms such as Unilever are now beginning to realise that only about 20 per cent of their available 'in-house' knowledge is being utilised (Ashworth, 1999). We would argue that knowledge work requires employment relationships and task structures that allow for creative application, manipulation or extension of employee knowledge. As a result, firms should be seeking to 'add value' through a matrix of competencies, knowledges and skills of their employees. That is not to say that business rhetoric about the learning organisation is matched by practices on the ground. Most firms are still opting for the 'low road'; that is, to identify, formalise and utilise workers' tacit knowledge to create new regulatory systems, rather than the 'high road' of utilising that same knowledge to improve those firms' products or processes (Applebaum and Batt, 1994).

Policy Implications
If we are right, policy-makers have to look beyond the knowledge economy to pursue a comprehensive strategy for

Scotland's economic development. Highlighting the importance of knowledgeability is not to argue for a new panacea for Scotland's policy-makers to fill the gap left by their realisation of the limits of 'real' knowledge work and the importance of interactive service work. But accepting our argument does make debates about knowledge in work pertinent for more employees in the Scottish economy, and it enables a more feasible response to the DTI's (1998b) call for a knowledge-driven economy that is applicable to all sectors in the UK — not just the usual suspects of pharmaceutical development and software design. It also signals what is required to enable the 'high road' strategy to innovation in the Scottish economy and workplace.

In this respect, our argument is significant not just for conceptualisations of work and employment, but for policy debates. There has been a welcome shift by left-of-centre governments to either renew or refashion active labour market policies in new political and economic conditions. What has not been achieved is an adequate balance between supply-side and demand-led factors.

While improving employability and enhancing human capital through training and other measures are reasonable objectives, current policy needs to shift so that, 'attention is paid to the demand side of the labour market, to issues like the quality of jobs, their availability, pay rates and so forth' (Peck, 1999: 7). State-led incentives to invest in progressive and innovative uses of human capital must be combined with policies to protect the employment conditions of what will inevitably remain mainly low skill jobs. On the other hand, supply processes themselves have to be re-thought. Existing training provision by agencies intending to make the young and unemployed attractive for firms has tended to be IT, IT and more IT. And yet there is some evidence that employers rank such skills very low as a criteria of employability generally (Hesketh, 1998). It is often the 'person to person' skills that determine employee selection at the point of entry to, and are crucial in, interactive service work (Keep and Mayhew, 1999). Vocational education and training needs to more seriously address the social competencies and skills that contemporary work requires, but which many school leavers appear to lack.

As Crouch *et al.* (1999) argue, public agencies must themselves be knowledgeable about the state of labour markets, and so be able to work closely with firms in the development of skills from a position of expert authority. Trade unions, too, have a role here contributing to the development of initiatives. Despite the debate on the content and delivery of public provision, most vocational training is currently provided by employers — which is worrying given Scottish employers' tendency for lower investment in employee training and development than the rest of the UK, plus the falling standards of Scottish school education (Peat and Boyle, 1999). Donald Dewar is right to argue that Scotland needs a skill strategy and that such a strategy must involve matching supply and demand. Unfortunately, current assessment of the actual skills required by employers and utilised by workers in the workplace is weak. The tendency is to use measurements of workforce pre-entry qualifications and levels of workplace training as proxy measures of workforce skill — a process distorted, as we noted earlier, by the rise of credentialism. Balance and co-ordination must be achieved, with the establishment of a Scottish Labour Market Unit a useful initiative.

A number of the above industrial and employment policy measures fall outside the remit of the Scottish Parliament. However, education and training, broadly defined, can be used as levers to enhance the country's economy. It is here that the much-vaunted 'joined-up' government can be made to work. Policy needs to be formulated that equitably shares the cost amongst the three main sources of skill development: the state, individuals and employers (Crouch, *et al.*, 1999). Clearly the state needs to invest more in schools and vocational education and training and, given the current squeeze on public finances, this might mean shifting resources within education and training budgets. Such decisions will be difficult, but it is with the difficulties of prioritising public funding that policy-makers are concerned.

CHAPTER 9

CREATING PARTNERSHIPS

PATRICIA FINDLAY

CHALLENGING SCOTTISH
BUSINESS AND TRADE
UNIONS

It is tempting to suggest that Holyrood will have very little effect on the relationship between employers and employees in Scotland. A key area of public policy, it will continue to be determined by Westminster and Brussels. All legislation directly relating to employment and industrial relations is a matter reserved for the UK Government, albeit shaped in important respects by EU law and policy. In addition, many other policy areas crucial to the context and conduct of employee relations will continue to be decided at UK and European level, such as fiscal, economic and monetary policy, as well as business regulation and competition policy. Thus, many fundamental issues in employee relations will remain beyond the remit of the Scottish Parliament.

However, it would be inaccurate to focus wholly on external drivers. The broader responsibilities of the Scottish Parliament for economic, industrial, education and training policy within the Westminster-established framework clearly includes a role for Scottish policy-makers in influencing employer-employee relations. The Scottish Executive can encourage, rather than prohibit or regulate, particular practices in Scottish industry, and it is its stated intention to do so in extensive consultation with employers and trade unions. A re-appraisal of this crucial area of Scottish life is, therefore, timely.

There is one direction to which Scottish employers and employees might be encouraged to turn. The process of establishing the new Parliament has stimulated debates on forms of governance in Scottish society and institutions. There is a strong case for extending the debate to the issue of workplace governance. Encouraging Scottish citizens to involve themselves more in the governance of national and local institutions will sit uneasily with conventional approaches to workplace governance. The responsibility for developing and encouraging new forms of workplace governance is not solely in the hands of politicians at Westminster and Brussels; it lies within the remit of an active and innovative alliance of Scottish policy-makers, employers, trade unions and employees.

Governance in the Workplace

Discussions of workplace governance are being informed by a number of distinct debates. Consideration of the much cited, if less clearly specified 'Third Way' and the extension of democratic principles within advanced economies, has emphasised citizenship and governance. Yet, many of these accounts do not explicitly examine citizenship from an industrial perspective (Undy, 1999). Important lessons can be learned, however, from the work-related policies and practices of social democratic governments within Europe which pursue greater social justice and more active forms of social partnership. There is also a clear recognition by the EU that an organised accommodation of the different interests of employers and employees should form the basis for regulating the employment relationship.

Recently, these ideas have converged with a more avowedly business-driven case for reviewing workplace governance. In both the UK and US, innovation in workplace social relations has been sought as a route to enhanced organisational performance. Many of these initiatives are focused on transforming work organisation. More integrated accounts address the need to link change in work organisation and task level participation to transformation of the employment relationship and workplace governance. Two important, and often linked, directions of organisational restructuring appear to be crucial to sustaining change. Firstly, the emphasis is on policies aimed at generating mutual gains or gain-sharing for management and employees, such as employment security guarantees, incentive based pay systems, increased investment in employee training and development, and extensive financial participation. Secondly, there are policies which focus upon the benefits of shared decision-making, on developing and extending collaborative, constructive forms of governance based on partnership between key organisational actors. Much is claimed in terms of the business benefits of partnership in particular. Yet there is little hard research evidence on what constitutes 'partnership', on the operation of partnership arrangements, and on the complexities of managing innovation in organisational decision-making (for exceptions see Findlay *et al.*, 1999; Marks *et al.*, 1998). Nevertheless, the promotion of partnership is a clear objective of the UK Government, and there are huge expectations that it will result in what Tony Blair has stated will be 'nothing less than [a] change to the culture of relations in and at work' (DTI, 1998: 2).

Developments in Scotland

An industrial relations settlement is already in place in the UK. Since 1997, measures have been introduced aimed at expanding individual rights and protection in the workplace. Most significantly, the passing of the Employment Relations Act in July 1999 will institute significant changes in employment law in terms of individual and collective rights and responsibilities. Its aim is to 'replace the notion of conflict between employers and employees with the promotion of partnership' (Blair in DTI, 1998a: 1). The legislation will not only compel reluctant employers to recognise trade unions for bargaining purposes; it will also impose a bargain upon them if they and their employees are unable to agree one. Through a Partnership fund, it will also commit government resources to the training of managers and employee representatives in developing partnership. The aim is to link economic competitiveness and growth with fairness and opportunity in the workplace.

Clearly, within the remit of the Scottish Parliament, there is no room for legislative departure from this framework. At this stage, however, the legislation is only a set of aspirations — it has to be made effective in the Scottish context and the changes desired by Blair are to go far wider than the legislative. Certainly, it is capable of generating widely differing outcomes. Whilst the various objectives behind the legislation are clear, the ease with which they sit alongside one another is less so. Rather than representing a unilinear trajectory from non-unionism to union recognition to union-based partnership, the provisions aim at distinct scenarios. Intuitively, it is unlikely that employers who resist or who are compelled into union recognition will be the most supportive of expanding employee opportunities in workplace governance. Neither should the potentially negative impact on employees of a hard fought and contested recognition campaign be underestimated. In this regard, the legislation appears to provide a 'carrot' for companies willing to enter into joint arrangements with their employees, and a 'stick' with which to compel employers unwilling to recognise employee rights in important decision-making spheres.

Yet a more complex range of outcomes is possible. Firstly, partnership arrangements could be instituted directly with employees and without trade union recognition, and many non-union companies claim to endorse such an approach, further claiming that their progressive and co-operative approach eliminates the need for trade unions. For these companies, developments in either or both union recognition and partnership might be on the agenda. Secondly, for companies who have, or achieve, union recognition, partnership may represent a progression from traditional bargaining agendas.

The point can be made more forcefully in the context of one of Scotland's key industries. The Scottish economy's dependence on foreign inward investment is typified by the electronics industry. The increment in real GDP gained through electronics in the 1990s outstrips that achieved by Scottish shipbuilding at its peak, and output in electronics is greater than traditional engineering ever was (Gibson and Botham, 1999). The industry is the largest manufacturing exporter from Scotland and is regarded as an important employer. It is, however, notorious for its non-union profile (Findlay, 1993). Non-unionism in part reflects the profile of segments of the industry worldwide (for example, semi-conductor production), but also reflects a deep ideological attachment to non-unionism within an institutional framework that has not challenged such a stance. There are long-standing concerns that the sector's non-union profile has been actively used to sell Scotland as a location for inward investment. Yet non-unionism takes two quite distinctive forms in the industry. On the one hand, some firms follow a policy of sophisticated paternalism, claiming leading edge employment policies, and arguing that they have developed effective employee representation in decision-making. These companies may wish to resist union recognition, but might still take advantage of moves towards partnership. However, there are concerns over the effectiveness of collective employee voice mechanisms which are not union-based (Findlay, 1992). Other firms in the sector are more overtly hostile to trade unionism, and are likely to provide some of the most orchestrated and vociferous anti-union campaigns. A statutory right to recognition in itself cannot create constructive employee relations — as the US illustrates.

What is required is an institutional framework and approach that deters employers from anti-unionism, which encourages trade unions to think imaginatively and constructively about their members' interest, and which actively promotes the extension of partnership. Public agencies, and Scottish Enterprise in particular, should be at the forefront of initiatives to link best practice criteria in employee relations to the provision of public funding for investment. This instrumentalism, more than any exhortation, is an avenue to real change in management attitudes.

The legislative framework not only creates scope for companies to position themselves in very different ways, it also creates a strategic tension for trade unions. While the provisions on partnership training encourage a co-operative role for unions, the statutory recognition procedures will stimulate a more active organising, and potentially confrontational, role for them. Relationships formed in the context of a bruising recognition campaign will take a long time to heal, and partnership is unlikely to arise out of strong employer resistance to recognition.

What is more significant from a Scottish dimension is the opportunity to use the legislation to change the culture of the workplace, and to convey and disseminate an alternative set of workplace values. The legislation has considerable symbolic importance, signaling the value placed on constructing collaborative and productive workplace relationships. Its coincidental timing with the establishment of the Parliament is fortuitous and has presented important opportunities to establish a distinctively Scottish approach. The size of the political, business and trade union community in Scotland facilitates close contacts at senior levels, aiding the dissemination of innovative ideas on governance. Both Scotland's industrial and trade union history, and successive opinion polls suggest that reforms to workplace governance would fall on receptive ears. Similarly, the disaffection of Scottish employees with the highly individualist orientation of current management practice (Millar and Donaldson, 1999), and their concerns regarding poor relationships between trade unions and employers highlighted in the 7th Annual Dibbs, Lupton and Allsop Survey (Rogers, 1999) suggest the appropriateness of a uniquely Scottish solution based on collective rights, rather than the wholesale adoption of US, and ultimately inappropriate, individualist management approaches.

The enticing language of partnership should not blind us to the very real conflicts of interests within the workplace. Capitalism will not support a partnership of equals. What partnership signifies in this context is a real expansion in the role of employees and trade unions in organisational decision-making beyond more traditional bargaining agendas. Partnership cannot be half-hearted with weak initiatives in employee involvement (Cully, et al., 1998), and the rhetoric of stake-holding alongside management unilateralism fools no-one. Effective forms of joint decision-making have much to offer the business community, but also demand much from them. Real extensions in governance will stretch managers beyond their comfort zones and challenge many of their cherished organising principles.

A statutory right to recognition and government endorsement of partnership offers hope to the trade union movement after two decades of membership decline. Yet we must remember that the primary aim is enhanced economic performance. Thus, new demands will continue to be made of trade unions. Unions have done much to re-shape themselves to new priorities. Traditional bargaining agendas have been expanded to include demands such as life long learning and work-life balance. Of more interest to the business community, trade unions and their members are increasingly knowledgeable about competitive realities, and productivity/efficiency considerations are real issues for their members. Unions have been willing to accept innovation in return for basic minimum standards and greater employment security. Clearly, Scottish trade unions will have to balance the often conflicting demands of aggressively campaigning, organising and confronting employers with attempts to develop bargaining relationships and, ultimately, forms of partnership with them.

Partnership raises many long-standing controversies about the nature of trade unionism. It is important to unions and to employers that partnership does not become equated with company unionism. Yet the line between company unionism and an innovative coalition with employers involving a mutual gains agenda will be difficult to draw. While it is important that unions show leadership to their members, it is in no-one's interest for them to identify too closely with managerial agendas legitimately opposed by employees.

A number of Scottish-based companies and trade unions are at the forefront of developing forms of partnership, most notably in the spirits sector. The economic and cultural significance of the spirits industry in Scotland is undoubted. It is consistently one of the UK's top five export earners, and is second only to electronics in terms of manufacturing exports from Scotland. It may be more significant than electronics in terms of its forward and backward linkages, creating 10,000 direct jobs and approximately 30,000 indirect jobs in Scotland (Danson and Whittam, 1999).

A number of companies in this traditional and highly unionised industry have responded innovatively to the continuing challenge of labour utilisation. Born out of company restructuring and concerns over long-term effectiveness, companies such as UDV (formerly United Distillers) and ADL have established, through negotiated processes, new types of relationship with their employees. The companies have experimented with new forms of work organisation, including greater task-level participation and decision-making, skill development programmes, expanded mechanisms for consultation and involvement at site level, streamlined approaches to pay and grading, and employee development initiatives. UDV's Leven plant was awarded Britain's Best Factory award in 1997 for its approach to work restructuring, instituting team-working, developing formal initiatives in partnership, and, of huge significance, investing in employee learning and development. Whilst examples of innovation in governance exist outside of the sector (for example, participation councils at Scottish Power offer opportunities for systematic involvement in workplace governance to its employees), the spirits industry has achieved an important profile in this regard.

These companies represent a combination of far sighted senior management and trade union officers who have been willing not only to consider new arrangements, but also to risk the scepticism of their peers, who argue that their stance risks either undue encroachment on managerial prerogative, or significant incorporation of unions. There are a number of senior managers and union officers operating in Scotland who have extensive experience in negotiating and managing partnership arrangements, and who are willing to promote the cause of partnership jointly as an example for other companies.

Delivering Partnership

The key question is what partnership produces. This is a difficult question to answer, given that the practical reality of reaching partnership agreements often requires a package of change, containing both significant re-constituting of work and of contracts, and elements of gain-sharing.

For companies, the primary driver towards partnership arrangements is obtaining employee co-operation in major change. Often, significant productivity improvements have accompanied the package of changes. Managers openly acknowledge the relevance of trade union and employee voice in decision-making. Being at the forefront of partnership initiatives has generated important public relations advantages, and much interest by policy-makers and by other companies. However, these agreements undoubtedly restrict managerial options, and challenge managerial views on their own roles, and the role of trade unions.

Trade unions, for their part, gain an opportunity to participate actively at the highest organisational levels, and to make advances towards long-established objectives, such as greater training investment and employment security. Importantly, they also gain in terms of institutional security for the union. For these reasons, there is strong support at officer level in Scotland for partnership agreements. This support is tempered, however, by perennial fears of incorporation and loss of independence, and by concerns at being outmaneuvered by management. For unions, the biggest concern relates to the role of workplace representatives. Whilst strategic level involvement guarantees the position of officers, and the expansions of lower level governance structures gives individual employees more direct access to decision-making, the impact on shop stewards is questionable. There are concerns that workplace representatives are being squeezed out at a time when they are most needed to mediate between levels of interest.

Partnership must be more than a formal agreement between senior managers and union officials — the major issue for unions, and also for managers, is to develop new and effective roles for workplace representatives, and equip them with the appropriate skills and abilities to make partnership work at the level of the shop or office floor. Some steps have been taken in this area (Millar and Donaldson, 1999). Greater public involvement in training for workplace representation could only assist, not only in developing workplace competencies, but also in developing a culture of active participation in Scottish society.

For most employees involved in partnership arrangements, the single most important gain is employment security. The attraction of greater training and development should also not be under-estimated, likewise increased task participation. Employees in this context are becoming increasingly aware of competitive realities, a development which challenges their managers as much as their union officers. In companies where partnership is at its most robust, it is clear that moves in this direction are often contentious. In a survey of two companies (Findlay *et al.*, 1999) employees agreed that moves towards partnership were, in principle, in the best interest of employees, and that unions should be involved in making companies more successful. However, there was a clear expectation/reality gap, with consequent implications for both managers and unions. Despite significant improvements in most indicators of organisational performance, employees believed that employee relations were worse than before and that actual moves towards partnership were limited. The language of partnership had advanced employee expectations more quickly than management's ability to respond to them. Employees were also concerned over the extent to which unions represented their views, and on whether unions were the best representatives of their interests. Yet this arose not from disaffection with trade unions in general, but from concern that developments in partnership were causally related to declining union power. Employees across the board believed that both union officers and shop stewards should be more influential than they were. A real concern remains that the consequence of shifting patterns of governance will be to squeeze out shop floor activism at a crucial time when developing more effective workplace representation might lead to a real and sustainable industrial settlement. The decline of workplace representation risks a gap opening up between members and the union as an active presence in the workplace.

There are important opportunities for public policy in Scotland to support the development of partnerships. But real partnership is not an easy option for either employers or unions. New formal mechanisms of workplace governance can add up to something or nothing, and workplace actors themselves will have very different definitions and expectations of partnership. Establishing effective and sustainable employee and union involvement in workplace governance is an attractive goal in terms of organisational effectiveness, the experience of work, and developing both an enthusiasm for, and an aptitude in, active participation itself. It will, however, pose major challenges to employers, trade unions and employees. This is an important time for Scottish employers and employees. While increasing trade union recognition has an important role to play in guaranteeing minimum standards and terms and conditions, rising to the challenge of new competitive, political and social aspirations will require from all parties considerable open mindedness, risk-taking, and perseverance. Partnership is only as strong as the weakest partner, and it is only as effective as the outcomes it produces.

CHAPTER 10

BRINGING WOMEN INTO BUSINESS

SARA CARTER AND
ELEANOR SHAW

Introduction

Over the past twenty years, entrepreneurship has become a central theme in the economic policies of all developed economies. In this respect, a prosperous and expanding small firms sector is considered vital, not only for employment and wealth creation, but also for innovation and technological development and the creation of new markets. In comparison with the rest of the United Kingdom, Scotland's economy is hampered both by low rates of new firm formation and the low rates of growth in existing firms.

A key element in strategies to expand the small firms sector has been the encouragement of entrepreneurial activities within groups not traditionally associated with small business ownership (Scottish Enterprise, 1996). The importance of women as a largely untapped pool of entrepreneurial talent has been widely recognised by economic development agencies. Yet, despite a broad awareness of the economic importance of women's business ownership and a number of initiatives designed to stimulate female self-employment, relatively few women are becoming entrepreneurs. Moreover, women starting in business have markedly different experiences of business ownership than men. In comparison with male-owned firms, female businesses are both financially under-capitalised and also suffer from poorer access to human and social capital. A growing weight of evidence suggests that these differences not only amount to discrimination on the basis of gender, but that these differences considerably undermine economic development at a national level.

This chapter starts by outlining the current trends in women's business ownership activities in Scotland, before discussing the experiences of women in business. The need to both encourage more women into business and improve the experience of female entrepreneurship impacts on both social and economic policy. The chapter concludes by arguing that removing gender inequalities in entrepreneurship would not only lead to a fairer society, it would also provide Scotland with a stronger and more dynamic economic base.

Women in Business in Scotland

Since 1979, there has been a dramatic growth in the number of women entering self-employment in the UK. Between 1979 and 1997, the number of women entering self-employment increased by 163 per cent, from 319,000 to 840,000 in 1997. In the same period, the number of self employed males increased by 67 per cent, from 1,449,000 to 2,421,000 (Labour Force Survey, 1997). The rate of female self-employment has increased to a lesser extent, however, from approximately 3.1 per cent of total females economically active in 1979 to 6.8 per cent in 1997. During the same period, the rate of male self-employment increased from 9.2 per cent of total males economically active in 1979 to 15.4 per cent in 1997.

In Scotland, the growth in female self-employment has been modest in comparison with the UK as a whole. Between 1990 and 1999, the number of self-employed women in Scotland increased by 6,830, from 47,957 in 1990 to 54,787 in 1999 (Table 1). Female share of self-employment has also increased, but by a relatively modest proportion. In 1990, female share of self-employment was 23.1 per cent. By 1999, this had increased to 25.7 per cent. During the same period, male self-employment in Scotland also demonstrated marked fluctuations, and actually ended the decade with an overall decline in numbers, compared with 1990. This, however, is the only year of the ten-year period when male self-employment dipped below the

Table 1   Self-employment in Scotland by gender 1990–1999

Year	Total Self-employed	Male Self-employed	Female Self-employed	Female Self-employment as % of total
1990	207777	159820	47957	23.08
1991	223851	173798	50054	22.36
1992	216373	171447	44927	20.76
1993	217708	160737	56971	26.16
1994	225216	166764	58452	25.95
1995	234630	174133	60497	25.78
1996	224997	161394	63603	28.26
1997	230915	168146	62769	27.18
1998	233883	172042	61842	26.44
1999	212888	158100	54787	25.73

Source: Labour Force Survey Quarterly Bulletin (1990-1999).

1990 base. Although the figures do not indicate consistent growth in male self-employment over the decade, in every other year there has been a growth over the 1990 base, and figures in excess of 170,000 in four years (1991, 1992, 1995, 1998) (Table 1).

Despite some growth in the numbers of female self-employment in Scotland over the past decade, female participation in enterprise is still low. These figures are particularly disappointing, given the range of current factors and trends expected to stimulate female entrepreneurial activity. The growth in the number of working women; unprecedented levels of female rates of remuneration; an overall expansion in the services sectors; the fragmentation and growth of local markets; the increase in 'feminised' markets; and the development and diffusion of home-based communications technologies — all appear to have had little impact on rates of female self-employment.

Women's Experience of Business Ownership

While the numbers of women starting in business is critical to the future development of the Scottish economy, statistical analysis of national trends offers only a partial insight into the problem. Of equal importance is the actual experiences of women starting and managing their own enterprises. Prior to the mid-1980s, the contribution women made to the small firms sector either as business owners in their own right, or more commonly as providers of labour to family owned firms, was largely unrecognised by academics and policy-makers alike. The growth in interest in the small business sector, coupled with a rise in the number of women moving into self-employment, triggered a number of important research studies investigating the issue of gender and enterprise. Despite this research re-orientation, research investigating female experiences of entrepreneurship is still scarce in comparison with the volume of work concentrating on the male-owned enterprise.

Early, exploratory studies of female entrepreneurship concentrated mainly upon the motivations for business start up and the gender-related barriers experienced during this phase of business ownership (Watkins and Watkins, 1984; Goffee and Scase, 1985). Overall, these studies presented a prima facie picture of businesswomen with more similarities than differences to their male counterparts. Like men, the most frequently cited reason for starting in business was the search for independence and control over one's destiny. The greatest barriers to business formation were difficulties in accessing capital and other start up resources. A key difference was found to be the sectors in which female-owned businesses operated. Studies found that female self-employment was largely confined to sectors, such as services and retailing, with a high concentration of female employment. The greatest barriers to business success were perceived to be financial discrimination and under-capitalisation, and a lack of training and business experience. Few of the early studies developed sophisticated taxonomies, preferring to identify female proprietors as a homogenous group, and there was an implicit acceptance that, beyond the start-up phase, few significant differences existed between male and female-owned companies.

More recent studies have started to explore the issue of the management of female owned businesses, and the field of study has developed to encompass more sophisticated methodologies, larger scale samples and more robust sampling procedures, in particular the use of both male and female samples. Importantly, the focus of investigation has evolved to concentrate on the effect of gender on both the experience of self-employment and the relative performance of small businesses (Rosa *et al.*, 1996; Brush, 1997; Carter and Allen, 1997). As a consequence, clear and unequivocal differences are starting to be revealed in women's experience of self-employment and business ownership. Gender differences are apparent in many aspects of female entrepreneurial activity from pre-venture experience; motivations for ownership; the level of constraints in accessing finance and other resources required for start-up and business growth; the management of the on-going venture; and in the performance of female owned firms.

The financing of female owned firms

Previous studies into gender and business ownership have resulted in conflicting evidence about whether finance poses problems for women starting and managing businesses. Several studies have suggested that it is both more difficult for women to raise start up and recurrent finance for business ownership and that women encounter credibility problems when dealing with banks. Other studies have not confirmed this finding. The debate has continued largely because of the difficulties for researchers in providing clear and unequivocal evidence. Four areas of the financing process have, however, been consistently noted as posing particular problems for women. First, women may be disadvantaged in their ability to raise start up finance (Carter and Cannon, 1992; Johnson and Storey, 1993; Koper, 1993; Van Auken *et al.*, 1993). Second, guarantees required for external financing may be beyond the scope of most women's personal assets and credit track record (Hisrich and Brush, 1986; Riding and Swift, 1990). Third, finance for the ongoing business may be less available for female owned firms than it is for male enterprises, largely due to women's inability to penetrate informal financial networks (Olm *et al.*, 1988; Aldrich, 1989; Carter and Rosa, 1998).

Finally, female entrepreneurs' relationships with banks may suffer because of sexual stereotyping and discrimination (Hisrich and Brush, 1986; Buttner and Rosen, 1989).

A large scale study of 600 UK firms, 300 owned by women and 300 owned by men, which controlled for location and business sector, provided clearer answers to these four issues (Carter and Rosa, 1998). This study demonstrated that women start businesses with only one third of the amount of capital used by men. Importantly, this initial under-capitalisation had a long term and deleterious effect on the performance of the firm. This result occurred in each of the sectors studied (manufacturing, services, hotel and catering) and in each location (Glasgow and the West Midlands) and can only be seen as a fundamental gender issue. Gender differences were also apparent in the use of on-going finance. However, the study found few gender differences either in the types of guarantees requested by lenders, or in perceptions of relationships with lenders.

Other studies have extended the gender and finance debate further by considering the role of banks in providing finance to female business owners. In a development of an 'asymmetric information' approach, researchers have attempted to determine whether banks have (unstated) differential lending policies to male and female business owners and, if so, whether these policies are a result of unwitting socialisation or outright discrimination (Fay and Williams, 1993; Koper, 1993). In New Zealand, Fay and Williams found some evidence that women encounter credit discrimination in seeking start-up funding, but concluded that 'the existence of discriminatory behaviour as a consequence of prejudice and stereotyping can be demonstrated only when all relevant factors up to the point of loan application have been equalised' (p.365). Researchers of female entrepreneurship are still a long way from being able to control factors so precisely. As a consequence, firm conclusions cannot be made.

Networks and female owned firms

Research that has investigated the management of female owned enterprises has often alluded to the important role of networks in the survival and success of individual firms (Carter and Cannon, 1992; Rosa and Hamilton, 1994). Gender differences in the way networks are created and used have been cited as having an influence on certain aspects of the management process, for example, enabling improved access to finance and the development of strong relationships with financial backers (Carter and Rosa, 1998). Some have suggested that distinct gender differences might exist both in the establishment and management of social networks (that is, the process of networking) and in the contents of social networks (that is, for what networks are used) (Olm et al., 1988; Aldrich, 1989).

The influence of gender on the networking activities of business owners has been subject to very little dedicated investigation, and remains a highly contentious issue. Not only is there debate regarding the relative influence of networking activities on the performance of small firms generally and on female owned firms in particular, researchers have yet to even conceptualise an appropriate starting hypotheses for research. Irrespective of the research issues, it is clear that profound gender differences exist. As Brush (1997: 22) concluded 'women are less welcome in social networks...and are left out of some of those loops, meaning they do not have access to as much information. So social structures and the way that women socialise influence the human and social capital endowments with which they start their businesses'.

The performance of female owned firms

Although many studies have made some mention of gender and business performance, most shy away from direct examination of quantitative performance measures, preferring instead to engage in discursive debate concerning gender differences in qualitative assessments of success. Overall, studies suggest that the determinants of performance (that is, the measures that are used by owners to assess their business performance) are similar by gender. Contrary to many of the earlier studies of gender and entrepreneurship, there is no evidence to suggest that men are more profit orientated than women, or less likely to value intrinsic goals. There are, however, significant differences in the performance of male and female-owned firms.

In a longitudinal study of 298 UK businesses, Johnson and Storey (1993) found that the 67 women proprietors in their study had created more stable enterprises than had their male sample, although on average the sales turnover for women was lower than for males. A more recent study of 600 UK firms (Rosa *et al.*, 1996) found that female owned firms substantially under-performed in comparison with male owned enterprises. Women's businesses employed fewer core staff, were less likely to have grown substantially in employment (more than 20 employees) after twelve months in business, had a lower sales turnover, and were valued at a lower level than male owned businesses. Men were significantly more likely to own other businesses (19.6 per cent compared with 8.6 per cent) and also to have strong growth ambitions in so far as they wanted to expand their businesses 'as far as they could (43% versus 34%)' (Rosa *et al.*, 1996: 469). As Rosa *et al.* point out, however, the complexity of the overall pattern of results suggests that a more sophisticated interpretation is required than simply attributing differences to gender alone. They did, however conclude that 'If female business owners have started from a much lower tradition of achievement in business, then this trend is encouraging and may provide support...that the gender gap in the UK is narrowing' (1996: 475).

Bringing Women into Business in Scotland

As this chapter has highlighted there are two key issues related to bringing women into business in Scotland. The first is to increase the number of women starting businesses, and the second is to improve the experience of business ownership for women. Both require quite different strategies. While the Scottish Enterprise Business Birth-rate Strategy has had partial success in improving the numbers of female self-employment in Scotland, it is clear a great deal more needs to be achieved. This strategy has been unable to address the more deep-rooted discrimination that affects the experiences of women entrepreneurs.

In part, women's experience of self-employment reflects the overall position of women in the labour market. Despite the increase in both the number of working women and in the continuity of their working lives, the position of women in the labour market has remained largely unchanged since the 1950s. Most women still hold low-paid, unskilled or semi-skilled positions. Employment is often part-time and concentrated in the service sectors. Twenty-five years after equal pay legislation was introduced, women still only earn on average 70 per cent of their male counterparts. At the executive level, only ten per cent of the UK's 200 largest companies have female board members. Until these inequalities are redressed, women will continue to enter self-employment with fewer financial assets, lesser experience in management and under-resourced in terms of their human and social capital.

This chapter has identified the issues and problems for women entrepreneurs as owners and managers of small firms. These issues and problems need to be addressed if the potential of Scottish women in business is to be tapped, with positive social and economic consequences for Scotland. For many, a modernised Scotland with legislative powers implies an opportunity to create a more equal society. In considering the position of women both in the labour market and in business ownership, creating a more equal society carries with it a promise of greater economic strength, prosperity and growth. By encouraging more women to identify business ownership as a viable career option and using Scotland's legislative powers to improve women's' experiences of business ownership, Scotland as a nation will benefit. By addressing these issues, Scotland's business base and social and economic environment will benefit from the sustainable employment offered by women-owned small firms. Moreover, by recognising that women's' experiences of self-employment and business ownership are fundamentally different from their male counterparts, Scotland will benefit from the opportunities which an expansion of the service sector, growth of local and 'feminised' markets and diffusion of home-based technologies have offered to women world wide.

To achieve this, a number of recommendations for policymakers, the Scottish banking industry, the Scottish Enterprise Network and the Scottish education system can be suggested. Using the legislative powers available to it, the Scottish Parliament should address the unequivocal gender differences described above and the subsequent discrimination faced by women considering and involved in self-employment and business ownership. In particular the Scottish Parliament should seek to introduce affirmative action approaches that have been so successfully deployed in the US. Related to this point British banks should be encouraged to recognise that as the financial history of self-employed women and business owners differs from that of their male counterparts, they are discriminated against when evaluated against traditional credit scoring measurements and that a more equitable credit scoring system should be introduced. Also, working with Scottish Enterprise, Scottish banks should make women aware of the implications that a smaller financial investment at start-up will have upon the future growth potential of their firms. Specifically, women should be encouraged to build their businesses from a higher capital base. For the purposes of accessing resources such as capital, information and advice, found to be contained within informal, social networks (Shaw, 1997), Scottish Enterprise should consider implementing mechanisms which will help women access and make best use of these networks as well as introduce initiatives which encourage women to develop their networking competencies. Finally, to ensure the future health of a progressive and modern nation, the impact which education can have upon men and women's perceptions of self-employment and business ownership should be investigated in order to ascertain the steps required to encourage the cultural and societal changes necessary if greater numbers of women are to enter self employment and business ownership.

CHAPTER 11

SCOTLAND'S PUBLIC FINANCES

GAVIN MCCRONE

The financial arrangements for the Scottish Parliament have to be seen to be fair, not only in Scotland but in the rest of the UK as well, if they are to prove long-lasting; and they must be sufficiently flexible for the new administration to decide its own priorities. At the moment they are not regarded as fair by an increasing number of people in England and Wales and attempts to make them so could create serious difficulties in Scotland as well as constraining the Scottish Parliament's freedom to set its priorities.

The White Paper on Scotland's Parliament said that existing arrangements would continue with only minor adjustment (Scottish Office, 1997). The Scottish Office would get the bulk of its public expenditure from the UK Exchequer in a block, and annual changes to this block would continue to be determined by the formula, known as the Barnett formula[1] which had been in operation since 1979. This formula has been widely misunderstood and has become invested with an air of mystery. But essentially this situation means that, while the Scottish Parliament is free to set its own priorities, the funding available from changes in the block will be related to changes in comparable services in England. If more or less is spent on a particular service in England there will be financial consequences for Scotland whether or not the Scottish administration has similar priorities.

The Scottish Parliament also has power to vary the basic rate of income tax by up to three pence in the pound. As a result of changes in the 1999 budget, one pence will now yield £230 million, giving a maximum of £690 million, roughly five per cent of the £13.8 billion block expenditure in 1996/97. In that year the Secretary of State's total expenditure, including block and non-block programmes, amounted to £14.9 billion and all locally identifiable expenditure in Scotland, including social security, for which the Secretary of State was not responsible and is not devolved to the Parliament, amounted to £24.7 billion (Scottish Office, 1998).

The key feature of Scotland's public finances is that locally identifiable expenditure per head is substantially higher than in England — 19 per cent above the UK average in 1996/97 and 24 per cent above the English level (Table 1). In an article published by the Fraser of Allander Institute, I examined Scotland's public finances since 1889 and showed that this has been the position for a great many years (McCrone, 1999). From the last decade of the nineteenth century, when the earlier Goschen formula for distributing resources was adopted, up to the 1920s, Scotland's contribution to UK revenue and its share of locally identifiable expenditure were both broadly equal to its population proportion. England contributed more in revenue than its population share and received a lower proportion of local expenditure, while Ireland (the whole of Ireland being then in the UK) contributed less in revenue and received more in expenditure. Since the 1930s, however, Scotland's identifiable expenditure per head has generally been some 15 to 25 per cent above the average for the UK and above England's level by slightly more (Table 1).

For many years differences in public expenditure levels between the countries and regions of the UK went largely unnoticed. Indeed statistics showing these differences were not readily available, and for the English regions they are still less comprehensive than for the four constituent countries. More recently, however, the position has become much better known. As awareness of the situation has grown, Scotland's higher level of public expenditure has attracted increasing attention in England; criticism has focussed, wrongly in my opinion, on the Barnett formula, and there have been increasingly strident

Table 1   Scottish identifiable public expenditure (per head)

Year	UK =100	England = 100
1986/87	122	128
1987/88	124	130
1888/89	123	130
1989/90	119	124
1990/91	118	123
1991/92	114	118
1992/93	118	123
1993/94	119	124
1994/95	120	125
1995/96	120	125
1996/97	119	124

Note: because of differences in definition figures for the first three years are not exactly comparable with other years and may be one or two per cent too high.

Source: The Scottish Office (1988-1998 editions) Government Expenditure and Revenue in Scotland.

demands for change, demands that have been supported by Lord Barnett himself.

There are of course some good reasons for Scotland's expenditure per head to be higher than England's; and there are wide variations also not only between the other countries of the UK but between the regions of England as well. Public expenditure is intended to provide broadly comparable levels of service throughout the UK, and both needs and the costs of providing those services vary from area to area.

With about a third of the UK land area Scotland has only 8.6 per cent of the UK population. The cost of providing services in sparsely populated areas is inevitably much higher: doctors lists, hospitals and school class sizes in such areas are smaller; the cost of road maintenance is higher; housing and many other local authority services are more expensive[2]. Furthermore, Scotland has a particularly poor health record; a high proportion of agriculture is in upland areas with adverse climate and topography; and more has had to be spent on economic development. But there are also services provided in Scotland, unrelated to Scottish needs, which serve the needs of other

Table 2   Scottish identifiable public expenditure per head excluding social security and agriculture, fishing, food and forestry

Year	UK = 100	England = 100
1986/87	132	141
1987/88	139	142
1988/89	139	142
1989/90	129	137
1990/91	127	134
1991/92	119	125
1992/93	123	128
1993/94	126	132
1994/95	126	132
1995/96	127	133
1996/97	124	130

Source: HM Treasury (1988–1998) Public Expenditure Statistical Analyses.

parts of the UK: in addition to their Scottish students, the medical schools, veterinary colleges and universities all have large numbers of students from south of the border.

But while justifications can be found, it is impossible to say if Scotland's higher expenditure levels accurately reflect need. And the arrangements that apply under devolution are not designed to take account of need. Contrary to what is often believed, the Barnett formula does not do so; it was never intended to be more than a population-based ratio. Rather than relate Scotland's expenditure to needs, it should therefore produce gradual convergence between English and Scottish expenditure levels.

The gap between Scottish and English identifiable expenditure per head applies in some measure to all programmes (Table 2). It is, however, negligible in law and order and less than ten per cent in social security and culture, media and sport; it is largest, perhaps not surprisingly, in agriculture, fisheries and forestry (85 per cent) and housing (62 per cent); and in the two largest programmes within the block — health and education, which make up some 65 per cent of the block total — it is 19 per cent and 26 per cent respectively.

Overall (as Table 1 shows) the gap between Scottish and English identifiable expenditure has fallen from a peak of 30 per cent in the late 1980s to 24 per cent in 1996/97, but there has been little change throughout most of the 1990s. These figures might suggest that a Scottish Parliament would have little to worry about. But the Barnett formula only applies to the 56 per cent of identifiable expenditure that comprises the block. If agriculture and social security, the main non-block programmes, are subtracted, the gap in the remainder is larger (because it is relatively small in social security) but convergence is more marked, the gap falling from 41 to 32 per cent over the same period (see Table 3 below). There has therefore been convergence in the block programmes which has been partially masked by the large expenditure on social security, a programme for which the Parliament is not be responsible.

Nevertheless it is surprising that the difference has not narrowed more with a formula that is based on a population ratio. In part this is because the formula was only revised once — in 1992 (the so-called Portillo recalibration) — to take account of the changed population ratio, although Scotland's population has continued to decline as a proportion of the UK. It became progressively out of

Table 3 **Scottish identifiable expenditure by programme (1996/97)**

	£ million	per head (UK = 100)
Agriculture, fisheries, food, forestry	751	185
Trade, industry, energy, employment	869	139
Transport	1,022	127
Housing	575	162
Other environmental services	1,249	144
Law, order, protective services	1,450	101
Education	4,026	126
Culture, media, sport	267	103
Health and personal social services	5,225	119
Social Security	9,142	109
Miscellaneous	172	—
TOTAL	24,748	119

Source: The Scottish Office (1998) Government Expenditure and Revenue in Scotland.

date therefore. But the major factor seems to have been the successful advocacy by successive Secretaries of State of what were regarded as particularly compelling needs; this action resulted in the formula occasionally being bypassed.

It would be unwise to count on Secretaries of State to continue this circumvention in the future. Under pressure from English MPs the Government have now given a commitment to adjust the formula annually in line with population. And as for bypassing the formula because of special needs, no doubt this will be attempted, but devolution will make this a much more transparent negotiation than it has been in the past. Not only will it now take place between different governments but also at some stage it is likely to be between Ministers of different political persuasions with less sympathy for each other's case than ever applied under the old system.

The outlook is therefore not reassuring. Even if the block, adjusted by the Barnett formula, can provide a reasonable interim arrangement so long as there is the goodwill to make it work, in the longer term it threatens a continuing squeeze on Scottish public expenditure. With a higher public expenditure base, the same per head increase for Scotland as England will amount to a smaller percentage increase. And if the increase in England is only just enough to compensate for inflation, in Scotland it could amount to a cut in real terms. Any notion that the Scottish Parliament's tax power might be used to fill this hole would not only give Scotland higher rates of tax, but as the tax power at maximum is only five per cent of block expenditure it would quickly be exhausted.

Some people have suggested that the answer to this problem is for Scotland to have the responsibility to finance its expenditure out of its own tax revenue, even in the absence of independence. This would have the welcome effect of reducing the danger of contentious financial negotiations between Holyrood and Westminster. But it would only make the problem more immediate. In the latest figures Scotland accounts for 8.7 per cent of UK revenues, approximately equal to its share of population or output, as measured by GDP excluding offshore oil and gas (Scottish Office, 1998). While some of the figures have been criticised, it is difficult to argue that it should be much higher, when Scotland's GDP per head is slightly below the UK average. Scotland's identifiable expenditure, however, which makes up 75 per cent of total public expenditure, is 10.4 per cent of the UK. It is hard to dispute these figures since they are derived from the annual public expenditure survey. One therefore has to make some very extreme assumptions about the 25 per cent non-identifiable expenditure to avoid a conclusion that Scottish expenditure as a whole is a higher proportion of the UK total than revenue. Since this expenditure is for services such as defence, foreign relations and interest on the national debt, the only sensible basis on which a share can be allocated to Scotland is by using a population or GDP ratio. That leaves Scottish expenditure at 10.1 per cent of the UK.

As Table 4 indicates, adding in oil and gas revenues improves Scotland's position, but does not solve the problem. As a result of research undertaken by Professor Alex Kemp of Aberdeen, it is now possible to make an authoritative estimate of the share of these revenues that might accrue to Scotland, if the North Sea were to be divided under international rules (Kemp, 1998). Whereas these revenues were very large indeed in the early 1980s, when the oil price was high, they are much lower now and the Scottish share for 1996/97 (the latest year for which revenue and expenditure figures are available) was estimated at £2.9 billion or 80.25 per cent, bringing Scotland's total revenue to £27.6 billion compared with expenditure of £31.4 billion. This would leave a deficit of £3.8 billion or 5.8 per cent of GDP, too high to be sustainable. To have got it down to three per cent in that year (the criterion for Economic and Monetary Union), taxes would have had to be raised or public expenditure reduced by about £1.8 billion.

For the future it is essential to find a system of financing Scottish Government that is stable and fair. The key to any solution must be based on a proper assessment of need. So far the only needs assessment undertaken was in 1979 when it was conducted by the Treasury with Scottish Office participation (HM Treasury, 1979). It

Table 4   Scotland's fiscal position 1996/97

| | Expenditure | | Revenue | |
	£ bn	% UK	£ bn	% UK
Identifiable	24.7	10.4		
Income tax			5.5	8.0
Scottish Office	14.9			
Social Security			9.1	
Nat. Insurance cont.			4.2	9.0
Non-identifiable	3.1	8.7		
VAT			4.0	8.6
Defence	1.9	8.7		
Other expenditure	4.0	9.7		
Local authority taxes	2.2	9.0		
Debt Interest*	2.5	9.2		
All other revenue			8.7	9.1
Total	31.8	10.1		
Total			24.7	8.7
(Deficit exc. Oil & gas 7.1)				
Privatisation	-0.4	8.6		
Oil & gas revenue			2.9	80.25
Borrowing requirement			3.8	
(as % of GDP			5.8)	
TOTAL EXPENDITURE	31.4	10.1		
TOTAL REVENUE			31.4	10.1

*Debt interest includes apportioned interest on the National Debt at 8.6% of UK and the actual local authority debt interest at 33.1% of UK.
Source: Kemp and Stephen (1998).

found that Scotland's needs justified a level of expenditure 16 per cent above England on services then proposed for devolution. This figure was less than the difference in expenditure that existed then, or still exists now. While there are no obvious reasons for supposing that Scotland's needs justify a larger difference now, a study that is 20 years out of date can tell us little that is useful about the present situation. The recent report of the Committee on Resources in the National Health Service in Scotland does however illustrate very clearly the higher costs of providing health services in remote areas and the greater needs arising from deprivation; similar considerations no doubt apply in education and in other services.

If a needs assessment were to be done again, it should not be done internally within Government but by an independent body of the highest standing; and it should cover not just Scotland, but the other constituent countries of the UK and regions of England as well. There are major difficulties in such an exercise and some subjective judgements cannot be avoided. It is quite likely that the conclusions would be contentious and unpalatable. And if they showed that Scotland's expenditure in relation to England was higher than could be justified, a strategy would have to be found for narrowing the gap at a pace that could be tolerated.

But the alternative is surely even less attractive. The present system provides no basis for justifying differences in expenditure levels between the countries of the UK; and the continued application of a formula related to population but not to need will impose an ever-increasing squeeze in Scotland. It may in the end result in levels of expenditure below that which could be justified on need. Yet in England dissatisfaction will continue because, so long as Scotland has a higher expenditure, it will still be thought to be unjustified. This is a recipe for increasingly raucous discontent in both countries and can hardly be considered a satisfactory long-term basis for financing Scotland's new Parliament.

Endnotes

1 So named after the Labour Chief Secretary to the Treasury in the 1970s.

2 See for example Scottish Executive (1999a) Fair Shares for All, Report of a Committee on Resources in the National Health Service in Scotland chaired by Sir John Arbuthnott.

CHAPTER 12

JOHN PEARCE

THE SCOPE FOR SOCIAL ENTERPRISE

In the coalition agreement for Scotland's new government in the re-established Parliament there is a stated commitment 'to support the development of Scotland's social economy to deliver local solutions to local problems' (Dewar and Wallace, 1999). Interestingly, this statement is to be found within the section 'Building communities' and not under 'Enterprise'. Similarly many of the development agencies in Scotland fail to include, let alone target, social enterprises for mainstream business support. Indeed, there is a real lack of interest expressed by traditional business support networks for entrepreneurialism in the social economy. Thus is the division between 'social' and 'economic' perpetuated. It this orthodoxy which the social economy challenges, its very name recognising that 'social' initiatives are part of the economy, can generate wealth and create employment, and that the 'economy' cannot, indeed must not, be organised without regard to society, to community, to people and to the planet.

What then is this 'social economy' whose growth the Joint Economic Strategy for Glasgow seeks to encourage (see Patrick, 1999)? And what are 'social enterprises'? This chapter seeks to offer some working definitions, to identify some of the key contributions which social enterprises can make to local development and community-based economic success, and to suggest some ways in which the Scottish Government can offer support within a policy context of cascading power and responsibilities down to local communities in a spirit of true subsidiarity.

Defining 'Social Economy' and 'Social Enterprise'

The term 'social economy' is relatively recent to the UK and its accepted meaning is still evolving. It is usually taken to include the co-operative movement, embracing the big traditional co-operative retail and wholesale societies, the mutual assurance and building societies, the agricultural and fishing co-operatives as well as more recently established workers co-operatives and credit unions. It also includes the Community Business or Community Enterprise sector, developed since the mid-1970s, involving neighbourhood-based initiatives which combine community development with local economic development. A popular form of this type of enterprise is the Local Development Trust. The Third Sector is additionally considered to be part of the social economy, embracing those organisations which are not part of the public or private sectors and including very small community groups as well as social and sports clubs, local leisure groups as well as the major national charities. Finally, the Social Housing sector (housing co-operatives and housing associations) is one of the strongest and longest-standing sectors of the social economy.

Within the social economy, 'social enterprise' has become a generic term used for a wide range of enterprises or organisations which have a clear social purpose and are non-profit distributing. Usually, social enterprises will have a local rather than a regional or national focus and it is on those locally-focussed enterprises that this chapter concentrates.

Core Values of Social Enterprises

Although only recently termed, the origin of social enterprises can be traced back to the Rochdale Pioneers of 1844. The development of social enterprises, however, gathered pace in the 1970s with high unemployment in the UK and other advanced economies with subsequent attempts to foster job creation, the voluntary sector, and local economic and community development and regeneration that is sensitive to community needs. A further boost has occurred in the last decade with the shift by local and central government away from the grant-funding of voluntary and community organisations towards contracting them to provide services, thus increasing their trading opportunities. This arrangement has fostered the business-like behaviour of the organisations and strengthened their self-perception as community or social providers.

The European Network for Economic Self-help and Local Development (1997) identified eleven key value statements which represent a 'charter' to which social economy organisations might be expected to subscribe. Briefly, these values are; contribution to the common good; the promotion of community; co-operation; the decentralisation of decision-making; democratic governance; the safeguarding of human and ecological diversity; the undertaking of socially useful work; a holistic integration of economic, social, cultural and environmental aspects of life; being socially inclusive; being people-centred, subordinating rather than serving the interests of capital; ensuring resource sustainability. Additionally, the University of Glasgow's Training and Employment Research Unit (McGregor *et al.*, 1997) emphasises the targeting of disadvantaged sectors in society — in terms of both employment and the provision of what might be 'uneconomical' services, and the involvement of volunteers alongside paid workers.

For the purposes of the debate in Scotland we might take the term 'social enterprise' to mean all those organisations which:

- have a local rather than a regional or national focus;
- have a clear social, ethical or environmental purpose; which
- is achieved at least in part by engaging in trading and income generation;
- are generally non profit distributing; and
- hold their assets 'in trust' for community benefit;
- seek to empower the local community by holding resources under local control; and

- involve local people/their members in the governance of the organisation.

The Scope and Nature of Social Enterprises

Social enterprises in the UK are a disparate body but may be characterised by a series of 'continua' which are not mutually exclusive but more a series of 'linked paths'. There are points of intersection along these continua such that neat categorisation is difficult. However, such an approach is helpful in distinguishing the scope and nature of different social enterprises.

First, is the continuum of what might be termed a 'voluntary enterprise' through to a 'community business'. The former is based primarily on volunteer labour and operates at the local community level while the latter is likely to be staffed entirely by paid employees. Along the continuum are those enterprises which depend to an extent on the voluntary input of members, directors or staff. Examples of voluntary enterprises include food co-operatives, thrift shops and community cafes.

Second, is the continuum which runs from the organisation which receives substantial public or charitable grant-aid or other subsidy and is totally dependent on such fund-raising through to the business which is entirely self-sustaining and competes unaided in the market-place. Along this continuum are enterprises in receipt of different types and varying levels of enabling support. Such support might take the form of 'peppercorn' rent for premises, donations, 'soft' contracts as well as unpaid labour or 'sweat equity'. Also, a number of social enterprises will be 'sustained' by a combination of fund-raising sources but will operate as businesses.

Third, is the continuum which runs from those enterprises which are primarily people oriented and providing necessary services through to those which put greater emphasis on the generation of profit — that is, however, profit which will be used for the benefit of the local community.

Fourth, is the continuum which goes from very small to large enterprises. Small (or micro-enterprise) include informal enterprise endeavours in local communities which in some way generate income (or reduce the cost of living) and thereby contribute to the domestic economy of disadvantaged people. Some of these enterprises may be operating in what is sometimes termed the 'shadow economy'.

Fifth, is the continuum which runs from the informal sector of Local Exchange Trading Systems (or LETS) and barter through to the formal part of the economy based on the exchange of money for goods and services.

Social enterprises are involved in a wide range of activities; services and manufacturing, finance and insurance, wholesale and retail, housing and community care, property development, import and export, mining, agriculture and fishing. Significantly, it is now possible to discern those activities to which social enterprises are suited and in which they are beginning to establish a strong track record. The New Economics Foundation (1998) identifies eight growth sectors in the UK social economy; care; energy and environment; micro-finance; ethical retailing; social housing; contracted-out public services; agriculture; new technology.

Hitherto associated with economic failure and social disadvantage or marginalisation, this emerging track record suggests that social enterprises might have a successful and positive contribution to make to the Scottish economy and society as a whole. Pearce (1993) has attempted to identify those activities at which social enterprises excel, listing eleven specific activities:

1. Creating infrastructure — facilitating enterprise (for example, managed workspace; self-employment advice; secondary marketing initiatives such as an organic veggie box schemes; visitor centres which attract people to use other local facilities; multi-functional community centres).
2. Care services (for example, child care; domiciliary care; homes for the elderly).
3. Commercial community services (for example, neighbourhood shop; community café; thrift shop; community transport).
4. Contracted community services (for example, estate maintenance; security; cleaning; graffiti removal; managing

swimming pools; managing leisure and recreation services; multi-functional community centres).

5. Job creation for the disadvantaged (for example, the disabled; the mentally ill; offenders; the long-term unemployed; using programmes such as 'intermediate labour market' or 'salaried training', 'New Deal' etc.).

6. Training programmes for example, self-employment; IT skills; life skills etc.).

7. Environmental action (for example, waste minimisation and management; recycling; composting; community gardens; city farms; energy efficiency).

8. Area development/renewal (including property management).

9. Running community service schemes and managing community projects.

10. Financial services (for example, credit unions).

11. Housing services (for example, housing co-ops; community based housing associations; 'foyer' projects).

It may be usual for a number of social enterprises to engage in more than one of these activities, for example, The Wise Group in Glasgow with energy, and training and work experience. Importantly, such combinations are what can make this sector distinctive and important, as private sector companies are unwilling to engage with such a complicated income generating area. For example, trying to match funding from different EU programmes with the New Deal initiative and council grants, alongside a tendered contract for a service which has to meet strict recruitment and selection criteria.

From the list it is also possible to suggest that social enterprises are likely to be engaged in activities which:

- provide infrastructure and services to make it easier for others to create small enterprises or establish income-generating projects;
- provide commercial and community services which meet important and immediate local needs;
- engage in trading activities from which the private sector

may have withdrawn and which are often not highly
profitable;

- undertake to provide some of the services which in the past
  have been part of public sector provision – 'communitisation'
  rather than privatisation;

- are labour-intensive, creating work particularly for people
  with few skills or other disadvantages;

- use local people to do local work; and

- are likely often to be multi-functional — that is, to engage in
  a mix of activities, some more commercial than others.

The Scale and Success of Social Enterprises in Scotland

Scotland has a long tradition of encouraging the development
of social enterprises. Glasgow was the home of the first community-
based housing associations in the early 1970s. In 1976 the former
Highlands and Islands Development Agency launched its scheme to
develop co-operatives as a means of stimulating local, community-
led economic activity. Later Strathclyde and other regional councils
followed, establishing units to promote and support community
business. The legacy of successes provides examples of what is
possible.

Clark and McGregor (1997) demonstrate that community
businesses have been successful, and cost-effective, in creating real
work opportunities for long-term unemployed people (especially
males) and in enabling the long-term unemployed to return
successfully to the wider labour market after working for the
community business. This research also signalled the importance of
evaluating such businesses not only in terms of their business results
but also in terms of their social value.

The successes include Govan Workspace, first established in
1981 to create managed workspace for small businesses — at that
time a radical idea, especially in its use of a former primary school.
Now with three properties, consistently let and profitable, Govan
Workspace can look back on having made a solid contribution to
reviving the economy of Govan and ahead to what it can do with the

surplus it is generating.

The Queens Cross Group includes a community-based housing association with a large portfolio of properties and continually engaged in new developments close to the heart of the city of Glasgow. Queens Cross Workspace develops and manages workshops and commercial properties for small business. Add to this activity programmes and projects to provide training, to provide care and support for the vulnerable and disadvantaged and there exists in Glasgow an example of a true, multi-functional, social enterprise.

Elsewhere, the community co-operative in Appin runs the local store and petrol station and has developed social housing for the elderly. In Papa Westray the co-operative runs the island store, the guest house and youth hostel and promotes tourism to the island. In West Ardnamurchan, the Kilchoan Community Centre offers office workspace and business advice, runs the tourist information service and offers tea-service for local people and visitors. It also hosts the doctor's surgery as well as providing for the recreational and leisure needs of local people.

The Four Acres Trust in Glasgow's West End has developed a theatre venue in the derelict Dowanhill church and turned the church halls into a thriving restaurant and bar. The Edinburgh Community Trust provides real work for people recovering from mental illness and for people with learning disabilities in their guest-house in Stockbridge, in their Rolls on Wheels business and in their laundry service.

Thus Scotland has examples throughout the country of people developing social enterprises, often unsung, often against the odds, often with little understanding or support from financial institutions and public sector agencies, and sometimes without realising there are others out there doing the same thing. In this respect, the true scale of the social economy in Scotland is unknown. Reports and findings vary - and are sometimes contradictory. It is likely that the scale across Scotland is substantial and probably largely under-reported. Furthermore, as indicated by the GDA (1997), the scale is likely to grow.

Preliminary analysis of a survey of Scottish community enterprise units and agencies, local authorities and local enterprise companies carried out by Community Business Scotland (1998) suggests that there might be more than 250 recognised community enterprises operating throughout Lowland Scotland alone and employing more than 1500 people. Research carried out by McGregor *et al.* (1997) estimates that the social economy in Lowland Scotland comprises 3,700 organisations employing 42,000 people and engaging 60,000 volunteers in their activities. The aggregate social economy income is calculated to be £1bn. Unpublished research carried out by Merkinch Community Enterprise and Alana Albee Consultants and Associates (1997) identifies 220 community enterprises in the Scottish Highlands and Islands of which 101 returned a survey form. These 101 enterprises have a combined turnover of £4.4m, employ 120 people full-time and 157 part-time. Additionally they employ 36 outworkers and engage 1100 people on a voluntary, unpaid basis.

It is also worth noting that the failures, too, offer lessons but that these lessons have yet to be even discerned. This is because these failures have perhaps not been as carefully examined as they might have been. In some cases the 'failures' were no more than enterprises coming to the inevitable end of their life cycle. So it is important that we understand that sometimes closure is not necessarily failure.

Some Concluding Remarks and Policy Suggestions

We need to appreciate the scale of the existing social economy and the potential contribution of social enterprises to Scotland's economy and society. The values which underpin social enterprises are distinctive and important, distinguishing these enterprises from their private and public counterparts. Indeed, it is the values which matter and not the myriad of names by which social enterprises are called. To assist the contribution that can be made by social enterprises, some further evaluation is required of past and current successes and failures. At this stage, it is important to recognise that even the smallest social enterprise at community level is worthy of support and encouragement, not least because it is from those small beginnings that something more substantial can grow.

As research develops, it is becoming possible to be more certain about what social enterprises are good at (and, therefore, what types of business activity are perhaps best left to other forms of organisation). Social enterprises have a strong focus on creating work opportunities for people who are in some way disadvantaged in the labour market. This has considerable impact on their ability to compete in the market place which sometimes needs to be 'adjusted' to take into account the social value achieved. Moreover, with many academics and politicians currently arguing the need for more flexible labour markets, it could be that, of necessity, many people in future will be employed in many simultaneous and contingent jobs rather than one full-time permanent job with a career. Social enterprises are well-placed to encourage and foster such 'portfolio working', but it requires recognition of social enterprise work and employment as legitimate and valuable.

Nevertheless, recognition should be made of the relevance of focusing policy on community income generation and the raising of that community's quality of life rather than solely the creation of employment as part of local community development and/or regeneration. Social enterprises are not just about creating jobs and businesses. Many social enterprises concentrate on the delivery of important services and the creation of local infrastructure, recognising that it is preferable for it to be managed as a community service rather than run solely for private profit. In many communities, 'development' needs to be about service provision at affordable prices; about quality infrastructure; about making scarce resources go farther; about encouraging people to experiment with enterprise. Social enterprises are at the cutting edge of this type of economic activity and development.

Local support networks are important in offering encouragement and services to people who want to try and develop some form of social enterprise. Much of the entrepreneurialism of the social economy is latent. Moreover, it must be said that much of this entreprenerialism does not look to mainstream business funding opportunities because of the binary divide operated by development agencies, for example, indicated in the introductory comments. The Scottish Government has an enabling role here, not least in encouraging the development of social enterprises. Practical policies are needed which recognise the important role of social enterprises at community level and the business areas which social enterprises are most competent to organise. A number of policy initiatives should be pursued;

— Social enterprises which adhere to the core values and which therefore operate exclusively for community benefit (for 'the common good') should be able to qualify for certain fiscal benefits which give them advantages which are not available to enterprises which primarily seek private gain from their operations. These benefits might include: preferential rates of taxation; exemption from some employment taxes; special quotas of public works offered through a special tendering process for social enterprises which takes into consideration social value as well as price competitiveness. The Charity Commission in England is currently reviewing the status of charities working in training that is related to the relief of poverty. A similar review might be conducted in Scotland based on the criteria of contributing the this 'common good'.

— If fiscal benefits are to be offered to social enterprises, then there must be some form of regulatory body which both confirms an enterprise as a genuine social enterprise and monitors its operation to ensure that it works for the common good and not for private gain.

— To aid accountability and transparency, recognised social enterprises should be required to report regularly on their performance in a way which demonstrates their social or community 'added-value'. This means adopting some form of social accounting and submitting these social accounts for external verification or social audit. Currently the savings in energy costs, for example, made by the initiatives of social enterprises are not reflected in the assessment of their funding utilisation. The Scottish Parliament would do well to first develop a more inclusive conceptualisation of 'value-added'. Thereafter, care must be made, however, to ensure that consequential auditing is not a bureaucratic burden on social enterprises which often, initially at least, have few and appropriately skilled professional employees or members. For the sake of accountability and transparency, audit trails are important but can be consuming of resources given the array of complementary funding often received by social enterprises. Currently, an initiative can be audited differently by the EU either by one of two secretariats in Scotland, the Scottish Executive, the Department for Employment and Employment, and the EU Court of Auditors — DGV or DGXVI!

Subsidiarity is about organising affairs at the lowest or most local level possible — 'reverse delegation' as Handy (1994) has put it. Devolution to the Scottish Parliament is but a first step in a process leading to a multi-layered system of governance and service provision for the country. Social enterprises, run by local people for the community, should have an important part to play in that process.

Endnote

1 This chapter draws substantially on research from a transnational project carried out in 1998 for the European Network for Economic Self-help and Local Development, entitled 'Employment Potential of Social Enterprises: Identification, analysis and determination of potential including support structures' (known as EPOSE 6) and conducted in six European Union member states. The editors would like to thank Allan Watt of The Wise Group for his comments on a draft of the chapter.

CHAPTER 13

SCOTLAND
THE
PRODUCT

RUSSEL GRIGGS

For most of the 1990s, business writers and politicians of all persuasions have accepted that the world's economy is now 'globalised'. With advanced telecommunications and transportation technologies the world has 'shrunk', the local and the global have become synonymous, and stateless, footloose transnational corporations now roam the world in search of resources and markets (Dicken, 1992; Holstein *et al.*, 1990; Waters, 1995). As a consequence, the nation state has been declared dead (Ohmae, 1995). National economic management is regarded as ineffective at best and superfluous at worst. Sovereignty has now passed to the customer, who increasingly chooses standardised and homogenised products designed for global markets (Levitt, 1983).

More recently, this perception has been revised. If the world's economy is 'globalising', even *The Economist* (1996; 1997) now accepts that nation states still matter. The number of nation states has increased dramatically in the latter half of the twentieth century as demands for national self-determination have grown and the old empires disintegrated. The establishment of the Scottish Parliament is but part of that process. Significantly, the nation state retains an important role in the management of the economy. Not only is this management existent, it is desired by firms as it provides them with export incentives, overseas investment aid, and the general industrial and social infrastructure — roads, education and health care, for example — that enables domestic firms to go about their business.[1] Indeed, having a strong domestic market and home government support seems to be very important for firms as a springboard to 'going global' — as the work of Scottish Trade International highlights. Moreover, for firms investing abroad, host governments too can provide a source of major incentives — as, again, Locate in Scotland exemplifies. Indeed, Porter (1990) argues that the role of the nation state has become more rather than less important.

The nation appears to have an important role in marketing too. Leading so-called 'global' brands have a strong national identity; IKEA and Sweden, Nestlé and Switzerland, Toyota and Japan, Microsoft, Coca-Cola and the US are but a few obvious examples. Successful brands seem to originate from successful countries and there is a strong transfer of imagery and brand equity between the two (Anholt, cited in *Managing Director*, 1998). It should surprise no-one therefore that Olins (cited in Powell, 1999) reports that 72 per cent of the world's leading companies in his sample cited the national image of the product's country of origin as important when making purchasing decisions. In an increasingly competitive market place, national identity can provide firms with not only a source of difference but also of advantage.

Devolution offers Scotland the opportunity to exploit its national image in the same way. The establishment of its first parliament in 300 years has raised the profile of Scotland throughout the world, especially amongst its huge ex-pat community. As Donald Dewar, then Secretary of State for Scotland and now First Minister, stated, 'The international publicity and higher public profile that devolution will provide for Scotland can be capitalised on and used to help us to create or reinforce favourable images of Scottish products and of Scotland as a desirable place to invest' (Dewar, 1998–99: 2–3).

Being able to exploit Scotland's image as a source of difference and advantage assumes that the country has a positive image that can be exploited. Anecdotal evidence would suggest this to be the case. One reason why so many call centres are being located in Scotland is the perception that a Scottish accent implies friendliness and reliability (Johnstone, 1997). Nevertheless, a systematic assessment is required of Scotland's national identity. This chapter reports research intended to fill this gap. Analysing Scots' and others' perceptions of Scotland, it suggests that Scotland the product has a positive brand image but one that must be refocused if it is to be attuned to a modern, globalising economy.

Researching Scotland's Identity

National identity is already important to Scottish businesses. These businesses would like a strong 'proposition' or statement that brands Scotland, enabling the country's identity to be encapsulated and carried forward for commercial benefit. The results of a recent survey carried out for Scotland the Brand (Clark, 1999) of businesses across all sectors found that:

- 75 per cent felt their business contained Scottish values;
- 77 per cent felt that having a Scottish identity was important to them;
- 67 per cent felt that their Scottishness gave them a distinct advantage in the marketplace;
- 77 per cent supported the creation of a Scottish proposition.

The task for Scotland the Brand was to identify that identity and assess how it might benefit Scotland commercially. Over the last two years, Scotland the Brand — in partnership with Marks & Spencer, UDV, Stagecoach and British Airways — has been carrying out large-scale qualitative research to identify Scotland's identity at the turn of the millennium. The same research has also attempted to identify the challenges and changes required to that identity and how any refocusing of the country's identity might be accomplished.

Project Galore was conducted by CLK, an internationally renowned specialist firm in brand research and development. It involved a literature review to discern the popular image of Scotland over the past twenty years or so. As a consequence, four core values associated with Scotland — integrity, tenacity, spirit, and inventiveness — were turned into concepts which consumers would understand. These concepts were then tested in focus groups in England, France, Germany, Spain, Japan, the US and Scotland.[2] The research had three dimensions:

- how Scotland sees Scotland;
- how Scotland thinks the world sees Scotland;
- how the world sees Scotland.

Research Findings

Scotland on Scotland — what the people living in Scotland today think of themselves

Scots believe that they have a clear identity and an identity that is envied by others. This recognition manifests itself in tartan (to which Scots have a huge attachment and pride when it is used properly but a huge distaste for when it is not), names, the landscape, music, voices, a distinctive culture, history, a democracy which is rooted in communities and folk tradition.

Scots also believe that they are a country, which matters both to themselves and to others. That country, they believe, is:

- a civilised, educated, skills-rich, astute, and responsible nation;
- a country with a small population and therefore not an industrial giant;
- an urban economy in which cities are more important than the rural community;
- a country with a huge ex-pat population throughout the world.

Despite the ensuing parliamentary elections, Scots dwelled much on Scotland's relationship with England, and the struggle Scots have to assert that identity in the shadow of England. Scottish people also believe that they are a country with values and there is considerable pride taken in the Scottish attitude to work, way of life, and moral philosophy. They acknowledge their restraint and silence, and the failure to blow their own trumpet — which is a major problem.

They have an unhappy and uncomfortable conflict, therefore, between dignity and pride. This dignity is also reflected in Scots' dislike or even loathing of dependency on others, especially others outside Scotland. This dependency is perceived to be manifest in:

- a disproportionately high funding allocation from Westminster;
- ailing industries that have caused this need for heavy subsidisation;
- a focus on jobs and not on indigenous business growth. The Scottish people commend and understand that inward investment can provide jobs but see prosperity for Scotland coming only from the growth of indigenous industry;
- Scotland being a tourism-dominated economy.

As to the four core values outlined earlier, Scots believe that they have strong integrity, and better ethics than most. They believe that they are very tenacious and that they deliver. They regard inventiveness as a major source of national pride but which is in urgent need of demonstrable application — they believe that they were inventive but are no longer so. They believe that they have great spirit but feel they are more 'poets' than 'artists' in terms of how that spirit is expressed.

How Scotland thinks the world sees us

Whilst Scots believe (wrongly as is seen later) that 'We're British not Scottish as far as the modern world is concerned', they hope that rest of the world sees Scotland as civilised, richly varied, lively, urban, friendly, highly educated, dynamic, inventive, modern, and entrepreneurial. Nevertheless, Scots believe that the world has a limited view of Scotland. That view comes through tourism, premium products, a Diaspora, from inward investment and from myth. Scots fear — and largely confirmed later — that the world sees us as dominated by the tourist picture: beautiful but empty, a small country happy to live off exporting whisky, salmon, shortbread, golf and fair isle jerseys. In other words, a country locked into the past and quaint.

They are very buoyant and confident about the admiration for Scotland from the old colonial countries to which many Scots emigrated. In terms of the overseas ex-pat community they believe that 'they all want to trace their roots back to Scotland'. While this is seen as a strong and confident attribute by the Scots at home it is also the key reason why Scottish ex-pats are not orientated to their country of origin in the same way as Israelis or the Irish, for example. Scots abroad are interested in an historical Scotland not the contemporary one. Ex-pats of Ireland and Israel on the other hand are more interested in helping their country as it is today than in investigating its history — which is why they currently add huge commercial and other value to their country of origin. Scotland is disadvantaged in this respect. Devolution for Scotland may provide the impetus for Scottish ex-pats and there are signs that the desire to engage with and learn more about contemporary Scotland is there. It will take commitment from both these ex-pats and the government to make this happen but it is crucial that it does if Scotland is to mobilise its potential 'overseas aid'.

Related to both points about ex-pats and the tourist picture book image, the Scottish people also believe that they export more people than products. They have much more confidence in the exported people of Scotland than the products and in how they do things than in what they produce. This feeling links strongly to the inability of the Scottish people to identify with indigenous companies and products.

The world on Scotland— how the world actually sees Scotland

It is important to state at the outset that Scotland is clearly identified as a 'country' by the world and is viewed positively by the world. As a consequence, I would suggest that there are more positive than negative aspects to Scotland's image and we should start from these positives rather than trying to reinvent Scotland for the world.

The key positive perceptions that the world has of Scotland are that the country is seen as a serious holiday destination and its landscape, heritage and, importantly, traditions are still intact. Again positively, Scotland is regarded as a rural economy which is clean, spacious and unspoilt. (There is little knowledge of the urban economy that the Scots in Scotland believe the country to be.) In terms of lifestyle, Scots are seen as having a high quality but slow pace of life. Scots are an honest, self assured and warm people.

On the negative side Scotland is seen as being unsophisticated in terms of the modern world. From a commercial and business standpoint the country is seen as having little technology or technological expertise and little commercial or logistical infrastructure. Most of the world is unaware of Scotland's industrial development in terms of either sunrise or sunset industries. The Scots are also seen as being inward-looking, and not interested in moving forward, or engaging with the world at large.

However the world has a real and large amount of latent respect for Scotland based on the world's dissatisfaction with elements of its own modern life and its own loss and lack of integrity, and its own loss of traditions. This sentiment was common to all of the country groups but was particularly voiced by the US and Japan where, for differing reasons, respondents feel that their rush to new technology and materialism has been at the expense of many core values. Comparatively Scotland is idealised as an 'island in the past' whose traditions and heritage are maintained, which still has its integrity, and a strong sense of self. It cannot be stressed strongly enough how important these values are to Scotland's place in the world and nothing should be done to jeopardise them as they are regarded as adding value to the Scottish identity.

In terms of the core values, the world sees Scots as tenacious, with this tenacity valued. It is, however, a value associated with historical rather than contemporary Scotland, therefore potentially backward-looking. Integrity is perhaps the strongest of all Scotland's values and indicates 'a country that believes in itself'. It is also the bridge to others, as Scots are seen as people who are honest. The world (outside of England) knows little of Scotland's historic, let alone modern inventiveness. A crucial gap therefore exists between what Scots believe of themselves and what others believe about them.

Inventiveness and creativity are seen at the heart of modern and prosperous countries. If Scotland is to take its place in a modern world then it will have to convince the world of its inventiveness. Nevertheless, it must do so in a way that does not mean the loss of the other traditional values that the world associates with Scotland. Scotland's expressive spirit was again strongly recognised. It adds a dynamic, welcoming, forward-looking and communicative side to the world's perception of Scotland and its people.

Moving Forward

In summary, the world has a strong desire to see Scotland take its place in the modern world but it worries that in doing so it could lose its values and traditions. Timeless tradition is at the heart of Scotland's equity so while Scotland does need to move forward it must do so in a way that does not jeopardise this equity.

The Scottish people agree with this view but feel that while their values have not changed, their lifestyles have and Scotland is a modern country. However the world thinks, and Scotland fears, that the country is in a time warp which stops this recognition. The people in the world who have never encountered the Scots feel they know and admire them and see them as the living product of an admirable past. The people of Scotland can therefore form the bridge between then and now. In the globalising economy Scotland's competitors are other small, inventive countries. Scotland is seen as having high educational standards and its known exports suggest sophistication but not inventiveness. The world requires knowledge about the country's infrastructure, and questions an apparent acceptance of exporting products that they have always exported, giving the impression that we are apathetic about marketing and have no modern technology.

In moving forward there must be a balance between old and refocused, and Scotland needs a strong proposition. I would suggest that the basis for this proposition and a subsequent reappraisal of Scotland by the world should involve a particular formulation of Scotland's core values:

- integrity — a country, people, products, and services to trust;
- tenacity — the reliable art of superb management;
- inventiveness — clever, educated, ingenious, imaginative problem-solvers;
- spirit — a country with soul, and people with distinctive style.

Of the above, the world knows, respects and believes three, but knows little of the fourth (inventiveness) and has concerns about how the fourth can be added without harming the other three. This formulation captures Scotland today as well as yesterday. The way forward for Scotland is not to 'reinvent' its identity but to develop, refine, and refocus what it already has with new images.

We know that Scotland can undergo a massive rebranding — it has already done so, and done so very successfully. As Devine (1999) notes, Scotland's image was transformed in the post-Jacobite period, aided, by the work of Sir Walter Scott in particular. Indeed, Scott could be argued to be the first branding specialist for Scotland as prior to his work Scotland's identity was viewed negatively. Following 1745, Scots were widely considered by those south of the border to be erratic, dangerous and unreliable. In the literature of the time the Scots were described as rebellious, violent, immoral, drunken, braggish and boastful, dishonest to a man, devoid of industry, and disloyal. Within half a century Scott's 'make over' had successfully established a new brand image for Scotland supported by a range of positive perceptions concerning the Scots. From that time on, Scots would generally be perceived as loyal, honest, god-fearing, humble, and industrious.

The problem is simple: Scotland is held in high regard by its people and the world but the values currently associated with Scotland are not those deemed contributory to a successful modern economy. Fortunately, the values which are contributory do exist in Scotland but have not been appreciated outside the country. They now need to be focused upon and presented to the world.

Gaining support for a new rebranding is not easy. That support does not entail us all using the same 'logo' or the same 'strap line', or having international generic advertising. However it does mean that we should all talk the same way about Scotland both as people and business, and to do that we may need some guidance. One suggestion might be the inclusion in every personal and corporate 'Brand Book' throughout Scotland of a few pages on how to refer to and articulate Scotland. A simple across the board generic story combined with one or two particular ideas for each sector would give strength and cohesion to the image of Scotland it appears we all desire but have not yet reached.

Over the coming months, Scotland the Brand will provide leadership in this respect through the production of the various Scotland inserts carried in the differing sectors' Brand Books. But the drive must also come from the government and the Parliament. Whilst control of the major economic levers is retained by Westminster, Holyrood must provide leadership by demonstration within the non-reserved matters. The responsibility for encouraging inward investment to the country lies with the Scottish Parliament, for example. To aid this investment, the new Scottish Government cannot just present an image of Scotland to the corporate world, it has a responsibility to shape that image. Just as national economies can be managed, so too can national images. To do so the Scottish Government must take on the role of persuader, encouraging a whole range of institutions, agencies and individuals which contribute to the country's identity to provide the intellectual and visible support for selling Scotland the product within the modern, globalising world. The consequence will be an enhanced source of difference and advantage for Scottish business.

Endnotes

1 For a review and critique of the globalisation thesis, see Warhurst, Nickson and Shaw (1998).

2 A full methodology can be obtained from the author.

CHAPTER 14

ANDY WIGHTMAN

LAND REFORM:

A LEVER FOR ECONOMIC
AND SOCIAL RENEWAL

Of all the topics to be addressed by the Scottish Parliament none perhaps more clearly demonstrates the value of the new institution than land reform. Historically a crowded Westminster agenda has precluded any meaningful change in the way land is owned and used, and the House of Lords has consistently resisted land reform to the extent that even a government committed to it would hesitate before committing valuable parliamentary time to a protracted struggle with the landed gentry.

That all changes now. Holyrood will have the time (albeit still limited) and the legislative capacity to deliver not only on land reform but on a host of other long neglected areas of public policy. But land reform stands out because, rather than simply being neglected due to time constraints of Westminster, it has been consciously marginalised and wilfully suppressed for the best part of a century as irrelevant and hostile to powerful vested interests.

Land reform is thus a completely new topic on the mainstream political agenda and is the only one on the Parliament's agenda not backed-up by the kind of information and analysis which comes from dedicated pressure groups, academic departments, think tank policy papers, or even (until recently) civil servants. But, alongside that, land reform has recently grown in importance on the non-mainstream agenda and amongst activists, eventually being pushed onto the formal political agenda (Callander, 1998; Wightman, 1996).

What is Land Reform?

Arrangements for how land is owned and used are social constructs expressed in law which govern how rights over land are derived, distributed and exercised. Historically our land laws have, as any cursory examination shows, been made by those who in the main have stood to benefit from them down the years. They have provided the means by which a system of feudal governance was transformed over time into a system of landownership (Johnston, 1909, 1920; Carter, 1975; Sillars, 1975).

This transformation has been carefully and assiduously protected and nurtured by landed interests for many centuries in the form of laws to protect property from creditors, to register and create real rights in property, to retain interests in land sold, to effectively privatise game, to secure the line of succession to land, and to protect landed assets against the onslaught of tax. Such formidable and discrete exploitation of political power has denied Scotland the kinds of reforms enjoyed by our West European neighbours. Indeed, as Sir John Sinclair, author of the first Statistical Account of Scotland pointed out in 1814, 'in no country in Europe are the rights of proprietors so well defined and so carefully protected' (cited in Callander, 1986: 5).

Land reform is itself a contested term with no consensus about what it should be attempting to achieve. One of the features of the debate over recent years is that the term has been used as a rubric for many topics, some of which have nothing to do with land reform at all. The conclusions of the Land Reform Policy Group set up in 1997 by the Scottish Office (which forms the basis for the Scottish Executive's programme of land reform) includes, for example, recommendations on national parks, codes of good practice on land use, and community planning (Land Reform Policy Group, 1999; Scottish Executive, 1999c).

There is thus a danger that the term is applied so diffusely that it loses any real meaning. Classical land reform involves the modernisation of land law, the redistribution of land and the provision of appropriate support systems to underpin such social change. What is happening in Scotland by contrast is that land reform is being used to cover changes or reforms to land policy as a whole.

Just as land law is about the derivation, distribution and exercise of rights to land, so land reform is concerned with changing the way in which such rights are derived, distributed and exercised. Land reform is about ensuring that the power conferred by such rights is:

- derived in a way which is properly constructed in terms of the balance between public and private interests;
- distributed in ways which promote social justice, opportunity and equity;
- and exercised in a responsible, accountable and sustainable way.

Land reform would not be necessary had Scotland enjoyed the kinds of reforms which swept Europe 100–200 years ago when feudalism was abolished, inheritance laws reformed, large estates broken up and economic power built up through powerful co-operative and mutual institutions. The process we are now embarking upon is therefore as much a catching up exercise as a modernising one.

The Politics of Land Reform

Land is political as it is about power, and it is here the more overt challenges for the political system lie. Scotland has the most concentrated pattern of private landownership in Europe and research has yet to reveal a country anywhere in the world with such a concentrated pattern.

This concentrated pattern of power associated with land is the core challenge for land reform. In 1872 around 100 landowners owned half the privately-owned land in Scotland. In 1970 this figure had risen to 313 and by 1999, to 343. At this rate, by the end of the twenty first century there will be 494 owners owning 50 per cent of the privately-owned rural land in Scotland (Wightman, 1999) — hardly a revolution! And it does not take an arithmetical genius to conclude that nothing much will change without a sustained and committed programme of reform.

But it remains one of the notable features of contemporary

political debate that whilst much rhetorical energy has been devoted to claims that land reform should benefit the many and not the few, and that monopolies of land are not in the public interest, there has been no serious engagement with the problems associated with the inequitable distribution of land and of the rights associated with that power.

The political right, for example, has been happy to defend private property rights but not to make sure that as many people as possible enjoy these, or to want to democratise them. Thatcher's property owning democracy only went so far, whilst at the same time decimating the public housing stock and making false promises about the virtues of homeownership — perhaps in a similar way to which we may now be in danger of creating false promises about community landownership.

The left by contrast, given its socialist roots, has been least comfortable with the notion of private ownership, hence the debates in the 1970s between nationalisation and private landlordism. Its failure of course has been in its historic thirlage to the statist model of social progress and its explicit rejection of the social economy model developed in agrarian society throughout Europe.

This failure meant that for too long the left's response to the land question was to nationalise it. Now is the time to re-evaluate the place of private ownership — both in terms of how it is defined and how it is distributed — in a liberal democracy. This is not something one might think that should be too problematic. But it is because it hits the most political of all issues — the division of land. Bluntly, can politicians remain disinterested in the remarkably concentrated pattern of private land ownership in rural Scotland?

The answer of course is that they cannot. But there is a fear in certain quarters that land reform becomes associated with what are now regarded as old-fashioned ideas of redistribution. The response to such fears is to view land reform as a process of modernisation of Scotland's land laws in order to redistribute power as part of promoting economic and social progress. Such a scenario hints at the potentially very wide coalition in support of land reform. Land reform in Scotland is an agenda for the left and the right. To expand private property, break down monopolies and promote opportunity is an agenda for the right. Redistributing power and increasing public accountability is an agenda for the left. Liberating and empowering the individual is close to Liberal hearts. And there is a longstanding concern for social welfare and environmental stewardship in the Green movement.

Land reform, in short, can be viewed as a process of creating a landowning democracy — a framework in which private property ownership is protected and cherished, where such privileges are widely distributed and where the framework (both legal and fiscal) in which those rights are enjoyed is accountable to the wider public interest. Such a philosophy provides a decisive break with the past as well as an ambitious and radical vision for the future. It embodies principles which are taken for granted in other areas of public policy (empowerment, accountability, public interest) and helps us to escape the barren ideology of private versus public ownership which has dogged what little debate there has been over the past few decades.

Taking the Debate Forward

Current proposals for land reform, and the debate that has accompanied it, have made some progress towards mapping out a way forward but remain ill informed and immature. In particular, we remain burdened by the legacy of the past both in terms of the system of land tenure and the pattern of landownership. 'The Government's approach to land reform has been to focus on the future, not the past', claimed Lord Sewel in his introduction to the Green Paper of January 1999 (Land Reform Policy Group, 1999:1).

This, it appears, is part of an attempt to remove from the debate the sense of historical injustice felt as a consequence of, for example, the Highland Clearances, and in a sense this is perfectly proper. But in a very fundamental way it is misguided, since the entire array of political, legal and economic factors which underpin the current system of landownership in Scotland are a product of history and of those who, in their own interests, have substantially made that history.

Moving forward necessitates understanding why we are here. A new Scotland is not an ad hoc collection of whimsical ideas about how we want to govern our country, but a vision that must be rooted in an analysis of why we are where we are.

In addition, land reform, encapsulating as it does issues of power, class, history, democracy, geography, culture and identity, is a topic which can attract potentially intoxicating oratory and given the long political dormancy of the subject its emergence into the harsh glare of public scrutiny demands that particular care is taken with how it is articulated. High hopes have been invested in the land reform process, but evidence so far suggests that political rhetoric and extravagant claims are in danger of raising expectations beyond what is to be delivered.

It is important that such rhetoric is contained because land reform is a sophisticated policy agenda that embraces urban and rural issues (tenement law/feudal reform, access), social justice and social inclusion, the environment and the economy. In particular, if land reform is to move forward as a platform for democratic renewal then it needs to move beyond its current portrayal as a Highland issue about big estates, bad landlords, crofters and downtrodden communities. Land reform is as much about helping the 30 per cent of households living in tenement property and the problems of rural homelessness as it is about dismantling landed hegemony in the countryside.

A Modernising Agenda

Scotland is now in a position to make radical changes in how the country is owned and used. A modernising agenda for land reform is one that updates outdated laws at the same time as promoting opportunity and enterprise, and building social justice and democracy. It is an agenda that brings together the essence of land reform — the redistribution of power — with the essence of modern politics — a progressive programme for building a better society. And it is this alliance of the political and the pragmatic which needs to be constructed if land reform is to be widely supported, and given the political support to see it through the challenges that lie ahead.

Those who argue that land reform should not be prosecuted to right the wrongs of the past are right. But land reform is about changing what we have inherited to make it fit for the future and that involves understanding and coming to terms with the past. In this respect, it is wrong to deny how the past has shaped the present. A modernising agenda must recognise this and be prepared first of all to do away with the archaic features of our current land laws. A long-overdue start will soon be made with abolition of the feudal system, but our laws of inheritance (children and spouses still have no legal rights to inherit land) and giving tenant farmers the right to buy their farms, are just two other areas where progress is needed.

These two modest measures would do much to balance the current emphasis on community right-to-buy by extending the scope for land reform beyond collective arrangements, to those governing opportunities for individuals. They would contribute to the vital goal of creating a more pluralistic pattern of ownership, a goal which, it should be stressed, will not be achieved by any one measure alone but rather by a range of measures including action on land monopolies, crofting reforms, more flexible powers of compulsory purchase, game law reform, residency obligations, offshore trusts, public access rights and so on.

A modernising agenda must also be quite clear about the imperative to promote social and economic progress and build democracy. Thus it must include measures designed (as indeed succession and tenancy law are) to break down landowning monopolies. The key to investment in the rural economy, as in the urban economy, is access to land. The current division of land frustrates investment through the monopoly power of large holdings. Breaking these down will promote investment and economic activity, rather than inhibit it as is so frequently claimed by those with vested interests in maintaining existing landowning power structures.

Building democracy through greater local control of resources, greater local democracy in decision making (introducing local democratic control over the Forestry Commission for example) and greater security for individuals and their families is the final challenge for a modernising agenda. Ideas have already been aired by the SNP for example on creating Locality Land Councils. Again evidence from Western Europe points to the crucial role played by communes and municipalities, co-operatives and mutual businesses, and local decision making in strengthening communities. Such land use bodies are not an ad hoc addition to existing structures but an integrated part of local democracy.

Conclusions

Land is political. Land reform is entirely appropriate and legitimate as the means to promote and defend the public interest in land, as well as the private interest. Land reform is as normal a topic of political debate as health, education or transport. Land reform is an issue for the whole of Scotland — urban and rural, lowland and Highland (Hunter, 1998; Wightman, 1996, 1999). To argue otherwise is to suggest that we as a society should remain entirely disinterested in how land is owned and used.

The development of a landowning democracy is long overdue, but provides unparalleled opportunities. From having one of the most primitive systems and patterns of private landownership in Europe, we could, if we are ambitious enough, move to a situation where we are amongst the most progressive. And we could do this in a matter of a generation or so. Now that Scotland has a degree of political autonomy, the time and will to deliver serious land reform, and the beginnings of a coherent agenda for doing so, there is no excuse for repeating sterile debates of the past.

Land reform is a lever for economic and social renewal and for cultural and environmental revitalisation. Its portrayal and presentation as a narrow rural agenda concerning crofters, bad landlords and the Highlands has confused and frustrated attempts to construct a forward-looking agenda. A modernising agenda based upon building a landowning democracy might begin to overcome the myths and stereotypes which still dog discussions and debates about the topic.

SECTION THREE: SOCIAL PRIORITIES

Chapter 15

TACKLING

POVERTY

Wendy Alexander

AND SOCIAL

EXCLUSION

The Challenge and the Vision

The establishment of the Scottish Parliament has created new opportunities for Scotland. The new Parliament's inheritance is challenging, particularly in respect of the high level of poverty that now exists in the country. The number of Scots living in relative poverty more than doubled from 1979 to 1997. The proportion of Scottish children living in households with relatively low incomes (less than half the average per capita income) is up threefold since 1979. Over a third of single pensioners experience fuel poverty (on UK changes, see Walker and Walker, 1997). Around 25 per cent of working age adults have poor literacy and numeracy skills. The Scottish Parliament, then, faces a tough challenge when it comes to tackling poverty and social exclusion.

New Labour is a government in both Edinburgh and London which is serious about creating a fairer society, a society in which all our citizens have the opportunity to maximise their potential and all can share in that society's growing prosperity. Indeed, new Labour is committed to creating a society within two decades in which no Scottish child lives in poverty.

Part of that strategy must be about alleviating the symptoms of poverty. Here many of the key initiatives will come through the UK Parliament; action on tax and benefits, together with our policies for work, which are already succeeding in raising incomes. But a comprehensive assault on exclusion must also tackle the root causes of exclusion which blight the lives of too many individuals and communities in Scotland. It is here, in attacking the roots of exclusion, that the Scottish Parliament can have a very real impact in terms of the policies that it pursues. (On the debate about social inclusion and exclusion generally, see Levitas, 1998; Lister, 1998; Perri 6, 1997a).

Alleviating Poverty

The three main causes of poverty in Scotland today are worklessness, the costs of raising children and old age. We are taking action on all three.

For most people of working age, the best way to avoid poverty is to be in paid work. Work is invariably the best route out of poverty. Two thirds of people who escaped from poverty in the early 1990s did so because someone in their household either started work or increased their earnings. So this is a government defined by its commitment to work. We make no apologies as a party of the progressive left for focusing on securing work. It lies deep in our roots. The Jarrow marches, UCS sit-ins and even the miners' strike were all struggles for the right to work. The New Deal, in particular, is working to help people into employment. Over 36,000 young people in Scotland joined the New Deal in its first 18 months. And in the two years since Labour came to power unemployment amongst 18–24 year olds has dropped by 55 per cent. It is an initiative too which is distributive of wealth, being financed through the taxing of the windfall profits of the richest privatised utilities.

In respect of the second cause, Labour recognises that children are the innocent victims of family poverty. Currently 10–15 per cent of families in Scotland fall into poverty following the birth of their first child. We have embarked on a range of measures to make work pay through introducing a minimum wage, new work incentives including the working families tax credit and up to £100 per week towards the costs of childcare. Families with someone in full-time work are now guaranteed an income of at least £200 per week. For pensioners, there is the £100 winter fuel bonus with a minimum income guarantee linked to earnings for the poorest pensioners.

But even in these areas of access to work, family incomes and security in old age, the Scottish Parliament can also play a vital role in ensuring that public policy interventions reach those most in need. For example, the New Futures Fund is a uniquely Scottish initiative intended to make sure that the New Deal reaches the most disadvantaged young people. Similarly, the Rough Sleepers Initiative is being extended beyond a narrow focus on housing to take account of the chaotic lifestyles of many homeless young people who sleep rough. And as we put in place the support structures to deal with issues such as drug abuse, we will also link supported housing projects into the New Deal to make it possible for the most excluded young people to enter the world of work.

Attacking fuel poverty is another area where the Parliament can boost family incomes by acting to reduce household costs for low-income families. The Warm Deal is a uniquely Scottish initiative designed to insulate 100,000 homes over the next four years. Average fuel bills can be expected to fall by over £100 per household. There will be a particular focus on pensioner households so the impact of the winter fuel bonus is not diminished by poor housing standards. A further uniquely Scottish aspect of the Warm Deal is the link to employment. Over 400 unemployed Scots will receive accredited training in home insulation as part of the programme.

The Scottish Parliament: Creating Opportunity

It is our ambition, however, to do more than simply alleviate poverty. The real challenge is to eradicate its root causes. And it is here that the Scottish Parliament can make a real difference. Parry (1997, 1998) has outlined the social policy context. The specific challenges that must be met by the Scottish Parliament are:

- tackling the causes;
- investing in people;
- investing in communities.

The problems inherited by new Labour and the Scottish Parliament are deep rooted. They are problems that have built up over a long period and they will take time to resolve, but we have made a good start through a number of wide ranging initiatives.

Tackling the Causes

Tackling the root causes of poverty means starting with our children to end the cycle of intergenerational poverty passed from one generation to the next. Our aim is to systematically attack poverty in the early years. Growing up in poverty effects, and often permanently damages, the life chances of children. Children growing up in families that have experienced financial difficulties are, on average, less likely to stay on at school, they have poorer attendance records and poorer attainment levels.

If there was a single big idea that could eradicate social exclusion it would have been tried by now. Often the solution is lots of different strategies and interventions, focused on the person and acting cohesively. So the solutions will sometimes be as complex as the lives they set out to support. But the Parliament can provide a new focus for accountability and public concern casting its light into the dark corners to ensure public policy reaches those most in need. For example the high profile commitment that no-one should have to sleep rough in Scotland by the end of the first Parliament's term. So, of course the old Scotland had pockets of good practice, but too often such good practice operated in isolation. We intend to ensure that in the new Scotland those pockets of expertise and the opportunities they provide will become the norm. Such practices include:

— Early intervention: a new network of family centres to help vulnerable families. By 2002, these centres will offer 5,000 new places for very young children and their families. And we need to do better in helping parents develop their parenting skills.

— Childcare: we are committed to high quality, affordable and accessible childcare. The new Scottish Childcare Information Line will be operational by December 1999. All three and four year olds will have access to a quality nursery place by 2002. At least 100,000 out of school care places will also be created during this Parliament. And as part of this initiative, we will train 5,000 new childcare assistants to work in this sector.

— A world class education system: too many Scottish children fail to obtain the education that they deserve. A child can only learn effectively at school if they are warm, dry, well fed and secure — and equally the school must help them to succeed. Our New Community Schools are meant to tackle some of the other barriers that stop children learning effectively at school. In schools, new attainment targets and reductions in class sizes will be complemented by the largest ever school building and improvement programme. With the arrival of the Digital Age it is essential that all Scottish school-leavers are 'communications savvy' — the information rich of today are invariably the income rich of tomorrow. Scotland's challenge is to create a wired generation universally at home on the net.

Of course, if young people are not in school they cannot learn. Consequently, we are also making firm commitments to reduce exclusions and truancy that are a primary cause of poor attainment. At present, 4,000 children leave Scottish schools with no qualifications. We have promised to halve that number over the lifetime of the first Parliament. This agenda for change is ambitious and it cannot be achieved without changes in how we organise the classroom and how teachers support tomorrow's learning environment.

— Helping vulnerable young people make the transition to adulthood: the New Deal is helping 18–24 year olds but too many young people fall through the cracks at 16 and 17. We are pledged to improve opportunities for 16–18 year olds to train and learn by creating 20,000 modern apprenticeships in Scotland during this Parliament. We also need a more level playing field to encourage 16 and 17 year olds to stay in education. So, we are piloting Educational Maintenance Allowances which offer targeted financial support to young people from low-income families.

By putting this range of building blocks in place over the next four years, from birth and throughout a child's school years we lay the foundations for the eradication of child poverty within a generation. And the imperatives of that information age in which our children will grow up requires a renewed effort in investing in people.

Investing in People

The Parliament must aim high. We should commit to the full participation of all Scots in the global information network. We can start by speeding the day when every child in every village, town or city in Scotland is able to reach across a keyboard and access 'every book ever written, every song ever composed and every painting ever painted'.

In the move from the 'industrial age' into the 'information age' the absence of learning, education or knowledge has an ever closer correlation with poverty and exclusion. And that information age is already upon us and so it is not just Scotland's children who must be equipped to learn: adults too must be encouraged to embrace lifelong learning (Scottish Office, 1999b). To this end we will create 100,000 individual learning accounts and a Scottish University for Industry will be launched. Our aim is for at least one in four adult Scots to be participating in one form of further, higher or community education at any given time.

However, if investing in people and their skills is at the heart of an inclusive Scotland there is also an agenda for early change around the most 'wicked' challenges, such as teenage pregnancy, rough sleeping, and drug and alcohol abuse. Here the response should involve joined-up action, allowing institutions and agencies to innovate across boundaries including the movement of budgets and staff, and often the development of personalised support services.

Investing in Communities

Yet creating an inclusive Scotland can never simply be about individuals — it is also about communities. And at the heart of those communities are the homes in which we live. The old solutions will not do. It is wrong at the start of the next millennium that some Scottish tenants are bearing a large debt burden through their rent payments for houses long demolished.

Embracing community ownership can both empower tenants and provide a new generation of investment for socially rented housing. No longer will council tenants be the poor relations when it comes to attracting new investment. By the Executive taking on responsibility for servicing Glasgow's outstanding housing debt the rent of the tenants can be freed up to support a new investment programme. Over £1bn of additional investment could be raised to improve Glasgow's housing. This would substantially improve the living standards of thousands of tenants by providing warm, damp-free housing. And community ownership brings other benefits. Tenants will, often for the first time, be directly involved in decisions affecting their own homes and it is estimated that this scale of investment could lead to the creation of 4,000 new construction and related jobs in the city. Without new investment in dilapidated council houses we condemn another generation of Glasgow children to growing up in some appalling housing conditions. Crucially, the choice must be with the tenants and in Glasgow, as elsewhere, it will be the tenants and the tenants alone that choose their own future.

But communities are often about more than place, they are about people who share a common interest or identity. The creation of a Minister for Equalities is recognition of just how far we have to go in creating an inclusive Scotland. Action on race, sex, disability and sexual orientation are all on the agenda of the Parliament and Executive. We need action over a period of years to tackle issues such as racism. However longer term ambitions should not preclude some early action on areas such as domestic violence.

Making it Happen

Many of the challenges cited above are all too familiar. Rising to meet those challenges requires a new approach. The halving of youth unemployment in Scotland shows the potential success of bold strokes. As the Minister for Communities I am determined that the

Scottish Executive should be the pioneer of new approaches which are characterised by:

- partnership, to ensure joined-up solutions to joined-up problems;
- results, requiring a focus on outcomes rather than inputs, and;
- empowerment of people and communities.

The Scottish Executive's own strategy will rightly come under close scrutiny to see how we live up to these objectives. We are already identifying key indicators of poverty and social exclusion by which we can monitor progress. New interventions will follow. And the power of government must be used to shape the actions and behaviours of other agencies — local government, the third sector and the private sector — each can do more to tackle exclusion.

The Executive itself must set an example when it comes to partnership working — results orientated and empowering local communities. Here, it is only possible to give a flavour of this new approach, for example:

- Partnership: in tackling drugs we will bring all those involved in enforcement, prevention and rehabilitation together with the communities most affected. We will work alongside employers in the creation of 100,000 individual learning accounts. And formally recognising the future policy development, service delivery and economic role of the third sector in Scotland including the infrastructure required to support such a role.
- Results: the Executive's Programme for Government, is built around a commitment to results. By making clear pledges and keeping those promises we can help restore the general loss of trust in government and politicians.
- Empowerment: we will listen to local communities by extending the use of people's juries and people's panels. And we will create a £2m national development fund to help local

people have their say over the spending priorities of the full range of public agencies in their area.

The Executive will be held to account for its actions and initiatives by the Parliament and the people of Scotland. Our whole approach signals a return to active government with a clear mandate for results and a strong focus on delivery within tight fiscal restraints.

In the new Scotland, structures should follow from strategy. Scotland's small size is our opportunity. It should be more straightforward to focus on outcomes and 'what works'. Success will require overcoming the low status afforded to implementation. We need to celebrate those individuals and agencies who can 'make it happen'. That means fewer and clearer goals, and imagination about means and boundaries.

To enable these new strategies to take root the process of government will also need to change. We need, firstly, to become serious about joining up activities. I do not minimise the problem: departmentalitis, silos, poor collaboration, and the dumping of problems. Yet solving the really wicked problems will depend on co-ordinated efforts by many agencies. Progress will require better joined-up budgets for areas such as community care (health and social work), around client groups such as children (New Community Schools) and around problem issues such as drug abuse.

Secondly, government — both central and local — needs to become better at learning and experimenting. Here we have much to learn from the third sector, as Pearce in this volume indicates. We need task forces, mixed background units, more secondments and the use of outside expertise. We need to be willing to learn from the international market in ideas, including from the private sector, in particular their ability to encourage risk and innovation.

Thirdly, we need to end the culture of blame and start to reward success. We can introduce risk money such as innovation funds for social entrepreneurship. Scottish Enterprise is already considering a Scottish School for Social Entrepreneurs. Finally we need to take citizens and customers more seriously. It is difficult to over-state the traditions of producer control and the poor systematic understanding of the public and their needs as consumers. The philosophy of community empowerment that underlies people's juries and panels and community capacity building will not take root unless there is a widespread commitment to cultural change in our public services.

In pursuit of these ends, government is at least aided by new technological developments. New technology opens a whole new set of opportunities to put the customer in charge and move away from the one size fits all services of the past. We must make government more personal, more high tech and more high touch. Important initiatives are already underway, there are now personal advisers in the New Deal, on-line government services and we are investigating a single online social housing register for Scotland.

Above all the challenge of this new Parliament is to combine its commitment to tackling social justice with a commitment to preparing for the future. Scotland must commit to modernisation and commit to breaking the chains of ignorance that bind so many to the past. The Scottish Parliament shares its infancy with the information age. For the new Scotland, the real opportunity of the information age is not simply technological or economic, but the opportunity to renew some of our most revered values of social justice and equality of worth.

The Executive and Parliament are not, and cannot, be alone in this endeavour. All around us, people are forging the new Scotland. It is a nation that is trying to live up to its future; at its best aspiring to be a beacon of progressive thought and community concern in a globalising world. We need the courage to match our tradition of community with a commitment to modernity. By committing to becoming a nation that is a leader rather than a follower in the information age Scotland can realise an inclusive community. We have nothing to fear but ourselves.

CHAPTER 16

BEYOND THE CLASSROOM:

SUE INNES

EQUALITY, DIVERSIY
AND LEARNING FOR
UNDER-16S

Each August, across Scotland, a rite of passage takes place, as self-conscious parents and small children walk to school with a mixture of anticipation and trepidation, to begin a journey of some 15,000 hours with an uncertain outcome. As those children start that journey, their right to equal educational opportunity and the support to achieve their potential, is generally accepted. No politician would stand at the school gate and say that since we know that some of these children will benefit less from education than others, that they should be offered less support. Instead the politicians are adamant: 'Education is our number one priority'[1] and 'Our children are the future of Scotland. We need to give them the best possible start in life' (Scottish Executive, 1999d: 5). It is hard to disagree with such sentiments. The issue, however, is ensuring that those sentiments are enacted as policies that deliver. This chapter assesses the learning of under-16s generally and how that learning can be supported by the Scottish Executive and Parliament.

Rethinking Education

'Modernising' is not a term that fits comfortably into the current schools debate, though it has become orthodoxy in policy-making. But radical, revitalising thinking is needed — drawing as much on established ideas and principles as from the new thinking that a modernising agenda demands, though no eager political adviser will make their reputation by saying so. Consultation and guidance documents are studded with words such as 'modernisation', 'improving', 'excellence', 'world-class'. This positions those who query the approaches proposed as old-fashioned, as unambitious for excellence, and as complacent about a second-class system. The distinction posed between today's schools, and education fit for the future is false. Workable solutions build on experience and reflection, are evidence-based, go with the grain of emerging ideas and create active partnership in developing those ideas (Swann and Brown, 1997).

Because government calls to modernise, and to form partnerships, have been accompanied by an apparent unwillingness to privilege the voices of educational professionals, fears of a hidden agenda have been exacerbated. Because a defensive profession repeats that none of the aims are achievable without mending school roofs, improving pay and attending to the conditions and morale of staff, it implies that there is nothing wrong with Scottish education that money cannot solve. But the good old days, when teachers were left alone to get on with it, were far from good enough. The polarisation between policy-makers and practitioners, each claiming to have the interests of children and Scotland's educational future at heart, more than anything damages those interests.

This is not to deny the need for change. Schools are populated by children who, given the chance, are the most demanding and modern members of our society. The emerging shape of the world in which they will live and work, calls for visionary and ambitious educational responses. Schools must also be stable, with a disciplined, encouraging and open ethos conducive to learning. We cannot waste the learning years of children by wrangling over them, and we cannot afford a demoralised teaching profession. Nor can we remove information from the public domain or repeal policy that widens choice for some. The challenge is to move on from a culture of numbers, driven by what is measurable, to a culture of meaning, within a more complex understanding of how learning is nurtured. Responding to this challenge means devising new, more subtle and more appropriate measures, aimed at achieving personal goals and life skills, as well as academic and vocational qualifications — that young people, parents and teachers can participate in setting (MacBeath, 1999).

We need to clarify the central question before we can find the answer — why do we value education and for what? Government calls for continuous improvement in performance and for raising standards are empty of content, and evasive on what constitutes acceptable performance. All schools will be challenged to achieve the best standards, but 'best' is neither defined, nor is there any acknowledgement that 'best' is contested and means different things to different people. Comparison and target-setting on a narrow band, without asking fundamental questions about what is measured and why, is self-defeating. We need to shift from narrow views of achievement that devalue life skills and reward conformity, to ways that recognise, manage, assess and reward diversity.

It also means shifting our thinking about the organisational unit of education — from the institutions where learning is organised, defined and contained, to the individual learner whose education comes from a variety of formal and informal settings. Public debate on learning is dominated by concerns about what happens in schools and colleges, to the virtual exclusion of what happens in families and communities. Formal education comprises around a third of a child's time during term, yet those hours are the overwhelming focus of our attention (Bentley, 1998: Innes, 1999).

Different Ways of Learning

Imaginative policy ideas are needed that locate the institutional basis of education as only part of learning, which create links both between families and educational provision. For example, well-planned family learning initiatives can be successful both for children and parents, who themselves may re-enter education. Similarly, links are vital between formal learning and a range of tools, and social and public organisations that can support learning and widen horizons. IT is a key agent of change, giving students greater scope to design and pursue their own learning programmes (Innes, 1999). This model is only one that could be developed, if the importance of learning outwith formal education is fully acknowledged. To do so emphasises connections not barriers, and takes education out of the classroom to work co-operatively across disciplines and old divisions.

The New Community Schools model aims to integrate a range of services for children and families, offering 'education plus' (Scottish Office, 1998a). The co-location on which most emphasis has, unfortunately been placed in discussions about these schools is much less important than the promised co-operation. If the main criticism of this idea has been the monumental task of creating multi-disciplinary teams, which is fraught with problems only if professional, adult interests are put ahead of those of children and young people, then the best aspect of the proposal is that it permits a degree of diversity, innovation and responsiveness to local needs. Such schools, the HM Chief Inspector promises, will be about the learning child rather than the school, about children's needs and development (Osler, 1999). All schools would benefit from such an approach — even highly academic pupils have social and emotional needs. If the initiative is aimed only at areas of social exclusion and not at schools that meet current attainment targets, and if simplistic targets remain in place, then New Community Schools will risk being stigmatised and further entrench a two-tier system.

Equality or Excellence?

The idea that has most eroded the foundations of state school provision in this country is that equality of opportunity and excellence in education cannot realistically co-exist. The idea that resources should follow success has influenced the centre ground of politics as well as the right. This belief has run alongside the notion that schools alone — and within them strong leaders, good teachers and maybe a few social workers — are all that is needed to redress social disadvantage and economic inequality; to suggest otherwise is simply to make excuses. If, in a society where what matters is adaptability, enterprise, imagination and learning to learn (rather than narrower strictly-vocational ideas of ability), we cannot find ways to develop the capacities and potential of all of our young people, we should resign ourselves now to a continued decline.

Equality in education is not about leveling-down or up, but about ensuring that the right people, structures and resources exist to offer all children and young people a good education that is right for them. It is about recognising diverse needs and aptitudes. It means posing questions that are far more fundamental and individually focussed than how to hike schools up the league tables and keep disaffected kids inside them, and off the streets. We could start by looking at those children starting school and ask, what happens to their excitement and energy? What happens to their creativity? What happens to children's inborn pleasure in learning? What do our schools, families and society do to kill it?

Introducing Meaningful Learning

New knowledge about processes of learning is reflected only marginally in debates on education and policy priorities, but it usefully refocuses questions of individual difference in cognitive potential and intellectual style and the consequent need for education appropriate to aptitude and need (Gardner, 1985, 1999). Such differences can be observed in any classroom, but what turns a straightforward-enough observation into a key to open potential is that cognitive science sees such differences as necessary and complementary, whereas most education in this country develops only a narrow area of competency and positions differences in learning styles and aptitudes in a hierarchy, which, put crudely, runs from physics and maths to domestic science.

The new thinking is unlikely to lead to any educational formula; it suggests a more demanding, specialised and multi-faceted approach to education. There are difficulties in putting such ideas into practice, but we are reaching the limits of what the current system can do. Even if it were to achieve targets for numeracy, literacy and other basic skills, questionable at the trailing edge of attainment, it still will not meet the needs of all pupils unless ways of radically opening up approaches to learning are found. Research into the needs of gifted children, and research into why young people leave school without skills or any form of qualification, shows intriguing parallels. It is hardly surprising that a mass education system is tailored to the needs of the average, well-motivated learner, but it is at a tremendous cost to children who do not easily fit in, or are unsupported.

Nor does current education always meet the needs of those deemed average, who may be far from that, given the chance. Such arguments do not offer the 'magic fix' apparently promised by the ideas of school improvement, but open new and longer lasting approaches, especially for children, including the most creative, the very able and those from disadvantaged backgrounds. At the centre of truly effective learning is education for understanding. Meaningful learning crosses the boundaries of experience, thinking and feeling, reflecting and acting. It facilitates health and well-being, and active citizenship, as well as passing exams and impressing interviewers.

Not that passing exams does not matter — arguably it matters most for children facing other inequalities. One of the less noticed aspects of recent research is that if people perform well in any one area, as long as they choose it and it engages their imagination, then it will lift their other skills. The more we 'cover the curriculum' and settle for surface and strategic learning, the more the process of understanding that transforms information into knowledge and into behaviour that demonstrates the deep-seated nature of what has been learned, becomes something for which we do not have time (Perkins, 1981). In parallel, the downgrading of art, music and drama within education has led to these subjects being seen as extras, and unaffordable luxuries. The common distinction made between academic subjects, and 'soft' subjects that serve to balance the curriculum, overlooks the value of creativity in itself and for the deep learning, transferable skills and personal development that it brings. The possibility of bringing together the arts and science, once part of the distinctiveness of Scottish education and a source of very rich understanding, has also been the casualty of subject hierarchies. The much-vaunted breadth of Scottish education can seem very narrow when it comes to choosing Standard Grades.

The uniformity and relative rigidity of how education is conceptualised is one reason why schools reinforce advantage for those who have it, and find it hard to break into patterns of disadvantage. Attainment, measured on the limited scales used, leads to a simplistic but influential distinction between well-motivated, middle class children who thrive in school, and the disadvantaged who cluster in failing schools. There are no gradations, no other children it seems — no fragile learners or troubled teenagers in the middle classes, and no working class or ethnic minority families that value education and support their children. This is 'under class' theory moving into the educational mainstream.

Education, Diversity and Social Inclusion

All children need the right opportunities and the support to achieve their potential. Some receive it from family, community and school in what becomes a positive cycle; others are so denied it that a negative and again self-reinforcing cycle sets in. Scottish schools have been relatively successful in reducing inequalities of class and gender in attainment, subject choice, staying-on rates and entry to higher education, but progress has stalled in the face of the social and economic polarisation of the past decade (Paterson, 1998b). The uniformity that has become so limiting began in a necessary determination to create equality. A balance must be found between new ways to enable and value diversity but also within overall provision available to all children, not least because those public services that are of highest standard are provided for and used by all social groups. That is not to deny that some children have more needs than others, or have special needs, but recognises that the greatest social and learning benefits accrue through universally available provision.

Diversity does not mean opting out but calls for a new kind of policy framework. Creating education that is uniformly of a high standard, defined in meaningful, participative ways and well-resourced, at the same time as moving away from uniformity in process and what counts as success, and to respond to the needs of all young people and of local communities within a vibrant social, economic and democratic future is a serious challenge. Meeting it was never going to be easy but if we value equality and excellence as we claim, it must be met.

Social inclusion is the other key outcome of education policy named by the Scottish Executive. Education, skills and qualifications are the most effective route to social inclusion, and conversely, low levels of educational attainment are a transmission mechanism for cycles of disadvantage. If education is the single most important means of liberating individuals from disadvantage, it cannot happen alone. Differentials of class and family culture, ethnicity and gender form a complex matrix that underpins learning and educational outcomes. Social disadvantage is not the only form of deprivation that can affect children's learning. Some risk factors cut across class and income group; including racism, bullying, abuse and domestic violence, for example, as well as the conflict for many parents between spending time with their children and being at work or coping with unemployment.

Having a child may tip a family into poverty, and pressures faced by parents are strongly exacerbated by poverty, isolation and poor environment. Since 1979 the number of children under 16 living in poverty more than trebled to 38 per cent; even more children under five (42 per cent) live in households defined as poor (Children in Scotland, 1999). There is a great deal of evidence that growing up in a family that has experienced the compound problems of disadvantage damages children's learning and life opportunities. Differences in cognitive perception, according to social group, are less significant in the early months of life but begin to widen as early as 22 months. In general they do not narrow but widen when children start school (Feinstein, 1998; HM Treasury, 1999).

Pre-school Considerations

Starting primary school is a crucial transition, but what comes before is even more important. Many parents facing great difficulties nevertheless give their children support. It is recognised, that alongside the risk factors for potential low achievement, important protective factors include strong early attachment to adults; parental interest and high quality pre-school provision. Pre-school provision has been an educational Cinderella; government recognition of its importance is probably the single most important positive step forward, but it must now be integrated, conceptually and organisationally, with other educational provision within a framework linking education and care. Rather than reinforcing a worrying trend towards earlier formal education, all young children must have the opportunity to play and learn in a safe, stimulating and culturally sensitive environment and to move to more formal learning when it is right for them (Penn and Moss, 1996). The extension of after-school care and study support provides new opportunities for informal learning and personal support. After a period in which schools have been pre-occupied by curricular and related matters, a re-emphasis on the welfare of the child as the business of the school is needed (Ball, 1998).

Widening the Learning Spectrum

Enabling and managing diversity within a commitment to high standards and equality is best conceptualised, as current good practice acknowledges, through a focus on the learner. To do so opens up a range of innovative practices, many piloted in local settings, but the rigidity and resistance to changing of the structural basis of education prevents them being introduced more widely; others overturn cherished orthodoxies. It means fully including children and young people in the debate, something many adults clearly find threatening, although schools that involve pupils in decision-making benefit from it.

Focusing on the learner means supporting children and young people in planning their own learning. Both IT and stronger links between different sites of learning, such as other schools, colleges, and institutions such as libraries, arts organisations, sports and community centres and voluntary agencies, offer individuals opportunities to pursue their own learning, with the support of teachers or other tutors. All possible opportunities, through and beyond formal education, to create strong learning links between schools and communities will be to the benefit of both. Learning can be facilitated by many people and in many settings. It may mean re-organising time for learning - a process already begun with breakfast clubs, after-school provision, study support and summer schools.

The transitions between stages of learning could be usefully revisited. For example, age five (as stipulated in the Schools (Scotland) Code) is too young for many children to begin formal learning; the introduction of early years provision opens up the possibility of the less prescriptive transition between pre-school and primary that is of evident advantage in the Scandinavian countries (Penn and Moss, 1996). Flexible transitions at school leaving age between school, college and work experience, voluntary activity and employment could be more widespread. Adaptive, and participatively formed, local systems of timetabling and curriculum management should be explored through applied research, drawing on success in other European countries (Trimaglio, 1998).

Developing policy to allow an environment which encourages innovation, and which responds to new voices and changing opportunities, need not mean unequal provision. Diversity can be framed within widely debated, clearly stated aims and principles. A national debate could bring a new sense of purpose and engagement to replace polarisation and resistance. It is a characteristic of Scots intellectual tradition to manage paradox creatively, to argue both/ and and to focus on the productive point where differing understandings meet. If ever that approach were needed, it is now.

Endnote
1 Sam Galbraith quoted from Scottish Executive (1999b: 1).

CHAPTER 17

LIFELONG
JANET LOWE

LEARNING:

FROM VISION TO
REALITY

The Current Vision

In the late 1990s, the UK educational policy environment has been characterised by a commitment to 'lifelong learning' and a 'learning society' (Hillman, 1998). A number of initiatives articulate this commitment. In February 1998 the Department for Education and Employment published *The Learning Age: A Renaissance for a New Britain*. This Green Paper reflects and builds upon the reports of a number of Committees:

- the 1997 report of Helena Kennedy QC (1997): *Learning Works*;
- the report of the National Committee of Inquiry (1997a); the *Dearing Report: Higher Education in the Learning Society*;
- the report of the National Advisory Group for Continuing Education and Lifelong Learning (1997): the *Fryer Report: Learning for the Twenty-First Century*.

In February 1998, the government also published its response to the Dearing Report, entitled *Higher Education for the 21st Century* (Scottish Office, Welsh Office and Department of Education for Northern Ireland, 1998).

In Scotland, the Secretary of State for Scotland published a Green Paper on *Lifelong Learning: Opportunity Scotland* (Scottish Office 1998b). A ministerial response to the Garrick Report (National Committee of

Inquiry, 1997b) was also included in *Higher Education for the 21st Century* published in 1998. *Skills for Scotland* (Scottish Office, 1999b) appeared early in 1999. Also in 1999, Scottish Enterprise published a new strategy for economic development in Scotland which places considerable emphasis on the development of the 'learning industry' and on a culture of learning within organisations and by individuals (Scottish Enterprise Network, 1999).

Each of these reports is predicated on an acceptance of the relevance of learning to the political, economic, industrial, social and technological changes which the reports expect to affect the UK, within a global environment and a 'knowledge economy'. Each accepts unquestioningly that lifelong learning and a learning society will contribute to economic success, social justice, competitiveness, prosperity, sustained employability and quality of life. The rhetoric is often visionary and inspiring, advocating sea-changes in values, culture and attitudes to learning on the part of individuals, employers and organisations.

The link, however, between rhetoric, strategy and initiative is tenuous, with the particular absence of any analysis of the need for systemic change. Most of the reports appear to accept that the emergence of a learning society has an inevitability and is a context within which specific initiatives require to be pursued.

Nor is there any shortage of initiatives and pilot projects, at national and local level. *Opportunity Scotland* (Scottish Office, 1998b) and *Skills for Scotland* (Scottish Office, 1999b) are good examples. They begin with impeccable statements of vision and aims and they then list a multitude of initiatives, from the University for Industry to Higher Still, from Investors in People to National Training Organisations. The reader is left to speculate on exactly how and why these initiatives, valuable though they are, will achieve the vision. The reader is also left to speculate on how it is all to be funded, especially if we are adding more to what is already there. The end result is a plethora of agencies purporting to collaborate but, in reality, jockeying for position to drive their own agendas through these initiatives. However, if the vision is to be realised, then some fundamental aspects of the current learning landscape need to be reviewed, before we set about channelling resources into projects.[1]

What Do We Mean by Lifelong Learning?

The idea, or ideal, of lifelong learning is not new. Tight (1996) notes that lifelong education was adopted as a concept by UNESCO in 1970 and by the Council of Europe in 1973 and 1975. Professor Frank Coffield (1997) similarly places the origin of debate about a learning society in the 1970s with the work of Torsten Husen who predicted that a learning society would be created by the year 2000. In the intervening 20 years, the concepts of lifelong learning and a learning society have been debated and appropriated by politicians, professionals, managers and academics, with a resultant variety of concepts, definitions and lists of characteristics. Whilst a good deal of progress has been made by various nations, no society has yet achieved the kind of systems advocated by these early proponents. No society has yet had the courage to change the things that matter.

In essence, this debate is about the role and purpose of education for individuals, society and the economy. It is not a new debate but it is particularly necessary at a time when the vision of a learning society is being used to determine and justify policy initiatives, to channel resources and energy and to influence the behaviour and choices of individuals.

To think of education as holistic, meaning integrated or inter-related, is one way to begin to give some substance to the aspirational notions of 'a learning age', 'a learning society' and 'lifelong learning'. It might enable us to define these aspirations in terms of outcomes such as:

- an open, accessible, flexible, integrated framework of learning opportunities and qualifications;
- learning entitlements for the individual which can be integrated with life, work, leisure, community and family;
- education and training systems which contribute fully to a prosperous economy, an inclusive society and a participative

democracy.

Coffield (1997: 450), in his role as co-ordinator of the ESRC Learning Society Project, defined a learning society in similar terms as:

...one in which all citizens acquire a high quality general education, appropriate vocational training and a job (or a series of jobs) worthy of a human being while continuing to participate in education and training throughout their lives. A learning society would combine excellence with equity and could equip all its citizens with the knowledge, understanding and skills to ensure national economic prosperity and much besides. The attraction of the term 'the learning society' lies in the implicit promise not only of economic development but of regeneration of our whole public sphere. Citizens of a learning society would, by means of their continuing education and training, be able to engage in critical dialogue and action to improve the quality of life for the whole community and to ensure social integration as well as economic success.

Schuller (1998: 11), more concisely, has suggested that a learning society must 'offer learning opportunities to all its citizens, and in such a way as to furnish a realistic chance of making use of them.'

Whichever of these criteria is preferred, they both suggest some areas in which strategic interventions need to be considered.

Options for Strategic Change

I suggest three areas for consideration:
- our current emphasis on full-time initial post-16 education;
- the bewildering and unco-ordinated arrangements for student support for non-advanced post-16 education and training;
- the absence of a national skills strategy for Scotland, at all levels, but especially at the higher skill levels.

At present, the predominant, visible and valued model of post-

16 education is comprised of one or two further years of schooling, followed immediately by full-time further or, preferably, higher education leading to one of a limited range of formal qualifications. Every year, for example, any debate about lifelong learning is overshadowed by media coverage of Higher and A-level results, followed by the annual frenzied scramble to match tens of thousands of prospective students with places on full-time degree courses. National news broadcasts images of joy and despair as young people receive their results are powerful reinforcers of what society values as educational achievement and progression. We are proud, in Scotland, that nearly 50 per cent of 18 year olds enter higher education. But how interested are we in the other 50 per cent? Where is the media coverage of these young people, their successes in getting into jobs, modern apprenticeships and traineeships? Where is the public concern about the ones for whom there is no obvious way forward because they have failed? If we are serious about lifelong learning, then we have to question the validity of directing so much of our resources and attention towards full-time university education for those in the 16–21 age range.

There can be no doubt about the need to change attitudes to learning if we are to improve participation in learning. Studies have shown that significant proportions of the population say that they do not participate in any form of learning and have no intention of so doing. We should not be surprised at this lack of interest. Outside the traditional safe route of highers and a degree, most learning is labelled as second class and second choice. Skills training, apprenticeships and vocational qualifications are neither valued nor recognised by a society which measures success in terms of the age participation index in higher education. Training opportunities for the unemployed, the disadvantaged and the excluded are presented as projects or schemes. We somehow expect these participants to value and demand opportunities for which eligibility is defined in terms of previous failure, failure to attain 'recognised' qualifications, failure to obtain and keep a job. So, before we rush into awareness raising campaigns to change attitudes to learning, it is worth looking at what these new learners will face.

They will certainly not yet find a fully open, accessible, flexible and integrated qualifications framework which enables them to fit learning into the rest of their lives, receive credit for what they have learned and choose from opportunities to progress. The Scottish Credit and Qualifications Framework, incorporating Higher Still, creates only the potential for change. A new system of educational opportunity will require serious shifts in attitude and behaviour on the part of those with vested interests in the status quo, primarily institutions and professionals. If we are serious about lifelong learning then we have to stop deciding who passes and who fails, and start valuing everyone's achievements.

Our new learners will also encounter a bewildering and discouraging array of potential sources of funding including benefits, bursaries, access funds, grants, training allowances, career development loans, tax relief, fee waivers and, in some pilot geographical areas, educational maintenance allowances and individual learning accounts. Employers encounter a similar array of subsidised and unsubsidised incentives to hire and train people who are labelled as low achievers. The urgent need for a radical overhaul of funding for all post-16 learning is of far greater importance than the much publicised debate about tuition fees for full-time higher education.

Holistic education requires that what people learn is fit for purpose and there is much to be said for a demand-led approach to determining priorities. No-one would disagree that well-informed learners should be able to choose what they study at whatever level and employers should have access to skills training relevant to their employees and their business prospects. Providers should respond flexibly and much has been achieved in recent years. Further education colleges, in particular, continuously extend, update and modernise their curriculum to respond to the demands of 400,000 learners, both employed and unemployed, per year.

An unsophisticated demand-led ethos, however, underplays the barriers which are created by qualifications frameworks, institutional and employment structures and societal obstacles. For example, Keep (1997) argues that a demand-led approach will succeed only if there are improvements to the responsiveness of the education system, changes in skills policies and the tackling of long-standing structural barriers to learning, such as lack of time, money and childcare. There is a myth of constant change in the education system. This disguises the fact that most change concerns the curriculum, not the structures which determine and influence who learns and why.

Even in terms of curriculum, the process of change is not consistent. The Scottish Consultative Council on the Curriculum is charged with advising government on the fitness for purpose of the school curriculum. There is no process for reviewing strategically the fitness for purpose, in social and economic terms, of the range of courses in post-16 education and training curriculum, including higher education. The Scottish Enterprise Network plays an indirect role and it is assumed that universities, colleges and training providers set their own standards of responsiveness on the basis of the best information they can acquire. It would be stretching a point to describe this as a national learning and skills strategy.

In respect of these issues, the Scottish Parliament has a new opportunity to consider how it might respond to some of these questions and issues, and in partnership with stakeholders.

Initial Post-16 Education: Time for Change?

It is time to reduce the period that some young people spend in initial full-time education. Mass higher education to degree level for young people is not compatible with holistic lifelong learning, either in principle or in the availability of resources. A phased reduction in the number of young people completing six years of initial post-16 education would release resources to support skills training, continuous professional development and part-time further and higher education for these and other young people and for adults. Although for different reasons, the Garrick Report (National Committee of Inquiry, 1997b) took a similar view, recommending:

183

- the widespread development of a three-year degree;
- staged completion of higher education;
- recognition of the value of one to two year HNC/HND programmes.

Neither the Dearing nor the Garrick Reports, disappointingly, advocated expansion of part-time higher education, nearly half of which is currently provided by further education colleges and which remains marginal in higher education institutions. It is difficult to understand how lifelong learning can be realised unless there is a considerable expansion in part-time, not full-time, post-school education.

There is another strong reason for a move in this direction. The Dearing Report and other studies found that entry to full-time university education for young people is strongly biased in favour of the higher income groups. Higher education for mature students, many of whom study part-time and at further education colleges has a bias towards the less wealthy. A reduction in the period some young people spend in full-time education (which may be preferable to a reduction in the number of young people entering higher education) and a redirection of resources towards adults returning to education in later life is likely to redress the balance in social terms much more effectively than the current attempts of higher education institutions to 'improve access' by encouraging young people from disadvantaged areas to participate in schemes which will reconfigure their educational achievements into something which higher education institutions can recognise as meeting their entrance criteria.

Accessible Student Support

There is also an urgent need to rationalise funding, including funding for student support, for non-advanced post-16 education and training and to create a learning entitlement linked to employment, not to unemployment. The thinking behind Individual Learning Accounts and Workplace Progression Accounts is sound.

The concept of a managed entitlement to funded learning for all, based on investment by the individual, by the public purse and by employers, linked to progression and to life transitions, would be a powerful way to motivate and to change attitudes and values. There is every reason to bring funding for all post-school education and training, including higher education, in to one integrated Learning Account system. This, of course, closes the circle. The visible and valued availability of funded lifelong learning at all levels would reduce demand for full-time initial higher education, not by imposing quotas, but by offering alternative options. The Scottish Parliament should begin by recognising and celebrating achievement for all learners as a counter to the current emphasis only on highers and degree graduation.

A fully developed Learning Account system would also be compatible with a lifelong learning record, linked to periodic 'health checks', linked in turn to entitlement to financial support. The well-established principle of a continuing professional development record is equally applicable at all levels of achievement and at all stages of participation in the labour market. It would shift the emphasis away from credit and qualifications as an end in themselves, towards valuing the intrinsic purpose of learning and its relationship to employment, leisure or community involvement.

Return on Investment

In addition, I believe that it is important to return to priorities in the post-school curriculum, in the social and economic sense. Intervention in the supply-side is also necessary and it is time to give thought to how public funds should be used. I would argue for a shift in emphasis to:

- basic skills training to address disturbingly high levels of functional illiteracy and innumeracy in the workforce;
- core skills in accordance with the EU principles of employability, adaptability, enterprise and equality;
- active citizenship;

- vocational skills up to level three for the whole workforce;
- high level skills across the full range of occupations within the current and predicted labour market and including highly developed core skills.

In advocating these priorities, I do not undervalue the broader purposes of education, to sustain intellectual development and to increase and disseminate knowledge and understanding, at all levels, for their own sake. I simply suggest that, in this case, the chicken does come before the egg. A high skill, high wage, low unemployment economy is better able to afford to sustain the pursuit of learning for its own sake.

The bold and imaginative step of establishing a ministerial portfolio of Enterprise and Lifelong Learning creates a policy environment in which the Scottish Parliament can debate these questions of priority. The new Parliament has the opportunity to create, in partnership with employers and trade unions, not a centralist planning model, but new strategic mechanisms to integrate economic and social development strategies with the development of the learning industry. The 1999 Scottish Enterprise Network 'cluster' strategy has already demonstrated how, in the microelectronics/semi-conductor industry, an integrated approach involving manufacturers, supply chain companies, customers, higher education and training providers can improve competitiveness and solve 'skills gaps'.

At the time of writing, the Department for Education and Employment (1999) has published Learning to Succeed, a consultation paper on the establishment of new Learning and Skills Councils which will fund all post-16 education and training (excluding higher education). This initiative is retrogressive. However important it is to improve basic and intermediate skills, one of our most urgent needs is to generate high level skills across the full range of modern occupations and technologies. This cannot be done without the enthusiastic involvement of employers, which the proposed Learning and Skills Councils risk losing. It presumably cannot be done by excluding higher education. In Scotland, we need to be more ambitious for the future of the economy.

Summary

It is now time to decide what is meant by lifelong learning and to agree that it will not come about through a series of initiatives and projects which define eligibility in terms of failure. Progress requires a new questioning of purpose, priorities and values involving all stakeholders. For the individual, learning must be complementary with work, with family life, and with participation in community affairs. It must be available at different stages of life and at times of transition, equitably and equally. The focus has to move from education and systems to learning and an active learning curriculum (see, for example, Bentley, 1998; Keep and Mayhew, 1997). All achievements must be visibly valued within a single system. For society and the economy, education must be integrated with the development of a high skills, high wage, low unemployment economy which can afford to channel individual and national wealth into supporting the broader purposes of learning.

Endnote

1 I have deliberately avoided the issue of new technology in this chapter but assume that it will also progressively transform education through the networked distribution of information and therefore of self-directed learning. The policy developments suggested here are highly compatible with these technological developments — so long as a national and not a piecemeal approach to 'wiring' the current educational infrastructure is pursued.

CHAPTER 18

ROSIE ILETT AND
SUE LAUGHLIN

MODERNISING

HEALTH:

THE PARADOXES AT
THE HEART OF
POLICY-MAKING

*Despite real improvements, Scotland's record of ill-health remains
a matter for serious concern and cries out for concerted action. Our
position at or near the top of international 'league tables' of the
major diseases of the developed world — coronary heart disease,
cancer and stroke — is unacceptable and largely preventable. Good
health is more than not being ill: we need to work on a broad front
to improve physical, mental and social well-being, fitness and
quality of life... Progress requires co-ordination and a lasting
commitment so that new ideas can develop and initiatives have
time to come to fruition. (Scottish Office, 1999c: 2–3)*

This quotation from the recent Public Health White Paper,
Towards a Healthier Scotland, demonstrates why the Scottish Parliament
has set itself the task of improving the health of Scotland. But, while
it has considerable powers to address some factors which affect
health, and the ability to determine the structure and function of the
National Health Service in Scotland, its power to affect overall the
macro-economic structures that determine health and ill-health in
Scotland are constrained.

This chapter will explore the tensions and difficulties that the
Scottish Parliament may face which could limit its potential impact
on the health of the public. It will propose that at the heart of the
matter — and firmly imbedded in *Towards a Healthier Scotland* — are

a set of paradoxes which unless understood and addressed, will inhibit the Parliament's potential impact.

Healthy Intervention

Over the past two decades our understanding of the determinants of health has undergone a profound change. In many ways, it has returned to an earlier Victorian wisdom when medical officers of health sought to address poor housing, access to reasonable diet and poor hygiene to improve the health of the public. A recent attempt to identify the fundamental reasons for inequalities in health and their physiological associations, highlighted three inter-related sets of research evidence (Wilkinson, 1996, 1999). Firstly, despite great financial and emotional investment, medical services provided by the National Health Service (including the National Health Service in Scotland), are not the major determinants of health in the population. These activities have minimal, if any, impact on health inequalities, as evidenced in the growing gap in health outcomes since the NHS's inception fifty years ago. Secondly, there is growing awareness of the fact that well-known behavioural risk factors leave most of the social gradient in health unexplained, and finally, social selection makes only a minor contribution to health inequalities.

This view is not surprising, as there have been a succession of official and influential reports, moving from a medical model of health to a more social model of health over the last few years, most notably *The Black Report: On Health Inequalities* (Townsend, Whitehead and Davidson, 1982). This was followed by *The Health Divide*, produced by the Health Education Council for England and Wales (Whitehead, 1987), and more recently the Acheson Inquiry: *An Independent Enquiry into Health Inequalities* (1998). The themes contained in the first two of these important reports were systematically ignored by the previous UK Conservative Government, but are now being adopted by the Scottish Parliament, following its recent endorsement of *Towards a Healthier Scotland*. There is still uncertainty, however, about the current UK Government's response to the Acheson Inquiry.

These reports encapsulate a broader thinking on health than

one concerned purely with the provision of medicine and clinical interventions to cure physical disease and ill-health. They recognise the role of material, environmental and cultural factors in determining health and accept that poor health results from all decisions made within society. They view inequalities as a social justice issue and as a social cost, and reflect the view that it is not wealthy societies per se that are the healthiest, as mortality rates in developed countries relate to income distribution and not to overall average income. Income distribution correlates with social status and the index of civic community, a lack of which has been shown to relate to poor health outcomes as the result of anxiety created by the experience of social disempowerment and lack of social support (Wilkinson, 1996, 1999). And again, evidence shows that the experience of inequality as determined by gender, race, disability and sexuality can also have a significant impact on population health. As Doyal (1995: 1) points out, for example, in relation to gender:

> There are obvious differences between male and female patterns of sickness and health. Not surprisingly, these stem in part from biological differences between the sexes... The situation is more complex than at first might appear. All societies continue to be divided along the fault line of gender and this too has a profound effect on the wellbeing of both men and women.

The implication of these points are that health improvements are only achievable by creating a more egalitarian society where social and economic policy is informed by its likely impact on health. This position should underpin all policy-making and legislative activity of the new Parliament, along with the belief that good health is a right for all the people of Scotland. The concept of joined-up thinking and holistic government is ideally suited to addressing health inequalities and advocating for health sensitive policy (Stewart, 1998).

Paradoxes in Provision

For change to be attainable, a number of paradoxes which are likely to inhibit progress need to be considered. We propose that there are five main assumptions which combine both long-standing myths and linear thinking to form complex and subtle barriers to change. These assumptions must be examined and dismantled for any modernising of governance and policy-making around health to be successful. We will address these individually.

Paradox1: doctors are regarded as guardians of public health
Who are the guardians of public health? In government, the primary formal guardian of population health is the Chief Medical Officer whose title exemplifies linkage between health and medicine. At a local level, the Scottish population is protected by Directors of Public Health within the fifteen Health Boards, who are medically qualified and whose objectives are undertaken mainly by consultant doctors in public health. In Scottish universities, heads of Public Health Departments are also medical doctors. Even the Health Education Board of Scotland, the main provider of lay health promotion and health education services, is currently headed by a doctor.

This is not to suggest that these individuals, or the resources and services which they manage, restrict their thinking only to medical matters, but indicates the power of medicalisation and the institutionalisation of the medical model. The entrenchment of this model has helped thwart or prevent the development of the role that others within the NHS, or outside it, have in taking responsibility for improving health. As a recent commission on health found, 'a broad public health approach that is not exclusively medical needs to be taken' (MacLeod, 1990: 2).

Paradox 2: resources, and accountability for health, are still seen as being within the NHS
The medicalisation of health has meant that both government and the public still place, and demand, resources for the National Health Service hoping that it can solve social ills much wider than the treatment of illness and disease. And, even more important than resource allocation is where accountability is placed. On the one hand, the health service has an accountability mechanism with

government, and is effectively accountable on interventions which are not designed to promote health (as opposed to manage illness). On the other hand, it is given responsibility for addressing inequalities in health for which it does not have the means. Even more paradoxically, there is no real onus on this structure to develop services which take health determinants into account.

Where the NHS could make a difference — in the patient's experience of ill health — there is no real impetus for improving the delivery of health care so that the diagnosis and management of health problems incorporates understandings of the social, as well as biological, factors which influence the reasons that people present to the health service, or for improving the interaction between professional and client. As the recent *Fair Shares for All: Report of the National Review of Resources Allocation for the NHS in Scotland* states:

> *Deprived groups may be less likely to use services for a variety of reasons...they may be less likely to seek diagnosis and treatment than affluent populations; they may not participate in screening programmes; they may be less effective at articulating their needs; or for various reasons the health care system may not ensure that they achieve access to the appropriate diagnosis, care and treatment... There has also been concern that ethnic minorities may not achieve a level of access to health services that adequately reflects their relative needs. (Scottish Executive, 1999a: 41)*

If we accept that agencies outwith the health service are crucial in determining health outcomes, then there needs to be clarity as to who ensures that local authorities, for example, make health improvement a corporate goal. Where is the push for ministers in the Scottish Executive, responsible for running non-health departments, to fashion their policies using possible improvements in health as criteria, and where is the accountability mechanism? Similarly, and resonating with the first paradox, why have COSLA, for example, who have expanded their strategic thinking well beyond the constraints of a medical model of health, just appointed a medically qualified person to take that work forward? Even though the appointee will be assisted by a soon-to-be appointed development officer, with a probable broad background in health and related activities, the message is still clear: the medicalisation of health continues.

Paradox 3: health interventions are seen as being most effective when targeted at the socially excluded

Towards a Healthier Scotland recognises the role of life circumstances in affecting health, but proposes interventions associated with risk behaviours or disadvantaged groups. Such interventions, however, are likely to have limited long-term effectiveness. The prioritising by the UK Government and the White Paper of teenage pregnancy and poor nutrition, for example, arguably falls within this category. These complex social issues will be addressed via changed life-styles and behaviours, rather than trying to take a root and branch approach which accomodates all factors that influence these forms of activity. And again, even though there is acknowledgement of the long time-scales required to deliver in these, and similar areas, funding of short-term projects is often the chosen way forward. Better funding of mainstream services to manage resources and activities in a way which really makes a difference or, alternatively, the mainstreaming of existing and successful innovative projects, are the only certain methods of achieving the required changes.

Funding is a major issue, but it is partly fudged in *Towards a Healthier Scotland*. This fudge is compounded by the general approval the report received from health professionals and the public. Pointing out this fudge is not to take the traditional argument that the health service only needs more money — to do so would contradict our proposition — but is to say that health sensitive policy is only achievable through the financially-enhanced activities of a wide range of agencies and stakeholders. There is little mention of the role of these agencies and stakeholders in the report. Moreover, asserting, correctly in our opinion, that the voluntary and community sector have a key role to play in addressing health inequalities is almost ironic given the financial constraints that many organisations and initiatives here are experiencing, dependant as they are on local authority money.

To illustrate these constraints, the only additional resource identified in *Towards a Healthier Scotland* is £15m for four Demonstration Projects, Starting Well (child health), Healthy Respect (teenage sexual health), The Heart of Scotland and The Cancer Challenge. If these are the key priorities, good practice already exists which could be awarded secure funding, rather than the development of PR-friendly, short-term opportunities, which will have arguably less effect. These four Demonstration Projects will be funded after open competition amongst Health Boards, who submit approved bids, which leads into our fourth paradox.

Paradox 4: allocating funding for health is best done through competition

Competition amongst Health Boards is mirrored by processes central to the Healthy Living Centre initiative. This funding opportunity is managed by the New Opportunities Fund, using Lottery money paid for by the public, and forms a major part of the rhetoric in the White Paper. Partnership and co-operation across statutory and voluntary agencies and across health and social agendas underpins the initiative, yet thousands of groups throughout Scotland are being set against each other, unclear as to the real criteria or time-scale, and uncertain as to whether their plans will ever reach fruition.

Many of these groups comprise people from deprived communities and socially excluded groups who have provided the very money for which they now hope to gain local benefit. They are competing for a total of £34.5m over five years for Scotland, with no evidence yet to suggest that the innovative projects which may eventually receive funding will achieve longer-term sustainability through local Health Boards or other resourcing organisations after the five-year period. There is also no evidence to suggest that any support will be available for the numerous projects being devised which receive no HLC funding. The demoralising and disempowering effects on many communities and groups is not difficult to imagine. Competition, in this context, is not healthy.

Paradox 5: scientific and medical health research is felt to be the most important

Finally, moves towards evidence-based health care and research are to be welcomed, as public monies need to be well spent to achieve the best possible outcomes, but the continued emphasis on medical and scientific research decreases their overall effect. Advocating this type of research as absolute, again reinforces the message that bio-medicine answers all the questions. There is scant reference within the White Paper and in public debates about the more complex investigations and processes which could inform joined-up policy imperatives and service planning, doing so by gathering together a varied span of evidence and information. As Whitehead (1997) points out, considering equity in health could, and should, be injected into policy-making at all levels, and epidemiological and health policy research can make a valuable contribution by helping to identify the most effective, efficient and equitable courses of action to tackle the health divide, rather than by concentrating only on adding to the medical body of knowledge.

We would suggest that the research remits of the Scottish Parliament should be broadly-based and draw from a wide spectrum of expertise and experience to better provide current, and plan future, services across all departments to improve Scotland's health. The acknowledgement of the role of health impact assessments does fulfil this recommendation to a certain extent, but there is extremely limited funding currently being made available to research the process, to identify the appropriate indicators of change or to facilitate a process of acceptability of their use by policy-makers.

Conclusion

Exploring these five paradoxes has indicated the difficulties that the Scottish Parliament faces in tackling ill-health in Scotland. The real challenge is to re-define health and to find ways of building structures which allow support for a social model of health to flourish, and to ensure that good practice which adopts this model is mainstreamed and made systematic. The good practice and ecumenical approach of many working in Scotland in the public health field, such as the Glasgow Healthy City Partnership, needs to be built on and replicated elsewhere, including within the Scottish Executive. Such models bring together key agencies across all sectors to plan health sensitive policy and to engage much more widely than the traditional thinking contained in the paradoxes that we have outlined here. If the Scottish Parliament can progress its thinking, and allow maximum participation by as wide a cross-section of the population as possible, national confidence will be boosted and a sense of achievement will be realised which will eventually show up as measurable improvements in morbidity and mortality. Scotland's population do not always have to be the sick men and women of Europe, but the way forward requires radical thinking and a re-direction of funding and prioritising, of which the ideas that we suggest here may only be the start.

CHAPTER 19

HOMES

ROBINA GOODLAD | # FOR THE

FUTURE

For the past twenty-five years, housing has been seen as a policy area appropriate for devolution to an Assembly or Parliament (Scottish Constitutional Convention, 1995). But in the twenty years between the two schemes for devolution in 1978 and 1998, the housing system and housing policy have changed radically, questioning the extent to which housing can be seen now as effectively devolved. This chapter traces the background to this paradox of centralised decentralisation, which Scotland has in common with other countries (Stephens and Goodlad, 1999). It reviews Scottish housing conditions, policies and institutional arrangements and then considers how we can reconceptualise the housing policy agenda to secure decent housing for all, taking account of Scotland's status within the UK.

Conditions, Policies and Institutions
Housing Conditions

Scotland has some serious housing problems affecting the health and well being of its citizens. These also have a potentially adverse impact on economic development, particularly in urban west central Scotland. Although the *Scottish House Condition Survey 1996* (Scottish Homes, 1997) reported a reduced level of below tolerable standard housing, from 4.7 per cent in 1991 to 1.3 per cent in 1996, it found serious problems of dampness and disrepair. One quarter (25 percent) overall and one third (34 per cent) of the public rented sector housing stock suffers from dampness and condensation and 16 per cent of public housing is in poor repair. Energy ratings are also a concern in all tenures, with more than nine in ten dwellings overall (93 per cent) not achieving the National Home Energy standard.

The worst neighbourhoods tend to also contain the largest concentrations of the most disadvantaged residents, suffering high levels of unemployment, isolation from amenities and other problems. These areas are dominated by local authority and housing association housing which generally house the poorest tenants. In 1996, median weekly income was £129 for housing association tenants and £135 for council tenants. However, private tenants had median weekly incomes of only £157 and some owner-occupiers, particularly outright owners, had equally low incomes (Scottish Homes, 1997). This demonstrates that no assumptions should be made about the quality and sustainability of the private sector. Relationship breakdown, a growing number of older owners and a reduced level of welfare support for mortgagors in arrears, demonstrate the vulnerability of some owners. Some ethnic minority groups occupy some of the poorest quality private housing.

Tenure

The most striking feature of the Scottish housing system in the post-war period has been the tenure structure, with a lower incidence of owner occupation — 60 per cent in 1997 — than in the rest of the UK. Although public (mainly local) authorities are still landlords on a large scale (28 per cent of the housing stock in 1997), this is only just over half the level in 1976 (see Table 1 below). This decline has arisen largely through the Right to Buy but also through stock transfer to housing associations and other non-profit landlords. In addition, some properties have been transferred to private developers for redevelopment for owner occupation. The significance of tenure change to the devolution settlement is that only one-third of the population of Scotland now live in the social rented sector over which the Parliament has most direct influence. In addition, that influence

Table 1   Tenure structure of housing stock, Scotland, 1971–97 (percentages)

Year authority*	local occupation	owner renting	Private	Housing association	Total (000s)
1971	52.3	30.5	17.2**	——	1,815
1976	54.2	33.6	12.2**	——	1,921
1981	52.1	36.4	9.7	1.8	1,970
1986	46.9	43.1	7.5	2.5	2,050
1991	37.8	52.4	7.1	2.6	2,160
1996	29.7	59.2	6.8	4.4	2,246
1997***	27.9	60.2	6.8	5.1	2,267

Source: Housing Statistics, Housing and Construction Statistics and Scottish Office Statistical Bulletin (Housing Series).

* includes new town development corporation and Scottish Special Housing Association/Scottish Homes
** includes 'other'
*** provisional

is qualified by the restructuring of housing finance in the last twenty years (Table 1).

Housing finance

If the Scottish Assembly had been created in 1979, it would have been responsible for a much larger capital and revenue housing programme than the Parliament has currently inherited. New house building and rehabilitation are now more concentrated in the housing association sector, and expenditure on Housing Support Grant (HSG), the 'bricks and mortar' subsidy for council housing, has been almost eliminated. Council housing capital allocations are insufficient to allow new building, or even to maintain remaining stocks in an acceptable condition. As HSG declined, personal rebates (housing benefit) grew. This is now the largest item of public spending on housing in Scotland, as Table 2 below shows. Public spending trends have also diminished the role of local authorities in relation to repair and improvement grants in the private sector, following the abolition of a separate allocation for housing in the name of local government autonomy.

In the social rented sector, Scottish Homes received a growing proportion of subsidy for housing associations (relative to local

Table 2   Public spending for housing in Scotland, 1997 (£m)

Local authority capital allocations (i.e. permission to borrow)	192
Local authority capital spending arising from 25 per cent capital receipts	57
Local authority expenditure on private sector	59
Scottish Homes capital and revenue	265
Housing Support Grant (i.e. to local authority Housing Revenue Accounts)	15
Miscellaneous	7
Housing Benefit Local Authority tenants	586
Housing Benefit private/Housing Association tenants	308
Income support to owner occupiers (MIRAS)	178
Total	1,697

Source: Convention of Scottish Local Authorities (1998).

government) in the period up to the 1997 General Election. Housing associations were required to borrow up to one-third of the cost of their development projects, so achieving more units per taxpayer's pound. Since the election, the balance has begun to swing back to council housing, through New Housing Partnerships, but only to facilitate more transfers from the sector by using public spending to lever private finance to assist the renovation of run-down housing and the funding of debt remaining after transfer. A sum of £323 million has been made available for 1997 to 2002.

The significance of these trends for Scottish devolution is to diminish the new Parliament's formal levers over the housing system. The reduction in public renting reduces direct control of the public sector over housing. Continued public spending restraint, and the attraction of using private finance to supplement public finance, makes it likely these trends will continue. In addition, the key policy instrument, housing benefit, is retained by Westminster. However, because policies open to the Parliament can have implications for the housing benefit bill, the Scottish Block will include expected expenditure on housing benefit and council tax benefit at the time the Scottish Parliament comes into operation (Dewar, 1998).

Given the continuing differences in the tenure structures of

Scotland, England and Wales, and the historical differences in rent levels, it is not clear how the Treasury will judge in the longer term what would be appropriate housing benefit expenditure in Scotland. This could become one of the most contentious features of the annual negotiations over block grant. There is a need here for Scottish interests to be represented in Whitehall and this issue alone justifies the continuing existence of the post of Secretary of State for Scotland. But the ministers and civil servants will be best able to promote Scottish interests if equipped with a vision of the housing system Scotland requires, backed up with evidence about the impact of different rent regimes, for example. This raises questions about the nature of housing policy in this new context.

Towards a Vision of Housing

Discussion of housing policy objectives often fails to get beyond the blandest statements such as Donald Dewar's 'Every household in Scotland should be able to live in a decent, secure and affordable home' (Scottish Office, 1999a: 3). The key words in this sentence — household, decent, secure, affordable and home — all need definition before a housing strategy becomes clear, and this still leaves open the means to be used to bring about change. For much of the post-war period the main means used to secure decent housing was council housing and for a period it achieved substantial success in providing security, improved health and affordability for a large proportion of the population.

Over the last twenty years this approach was challenged by the neo-liberal Right, seeking to restrict the role of the state to securing civil and political rather than social rights. The welfare state — a set of social rights, including council housing — has been defended by the Left, but the paternalistic welfare state is acknowledged as requiring modernisation. Within the Left, a contest rages between those who wish to continue to provide services and goods directly and those who wish citizens to play a more active role in a more pluralist society and economy. Those on the Left who identify social rights in housing with public provision are, however, ignoring the evidence about state support for private provision which created today's tenure structure — council housing was never the only means to influence housing conditions. There are many ways to use the state's resources actively in improving the quality of citizens' lives. The contest over the roles of the state, the market and civil society is illustrated in housing policy in the case of the switch from local authorities to housing associations as the favoured providers of social housing — a victory for a form of communitarianism, modified by the role of the state as regulator and funder.

The meaning of tenure is therefore contingent on particular histories, geographies and policies. State resources can be deployed in support of a variety of forms of private housing as well as public housing. The Parliament's task is to explore the scope for a variety of social rights in relation to different tenures to secure its conception of social justice. There are many more than two ways — public and private — to choose from in forging a new agenda for housing in Scotland.

A New Agenda

It follows from the democratic justification of the Parliament that it should have a housing strategy. It is crucial that this strategy is comprehensive: no housing strategy is credible if it does not take account of the nature and incidence of owner occupation, the impact of housing benefit or the role of financial institutions, for example, all issues that might be seen as dealt with by the UK government. In the past, the Scottish Office took such a comprehensive approach in housing policy but the Green Paper published a few weeks before the Scottish elections (Scottish Office, 1999a) was largely silent on the tenure forms that house two-thirds of the population — owner occupation and private renting. Such timidity may be understandable in the lead up to the Scottish elections but represents a serious danger for the Executive and the Parliament if it continues.

The housing vision of the Executive should in part contain references to policy instruments controlled by Whitehall. The Executive and Parliament must see the limits to their role as a challenge not a problem. This requires innovation in the development of new policy instruments, and lobbying of Whitehall departments in relation to UK policy instruments that require change or variation. The Scottish Executive will need to be able to back up such requests with strong evidence. The support and lobbying role of the Secretary of State for Scotland in the British cabinet will be crucial while Whitehall learns that the devolution settlement does not end the tradition of territorial interests being represented in UK decision-making.

Three other dangers are present in existing debates about housing policy:

- that debates will be dominated by the search for clarity about the shape and role of the key institutions involved in the governance and management of housing;
- that inter-relationships between housing and other areas of public policy will be neglected, and in particular the definition of housing as social policy will lead to a neglect of housing as economic and urban policy;
- that the current obsession with stock transfer will distract policy-makers from other issues.

Housing Governance and Management

There are some key institutions in Scottish housing policy whose role needs to be clarified — primarily local authorities, Scottish Homes and housing associations (Goodlad, 1999). These can and should be dealt with quickly but the fact that the destiny of many housing professionals will be determined by decisions to be taken will make securing consensus very difficult. Local authorities should be granted the status and relationship with the Parliament suggested in the report of the McIntosh Commission (Commission on Local Government and the Scottish Parliament, 1999). Scottish Homes should be recast as a regulator and supervisor of social landlords and its policy staff made accountable to the Scottish Executive. Housing associations need to be reassured of their key role in the new Scotland, even though they may not be seen by all local authorities as automatic inheritors of the former council housing stock. Tenants need to have, at last, the statutory rights to participation heralded in a recent consultation paper (Scottish Office, 1998c). Getting the roles and relationships clarified is important now, and in the future, but the substance of policy will be neglected if too much time is spent on this process.

Housing as Social, Economic and Urban Policy

That housing has been located in the Executive ministry responsible for social inclusion is neither surprising nor inappropriate. From that base the contemporary role of housing in community development, community care and health policy can be developed. The programmes, such as the rough sleepers' and the empty homes' initiatives, started or expanded by the Blair Government can be developed, as can ways of improving the design of housing and the support provided for people in need of community care. Complex links between homelessness, health, educational attainment and social exclusion can also be addressed without adopting over-simplistic models of cause and effect.

Welcome as this approach to holistic government is, it is in danger of not being holistic enough and neglecting the relevance of housing to economic and urban policy. The economic difficulties of Glasgow and other urban areas have been compounded by the dereliction that characterises the urban environment and by the scarcity of housing that is attractive to the middle class. This in turn has exacerbated the flight from the city to the suburbs where schools as well as the environment are perceived as more attractive. This has primed a vicious spiral in which the location of jobs close to attractive residential areas has further compounded the difficulties of the poorest areas. In addition, the absence of new building and adequate modernisation work in the public sector in the last twenty years has meant the loss of jobs and apprenticeships and the multiplier effects they bring — experienced most severely in the poorest areas of public housing. Planning, urban, economic and social policies all have to work together to tackle this set of problems as they apply to the largest urban area of Scotland, west central Scotland. The Glasgow Alliance has made a good start with this task.

Stock Transfer

If newspaper headlines are taken as a measure of housing policy debates then the issue dominating in Scotland currently is the proposed transfer of council housing to new non-profit landlords in Glasgow and elsewhere. To senior housing professionals, the combination of disrepair, inadequate investment, high debt and dissatisfied tenants points unambiguously towards transfer on the basis of the evidence of workable models for investment, tenant involvement and common ownership. To trade unionists, some tenants and some political activists, the issue is about privatisation and the danger to job security, tenants' rights and accountability. The debates are consuming enormous amounts of time and this carries the danger that other issues will be neglected. For professionals well versed in the issues there is a particular need for patience with those less well informed. Civil servants, ministers, local government officers and councillors cannot afford to neglect this issue but need to strike a balance with the other housing issues and tenures — including the most troubled of all, private renting — that should command their attention.

Conclusion

This chapter has argued that Scotland has some serious housing problems and that changes in housing tenure and finance over the last twenty years mean that the Parliament has less direct leverage over the housing system than was envisaged in the 1978 scheme for devolution. The Scottish Executive and Parliament need to take a wide view, not just to secure the holistic government required to tackle housing and related social, economic and urban problems, but to ensure that policy takes account of UK as well as Scottish policy levers. This should be based on an understanding of housing policy as more than the provision of social rented housing. A variety of new and old methods must be used, including lobbying Whitehall departments with a continuing role in the tax, finance and housing benefit systems that affect housing. There are dangers that the Executive, Parliament, local authorities and others will neglect their comprehensive role in the search for clarity about the shape and role of the institutions involved in the governance and management of housing. A vision of an active and varied role for the state in securing the Scottish people's entitlement to decent housing in all tenures should inspire the parliamentarians as it inspired the citizens of Scotland to vote for the Parliament in 1997.

CHAPTER 20

COURTNEY PEYTON
AND IAN THOMSON

TOWARDS A SUSTAINABLE SCOTLAND

New thinking for the new Scotland needs to be 'sustainable' thinking. Based on concepts of interdependence, partnership, flexibility, recycling, diversity and learning, a sustainable Scotland will deliver the quality of life we expect from our new devolved status. Sustainability is a new driver providing an overarching framework for developing a new Scottish identity while eliminating the present waste of:

- peoples' talents and abilities due to poor education, social exclusion and discriminatory practices;
- human health potential due to poor housing, urban planning and poor public health;
- the many resources of our land, sea, lochs and rivers;
- indigenous flora and fauna and the ecological diversity which they possess;
- energy and resources caused by poor building design and construction, and by inefficient production, distribution and retailing across industries.

Scotland has a wealth of assets, but as with most developed countries it has been wasteful in their use. A modern sustainable Scotland will:

- emerge from an interweaving of all economic, social and environmental objectives and thinking;

- build a healthy and diverse economy adapted to change, that provides long term security to its people and recognises social and ecological limits;
- be locally reliant with a minimal ecological footprint;
- be a learning society, willing to openly share both its successes and its failures to the greater benefit of all.

This is not a utopian ideal. Technologies, processes, products and services are developing consistent with the fundamentals of sustainability. In addition, effective models of regulations, industrial development and planning have already been developed. Models of sustainable businesses and economies are gaining acceptance as practical and achievable, and superior to the current concepts. Information, knowledge and management decision support tools are now available to help decision-makers at all levels, and there is evidence of a change in basic values and morals moving towards sustainable living.

Applying the Process of Sustainable Development

Many have offered definitions of sustainable development, capturing in a sentence the essential attributes of sustainability. The Brundtland Report (World Commission on Environment and Development, 1987: 63) defines the essence of sustainable development as 'a process of change in which the exploitation of resources, the direction of investments, the orientation of technological development, and institutional change are all in harmony and enhance both current and future potential to meet human needs and aspirations'. Others have offered different definitions but a sustainable Scotland would not spring to life even if we had an agreed definition. It will emerge from a complex interaction of seemingly trivial actions, attitude shifts and symbolic political events. Sustainable Scotland will not depend upon multi-national sustainability treaties, but on the synergistic impact of decisions at individual, organisational, business and governmental levels.

At an individual level, it will emerge from changes in our attitudes and lifestyles:

- what we buy and where it comes from;
- how we work and who we work for;
- what we teach children and how they travel to school;
- where we buy our new house or how we renovate our existing one;
- buying locally produced food and products which keep money within our communities;
- valuing resources for what they are worth, not what they cost.

At business and organisational levels, it will require consideration of:

- employment practices, remuneration packages and incentives;
- location, flexibility and design of healthy premises;
- training and learning opportunities, especially from cluster relationships with others, including 'competitors';
- what to make, how to make it, who to buy from, where they sell it, how they transport it, how much they charge, who has it when it is no longer useful, what can be made of it next.

At government levels, it will require:

- major legislative measures and small administrative changes;
- transparency of the civil service and partnership with outside bodies;
- overhauling building standards, controls, regulations;
- changes in what and how we tax;
- incentive and grant schemes encouraging ecological entrepreneurs in business and industry;
- environmental restoration rather than protection regulations and spending on prevention rather than response;
- changes in enforcement regimes and a trans-disciplinary approaches to legislative and regulatory change.

SECTION THREE: SOCIAL PRIORITIES

Sustainable systems echo natural systems and there appears to be an evolutionary advantage in co-operation. Capra (1996) suggests that complex life forms evolved not by competition but by networking. Partnership and co-operation are the tested models which should underpin our thinking about how to build sustainable anthropological systems — from processes to communities. To foster these systems sustainable Scotland requires a new infrastructure to link economic, social and natural environmental networks (Thomson with Talbot, 1998).

Sustainable Communities and Industrial Ecologies

Enabling Scottish communities to become sustainable represents one of the greatest long-term planning challenges in the twenty first century (Talbot, 1998). Defining characteristics of sustainable communities are increased local self-reliance, diversity as well as equality of opportunity, an equitable distribution of resources, a guarantee of participation in civic activity and an acceptance of responsibility and accountability for the direction and outcomes of that activity. A sustainable community is a community that uses and conserves its resources in such a way that the integrity of ecological processes are maintained and enhanced. This means:

- using renewable resources at a rate that can be maintained over time;
- gradually reducing reliance on non-renewable natural resources;
- limiting the release of toxic substances that do not readily break down in nature;
- using all resources — including land — as efficiently and fairly as possible;
- preserving biological diversity.

Sustainable communities of the future will possess the culture-specific knowledge and capacity to manage their resources in ways which are analogous to those of natural, ecological systems. Communities that successfully make the transition to becoming

210

sustainable will be learning communities — educated in the essentials of sustainable development and environmental stewardship and equipped to monitor and evaluate their own environmental performance.

Learning communities will be those able to adapt their social structures, their cultural values and their patterns of resource utilisation in response to the demands of sustainability and to share their learning experiences. Some models for sustainable communities can be found by examining Scotland's history. Although circumstances will have altered, learning from the past within the context of the present can be an educated means of travelling forward (Peyton, 1996).

Analogous to the development of sustainable communities is that of industrial ecologies, which apply similar metaphors and systems approaches to the industries of people and process. Just as nature works in eco-systems, where processes feed into each other and by-products of processes are not waste but feedstock into other symbiotic processes in the network, so can we inform our actions and choices on both personal and commercial levels. Industrial ecology, 'the study of the flows of materials and energy in industrial and consumer activities, of the effects of these flows on the environment, and of the influences of economic, political, regulatory, and social factors on the flow, use, and transformation of resources' (White, 1995: iv), can work at many levels. It may be as complicated as its most famous example in Kalumbourg, Denmark (which interconnects a power plant, a cement producer, a fish farm, community housing and farmland among others) or as simple as the traditional relationship in Scotland between breweries, distilleries and livestock farms. It is all systems thinking and be it a building, a process, a community, an industry, or a network, approaching it sustainably is key to long lasting and far-reaching success.

Can We Afford Not to Go this Way?

Sustainability is universally assumed to be unaffordable. While some components may appear expensive in the short term, for example major public transport programmes or other transitional investments, in many cases the costs over the life cycle of a sustainable solution will be less than an unsustainable one. Sustainability is about being less wasteful and having less waste costs.

Business and planning strategies such as cleaner technology (Clayton *et al.*, 1999), industrial ecology, eco-design, life-cycle costing cut out waste and pollution and improve profitability. Industrial pollution and waste is beginning to be seen as the result of poor management and bad business practice. Better product design, improved production methods, better material sourcing and improved distribution methods can reduce environmental impact, reduce costs and improve product value.

Sustainable business ideas question many current practices: paying to dispose of waste rather than selling it; buying expensive raw materials rather someone else's waste for a fraction of the cost; paying to dispose of waste rather than developing it into a new product. Dematerialisation, strategies where firms move away from making and selling a single product to providing the same functionality to their customers by service provision (for example, Interface and Rank Xerox) offers cost and value opportunities to both parties, whilst reducing the environmental impact and increasing employment.

In their ground breaking book *Factor Four*, von Weizasäcker *et al.* (1997) demonstrate practical ways in which we can half our resource use whilst doubling wealth and should be compulsory reading for all decision-makers. The answer to the question of whether we can afford to become sustainable, is actually another question, can we afford not to? Below, we outline some of the ways that sustainable thinking makes positive contribution to our working and living.

Application to Specific Sectors
Health Care

It is not only business that is wasteful, but also many broader areas of human industry and social patterns. We are all aware of the cost benefits of preventative health care compared with treating ill people. The financial cost savings themselves are significant but there are also the hidden costs of lost productivity and the physical and emotional debilitation of the patient and their family. Paradoxically many public health initiatives are linked with issues of sustainability: improved housing quality and urban planning, healthier diets, reduced environmental pollution, better sewage systems, eliminating social exclusion, improved educational opportunities. Sustainable Scotland will be a healthy Scotland.

Building
The energy saved over the lifetime of a well designed and constructed building can be more than the cost of the initial building. The cost benefits of the increased efficiencies of a workforce operating in a sustainable building can exceed the value of the energy savings. The holistic approach required includes considering: siting and orientation, material selection, elimination of toxins, reduction of embodied energy and energy in use, indoor air quality, designing out mechanical systems, flexibility, opportunities for re-use and disassembly. Buildings constructed using sustainable construction methods can cost less than 'conventional' buildings, they tend to last longer and are better. They are therefore a sounder investment, as insurers and lenders are beginning to realise (thirdwave, 1999). The tragic waste of life, human suffering, damaged physical resources (and related costs) following the recent Turkish earthquake could have been avoided with a construction cost increase of just three per cent.

Land Use Planning
Re-use of brownfield sites and the protection of the greenbelt are seen to be positive environmental choices because in addition to encouraging the increase of urban densities, such action decreases toxic land quantities and safeguards the green spaces separating our cities from the developing surrounding communities. But these are often limited approaches to large opportunities. Detoxifying land

only to then cover it over again with building complexes with large footprints, tarmac and paving undermines the opportunity to allow the land to contribute to human systems. Likewise, protecting greenbelt land in its current state rather than accepting that it is industrialised land (by virtue of past generations use of it for agricultural purposes — at the very least) and proactively returning it to greater ecological benefit through the reintroduction of past eco-systems is a true loss.

Taxes

Sustainable tax reforms are met with a knee-jerk opposition to the cost impact on poor, over-taxed business (particularly SMEs) and individuals. This is not always the case. Sustainable tax reforms utilise two corrective mechanisms. Firstly, they correct the current distorting effect of existing taxes and subsidies and, secondly, they introduce new taxes that support the basic principles of sustainability. Sustainable tax reform is about shifting from taxing goods to taxing bads. Existing tax systems penalise 'goods' — in particular human labour — and reward 'bads' — excessive resource use, pollution, inefficient use of energy, and destruction of communities. Ecological taxes have the potential to alter perverse incentive structures, reducing other taxes and deregulating environmental issues allowing prices for goods and services to tell the ecological truth about their lifecycle and impacts. Sustainable tax reform is a way of tackling unemployment and related social problems, by redistributing the balance of taxation away from desubsidising resource use in favour of labour and employment

Promoting Sustainable Enterprise

The true costs of unsustainable business practise are often under-estimated. Elkington (1998), Hawken (1994) and others argue that the costs to businesses of ignoring sustainability are substantial and that integrating sustainability into business strategy and operations is beneficial. Firms, in their decision-making, do not include the full costs and benefits of their actions (Gray et al., 1993).

They are dominated by a short-term bottom-line accounting culture, and are actually making decisions that are bad for themselves. Their decisions ignore many real business costs and real sources of value. Businesses should change their strategies to those mutually beneficial to themselves, society and the environment.

Successful business will be (and always has been) based on values and ethics. This is not the much-hyped and faddish 'corporate culture' promoted by business writers such as Peters and Waterman (1982) but the ethics which underpin management and organisation. Companies that are able to identify, understand and respond to those underlying values are more likely to be successful. Companies with clear values invest more in training employees and put money back into the communities buying their products. It is these companies that will have more success over the long term than those still caught up in a single bottom-line culture.

Firms can lose out if they ignore the changing underlying values of society. Business success depends on a strong sense of purpose and values within an organisation and the congruence of these values with external stakeholders. Financial markets react negatively to companies perceived to ignore these values. Recent examples include response to:

- Shell — attempted dumping of Brent Spar oil storage buoy (environment);
- Mark and Spencers — offshore manufacturing (commitment to local communities);
- Nike — use of child labour making trainers in the Far East (ethics);
- Bank of Scotland — partnership with right-wing TV evangelist Pat Robertson (ethics);
- Monsanto — aggressive promotion of Genetically Modified foods (environment and health).

The Way Forward

New vision will be required to evaluate the consequences of changes in economic, social and environmental systems. Business and social reforms can no longer be regarded in isolation, just as environmental reforms cannot be implemented without the social and business impact being taken into account. A sustainable Scotland will consist of three inter-related, mutually dependent elements: a sustainable economic system, a sustainable social system and a sustainable natural environment system. This relationship will form the basis of an eco-infrastructure.

The development of a Scottish eco-infrastructure (Figure 1) involves holistic perspectives, but there is also a need to concentrate on tangible day-to-day reforms and improvements. These reforms will be many and varied, reflecting the diversity of life in Scotland and its ever-changing nature. As long as these diverse changes are implemented in the spirit of the Scottish eco-infrastructure, progress towards sustainability will be achieved.

Sustainability may appear complicated. However, the solutions are often simple — it is our thinking that has to be different.

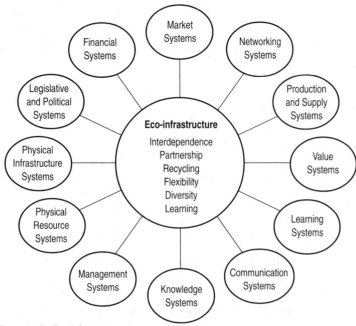

Figure 1   **An Eco-infrastructure**

Knowledge is a critical part of the move towards a sustainable Scotland. New knowledge systems need to be developed:

- ecological footprints of material and energy flows scalable from products to city-regions and beyond (Giradet, 1992);
- bio-regional mapping of industries developing closed loops (Alexander, 1998);
- sustainability potential assessments for contributions by the built environment to their context (thirdwave, 1999).

Knowledge is needed on how to:

- identify how such changes will impact upon existing structures;
- identify groups that will gain and groups that will lose;
- ascertain who would be more significantly affected than others, and the need for programmes of help or compensation;
- determine the combination of penalties and incentives that would best encourage innovation and development in the appropriate direction.

The way forward is to create an eco-infrastructure, such as the one above. As with all systems approaches, applying sustainability is much more about the process than it is about tactics (Talbot, 1998). One effective strategy is to identify and use 'leverage points' — places where a small shift in one thing can produce big changes in everything. This is doing more with less, achieving maximum results from minimum effort. The most powerful and effective way to intervene in a system is by changing the mindset or paradigm which gave rise to the system structure in the first place. The least effective is fiddling with the numbers (Meadows, 1997).

A real and lasting strategic advantage for Scotland can be gained from the integration of the principles and practices of sustainable development into all aspects of Scottish life and work. The goal is to create high quality jobs in environmentally sound enterprises based in sustainable communities which proactively benefit rather the merely safeguard the planet. The time is at hand.

Chapter 21

Racial

Rowena Arshad

Inclusion

AND THE STRUGGLE

FOR JUSTICE

*'We can educate the next generation to solve many of our problems
if we are courageous enough to free them from our own prejudices
and anxieties.' Charlotte Epstein (Quoted in Rudduck, 1986: 11)*

Charlotte Epstein made this statement as a teacher in
Pennsylvania in 1972, working with young people in the classroom
on controversial and sensitive issues of racism, sex and drugs. She
recognised that too often issues were not discussed because figures
of authority were afraid to be questioned, thereby creating a climate
which closed the potential for open dialogue and values growth.

As Scotland reclaims its identity and looks to the more
democratic participation of its entire people, a principal dynamic it
will need to grapple with is an 'assertion of difference'. The flowering
of different ethnicities and cultures are an expression, not of social
discord, but a new form of democracy through which the voices of
the previously silenced can now be heard.

It is an attractive proposition, to those who seek to lead our
new Parliament and Executive, that groups should have a right to
speak for themselves, in their own voice and have that voice accepted
as authentic and legitimate. There is some urgency about 'becoming
multicultural' now that policy makers and politicians are open to
being embarrassed by the lack of black/minority ethnic presence in
national bodies. The Stephen Lawrence Inquiry precipitated an

urgency to include those who have been marginalised and excluded. There is a desire to encourage civic participation and to make formal politics more open and participative, to be champions of social justice and to challenge discrimination and bigotry while maintaining an economic base that is buoyant and competitive.

In Search of Representativeness

On the journey towards inclusion of diversity, there are many dead ends and false starts. In an attempt to be inclusive, service providers and policy-makers may seek to ensure all communities (majority and minority) are included and consulted. This approach is to be commended. Unfortunately, many see this approach as an end to itself. Open consultation is the beginning that should lead to action. Open consultation in itself is not an indicator of anti-racist or culturally inclusive work. It may be an indicator of better communications procedures.

In addition, in the search for 'community representation', once there are definitions of which groups should be included, others are excluded. 'Community representatives' are often self-selected and may not be committed to principles of equality and justice, instead serving sectional interests. 'Community representation' can easily become a colourful cosmetic exercise, even more divisive than the former neglect.

What is more important is to seek dialogue with those that genuinely wish to see racial and cultural exclusion end for the benefit of all. It is critical that those who shape policy and strategies to challenge exclusion and bigotry are themselves accountable to people whom are marginalised and discriminated against. A strategy of dialogue would lead to learning about the reality of discrimination and exclusion on grounds of colour, ethnicity, culture, language and religion. As it advances, this process would lead to action to eliminate discrimination and advance inclusion. In doing so, there is a need to ensure that consultation has crossed ethnic boundaries. The voices of various groups should help guide future action.

Consultation also requires a move beyond the usual suspects

such as the Commission for Racial Equality, and well known black/ minority ethnic organisations and individuals, to include those that often do not have seats at the table. This may mean those who consult need to go to those being consulted, rather than the usual practice of requiring those being consulted to come to the table of the power holders.

Redefining Multiculturalism

The journey demands new maps, rewriting the notion of cultural so that all ethnicities, colours, religious groups and traditions are drawn into concepts of 'Scottish'. This change would mean deconstructing the notion of 'white' which is often presented as a fixed asocial but 'normal' category (Bonnett, 1999). By inference, all other colours that have been denied the privileges of normality/ normativity, are marked as marginal and inferior or not perceived to be 'Scottish'. How do we ensure that this is changed to accept brown and black faces as being 'Scottish'?

Multiculturalism has for too long been a code word for 'racial' issues when its definition should include socio-economic class, gender, language, culture, sexual preference, age and disability. This would mean accepting that cultures and ethnic categories are neither static nor stable. No two experiences or understandings are identical, because the formation of identity depends minutely on interaction within contexts. Therefore inclusion strategies need to recognise many interpretations and subjectivities. New Scotland needs to engage in debates that would allow all ethnicities/cultural groups to be visible and exposed for critical inspection. No single group should enjoy a predefined status or category.

The project for the next century should be for each group to examine how they can contribute to a tapestry that unites us all. But, the examination must debate how prejudices, intolerances and bigotry within each group are challenged and eliminated to prevent further oppression and discrimination. Racially inclusive strategies need to cross boundaries and revisit concepts of universalism, collective provision and citizenship. A strategy that satisfies the needs of specific identity groups will become a double-edged sword. Such a strategy might achieve results for particular groups, but it allows others to remain marginalised and for mainstream provision to abdicate a wider sense of responsibility.

New Scotland should also ensure that different cultural and ethnic groups find a way to express their opinions and bring forward examples that demonstrate how each group experiences discrimination and injustice. The congruence of experiences needs then to be highlighted but the specificity of each should assist policy-makers to develop appropriate action plans to meet the different experiences.

Placing Racism on the Scottish Agenda

It would be wrong to seek to foster cultural inclusion without explicitly addressing racism. Racism and racial prejudices prohibit genuine cultural inclusion and therefore those who work for cultural inclusion would be walking into the kind of problems that the Metropolitan Police has faced because they avoided the rough terrain of the facts of racism. Some of the most effective forms of racist exclusion lie within longstanding custom and practice rather than the crudity of a fist in the face.

Scotland has avoided the realities of confronting racism as a door-step issue as most reports on racial harassment and racial crime have been largely drawn from evidence in England and Wales. As statistics are now being disaggregated and comparisons can now begin to be made with other parts of the UK, the belief of Scottish egalitarianism and friendliness may well become another national myth.

The recent report *We Can't All Be White* (Rowntree, 1999) is important as it is one of the first few reports on racial bullying and harassment to have included Scotland. This report found that racist bullying is endemic in Britain but is unrecognised by officialdom and unchallenged by wider society. One black interviewee summed her experience up by stating: 'As far as casual, unprovoked verbal racism is concerned, we just take it as part of living in Glasgow' (Cunningham,

1999). The latest Commission for Racial Equality figures on racist incidents showed that Scotland's black/minority ethnic groups were at least three times as likely to suffer racist incidents as black/minority ethnic people in England and Wales (Booth, 1999). Yet, a recent televised programme 'Bhangra and Bravehearts' (Network East, 1999) hosted by Anvar Khan, one of the few prominent Asian Scottish journalists, found that the notion of Scotland being a tolerant nation with few racial issues continues to dominate.

What cannot be denied is that racism and racial bigotry should now be a matter of grave concern for Scotland's parliamentarians and policy-makers. The following catalogues some recent high profile incidents and publications related to racism and race equality which has affected Scotland:

- the tragic death of schoolboy Imran Khan in Glasgow;
- the acknowledgement by an industrial tribunal of gross racism in the case of PC Lawrence Ramadas from Strathclyde Police;
- the publication of the MacPherson Inquiry into the murder of Stephen Lawrence;
- the continuing campaign by the Chokkar Family and their Justice Campaign to seek justice and a fair trial for the murder of young Scots waiter, Surjit Singh Chhokar in 1998;
- the election of an all-white Scottish Parliament;
- the release of statistics from the CRE showing that in relative terms, racial incidents were far more likely (up to three times) to occur in Scotland than in the rest of the UK;
- the on-going debate on whether institutional racism exists in Scotland, most notably through comments by Lord Hardie the Lord Advocate and the refusal of the Scottish Police Federation to acknowledge the existence of institutional racism within Scottish Police Forces;
- the aforementioned Rowntree report *We Can't All Be White* based partly on Glasgow data which showed that 'racist' bullying is endemic in Britain, unrecognised by officialdom

and unchallenged by wider society;

- the Scottish Qualification Authority's use of a racially offensive passage in the 1999 Standard Grade English Exam causing a major public outcry (the book from which the passage was taken seeks to challenge racism, but the passage with the offensive terminology was used out of context);
- the recent reports in Scotland which indicate racism and racial harassment to be alive and present (Hampton, 1998; EIS, 1999).

The challenge to those taking forward the larger racial and cultural inclusion project is how the social construction of race and especially racism becomes a central feature of any inclusion project. Such a project would need to identify and dismantle power structures that have helped construct the racialisation of Western societies.

Guards and Gatekeepers

After nearly a quarter of century of the Race Relations Act 1976 and countless pounds spent on 'cultural awareness' or 'anti-racist training', the pace of change has been varied from zero to a canter. Within some local authorities, work in multicultural and anti-racist issues has been evident. In others, there is not even an acknowledgement that racial equality issues matters. Many professionals and practitioners have now learnt the 'jargon' of equality. Many can engage in verbal cleverness, using up-to-date terms to generate a veneer of tolerance, inclusion and respect. Differences are not denied but, the concept of different but equal remains just that — a concept. To counter this veneer, Scotland requires politicians and policy-makers who are informed and grounded in the reality of peoples' experiences, who are astute and prepared to analyse documents and policies to ensure that behind the jargon of equality that suffuses these initiatives there does not lurk an assimilationist agenda which is essentially an exclusionalist agenda.

The assimilationist agenda of the twenty first century is not very different from the assimilationist agenda of the 1950s and 1960s. It is however more sophisticated than its predecessor of forty years. The new agenda will appear to celebrate diversity and will profess loudly its intention to work towards a harmonious society. It may agree that mainstreaming the equality agenda must be the way forward. Short-term funded projects to help intercultural education or cultural exchanges are likely to be encouraged and funded but research or projects which set out to critically examine the reality of racial discrimination are unlikely to be resourced. It will be resistant to close scrutiny and unwilling to discuss key issues around the nature of piecemeal and short-term funding for work with the black/minority ethnic communities.

Contemporary Scotland is predominantly white, speaks English and is Protestant. Anything that might fundamentally challenge this status quo will be treated with caution or resistance. Those that attempt to create change will face an uphill struggle.

Who are the Guards and Gatekeepers within Scotland?

It is difficult and possibly unfair to point to any one grouping. However those that shape the business of politics and government — particularly the Civil Service, the media, those who develop educational curricula, those who inspect for quality and standards in our public sector provision, those that caretake our justice system — should be the most alert to the challenge of doing things differently. Those that are intransigent to change will become more exposed and isolated.

Those of us that purport to take forward the race equality agenda in Scotland, whether from the statutory or voluntary sector, or white or black/minority ethnic led groups, must also be self-critical and examine our 'gatekeeping' potential. The credibility of those who take forward race equality work should be based on the ability to analyse and challenge racism, to network constructively across ethnic and cultural groups, and to enthuse colleagues and communities to action.

Opening Pandora's Box

If racial and cultural inclusion is to become a reality there are hard questions to be asked. New Scotland needs to be brave enough to open Pandora's box and grapple with controversial and sensitive issues as did Charlotte Epstein.

Why does Scotland continue to marginalise issues of multiculturalism and racism? We need to ask what it is that generates complacency on racial issues in Scotland. When will we stop playing the numbers game? When will we stop questioning whether Scotland is multicultural or not? Multiculturalism is now a reality, it is not something in which we might believe or with which we might agree: it exists. For New Scotland, the question is how we might choose to respond to this reality and to devise strategies to redress the imbalances.

Double Standards?

There are key examples of double standards — particularly in the area of socio-economic class divisions. Two examples are explored here: the issue of denominational schools and the issue of recognition of languages spoken in Scotland .

Denominational Schools

Why do we have state-funded Catholic schools, yet deny the same to other faiths? Why are all other faiths accused of 'fragmentation or divisiveness' if they pursue state-funding for a school? Politicians have to be challenged about separate schooling in a way which encourages them to be imaginative in creating policy to reduce denominationalism. Kelly and Maan (1998) suggest that one way forward would be to bring religious instruction into specific periods, thus permitting the secularising of the rest of the school week. Would New Scotland dare to consider this as an option?

The reasons for the start of Catholic education — to prevent alienation, isolation and to provide a safe place to learn — could be applied to Muslims in Scotland today who experience Islamophobia and demonisation. One of the most prominent examples of media

Islamophobia was how the Mohammed Sarwar incident was covered. Sarwar, MP for Glasgow Govan was often referred to as 'the Muslim MP Sarwar'. What had his faith to do with his responsibility as Member of Parliament? What was the point of describing Sarwar in this way if not to subtly engage in Islamophobia and ethnic division?

Community Languages

Scotland is a linguistically complex nation. Several languages are first languages of Scottish citizens: English, Gaelic, Scots and other community languages, for example, Punjabi, Urdu, Chinese, Bengali, Arabic, Hindi and Gujerati. This diversity has often been viewed as problematic for the delivery of education and other public services, and as a threat to national identity and cohesion.

Urdu is now the second most commonly spoken language after English in Edinburgh and Glasgow. It is highly probable that Urdu is more widely spoken then Gaelic. We have Gaelic-medium primary schools in Edinburgh and Glasgow but no Urdu-medium primaries. It is argued that Gaelic is the heritage language of Scotland and an essential part of Scotland's cultural heritage. It is also argued that if Scotland does not nurture its continuance then the language will be lost, where Urdu will be nurtured in Pakistan. There is no dispute with this fact. On the contrary, a progressive Scotland would look to see how positive benefits of bilingualism demonstrated by Gaelic-medium education, can be extended to the recognition, maintenance and development of Scotland's other community languages so that the New Scotland can see the flourishing of all within it. If we believe that language is important in shaping culture, identity and self-esteem, what then are the educational and social rights of Scottish Urdu speakers or other community language speakers?

Creative Policy Development to Aid Inclusivity

The Parliamentary Equal Opportunities Committee will need to be vigilant as they scrutinise internal proceedings and White papers that racial equality does not become such a discrete part of the equalities debate as to become insignificant. The Commission for

Racial Equality Scotland has recently submitted *Racial Equality Matters: An Agenda for the Scottish Parliament* which tables a list of actions for parliamentarians to consider (CRE Scotland, 1999). There are useful suggestions in this document that could be used as a starter list for action.

However, will Parliament be creative in developing new policy to assist racial and cultural inclusion? Will the Scottish Executive be creative in their advice to parliamentarians? For example, it is now timely, to consider the development of a distinctively Scottish language policy. The aim of such a policy would be to provide national and public bodies with a clear and coherent framework for supporting the development and use of Scotland's languages. It would also stress the importance of the teaching and learning of other world languages, especially the languages of Scotland's European partners, for purposes of commerce and harmonious relationships. Currently, policies and practice with regard to language use in public services and language in education in Scotland are fragmented. It would also address the need for more coherence in the funding and delivery of interpreting and translation services in Scotland.

What would be the point of not allowing recognition and support for all our languages, other than to engage in cultural racism? Will we be astute enough to embrace multilingualism as a feature of a nation that can function competently in a global society both socially and economically, as suggested by CERES (1999)?

Change and the New Scotland

We need to have courage to dismantle institutional racism as well as confront the prejudices and bigotry that exist within all communities both black or white/majority or minority. We need to speak out against bigotry, masquerading as 'cultural or religious traits' in the interest of human rights. We need to ensure that disinformation on race or immigration in the media is swiftly rebutted.

Any progressive nation that remains silent in the face of controversies and division over who should be part of Scotland, that does not discuss what shape Scotland needs to be to include everyone, is bound to fail. The challenges of racial divisions we face today are different from those of earlier generations but all of us will be measured by how much we promote the causes of a common citizenship and justice for all.

If we have the political will to continue the journey, then I believe we will begin to unite the public behind a new, inclusive vision of Scotland. People will begin to feel the change — our choices will determine the shape of Scottish politics for the next century.

Endnote

I wish to thank Dr. Elinor Kelly, Malcolm Parnell and John Landon for assisting me in shaping the ideas in this paper.

CHAPTER 22

CHANGING GENDER RELATIONS IN CONTEMPORARY SCOTLAND

ESTHER BREITENBACH

This chapter is concerned with the nature of gender relations in contemporary Scotland; that is, the structural inequalities in access to power, decision-making and resources that continue to exist between women and men. Gender issues are often seen to be synonymous with women's issues, yet this is not so. To look at gender relations is to look at the changing relations between women and men, and to ask not only how women are responding to social change, but how men are doing so too. Nonetheless, given the inequalities that women face compared to men in general, the major focus here remains the position of women, how that position is changing, and the aspirations of women.

It is important to acknowledge that women are not an homogenous group. Nor are men. Differences of ethnicity, able bodiedness or disability, sexual orientation, class or socio-economic status, religion, rural or urban conditions, age, and so on, combine in different ways to shape the experience of men and women. Different characteristics and/or experiences may therefore have more or less significance for individuals in defining their identities, but may also permit fluid and changing identities for individuals. If Scotland is to be a tolerant and inclusive society, and if government and other public agencies are to be responsive to the varying needs of different sections of the population, sensitivity to and awareness of this difference and diversity in society is something to be encouraged,

As we approach the end of the twentieth century women's aspirations to equality occupy a salient position on the political agenda not only here in Scotland, but throughout the world, as widespread commitment to the UN Convention to Eliminate Discrimination Against Women indicates. Yet the twentieth century also opened with mass campaigning for women's rights, in particular the right to vote. If significant changes have occurred in the course of the century, the road to full and active citizenship has proved to be a long one.

Despite major social and economic change the persistence of inequalities and gender divisions is striking. Historian Arthur McIvor has summarised the major changes in the position of women in Scottish society in the twentieth century: fertility rates have fallen and average family size is much smaller, while at the same time life expectancy has increased, with the consequence that a far smaller proportion of women's lives is taken up with childbearing and rearing; divorce and cohabitation rates have risen considerably since the 1960s, and there has been a growth in the number of lone parent families; the availability of contraception and abortion have allowed women greater control over their fertility. While these changes have expanded the range of opportunities open to women in their working lives, and have reduced the burdens of domestic labour and child-rearing, lack of systematic research means that, as McIvor puts it, 'the internal life of the Scottish family remains relatively mysterious'. Indeed, he takes the view that changes in the private sphere in women's lives have lagged behind changes in the public sphere, 'Female subordination and economic dependency within the home, the persistence of a marked sexual division of labour, the maldistribution of resources within the family and the survival of chauvinist attitudes and patriarchal values continue to characterise the Scottish family' (McIvor, 1996: 195).

This view may seem bleak, but if surveys of young people's attitudes towards traditional sex roles suggest a change towards a more egalitarian view (see Siann, Wilson, Rowan, 1998; Wilkinson, 1994), a gap appears to remain between the expression of these attitudes and the actual experience of men and women. And, while the point has been made above that gender relations includes the experiences of men as well as women, within a Scottish context the extent to which men are re-examining their attitudes and behaviour, and their conceptions of masculinity, remains limited. At best it can be said that there are tentative beginnings, whether in academic literature or in fiction (see, for example, Howson, 1992; Littlewood, 1998; MacInnes, 1998).

Changes in women's role in the labour market have been significant, yet gender inequalities have continued. If more women carry out waged work as well as unwaged work in the home, and if in particular the participation of married women in the labour market has greatly increased, gender segregation in the labour market remains very much in evidence.[1] As a consequence women earn on average far less than men (full-time working women's weekly earnings are on average 72 per cent that of men), with part-time workers being particularly disadvantaged in terms of low pay, low status, and unsocial hours. Women remain more vulnerable to poverty than men, in particular as lone parents or pensioners, though married or cohabiting women in households experiencing poverty often bear the brunt of this, carrying the responsibility of caring for partners and children on low incomes and often sacrificing their own well-being to the interests of others.

Though there have been significant changes in girls' educational performance, with girls now out-performing boys in school examination results, and making up just over half of under-graduate entrants to Scottish universities, gender stereotyping remains in evidence in subject choice, and academic success has not yet carried through to the labour market where young male graduates very quickly earn more than their female counterparts (see forthcoming Scottish Funding Councils for Further and Higher Education Study, 1999).

Progress towards equality for women has tended to be incremental and slow. Despite equal rights as citizens, equal access to higher education, and wider (but not yet equal) access to job opportunities, women are still under-represented in political and public life and in senior positions in their working and professional lives. This under-representation is not solely a result of interruptions to employment and career for childbearing and rearing, but is the product of a variety of processes that work against women. These processes can range from direct discrimination, to the unthinking and unconscious reproduction of 'macho' working styles and practices.

Explanations for the under-representation of women in senior positions in the professions, and in political and public life, are likely to be similar to those advanced for other parts of the UK and other Western industrialised countries, although it is worth making the point that Scotland is less well served in terms of research than many other countries (see Brown, Myers and Breitenbach, 1994; Breitenbach, Brown and Myers, 1998). Qualitative studies have suggested that all the following factors play a role in acting as barriers to women in politics, public life and at work: methods of selection, recruitment and promotion; competing demands of family and working lives; gender stereotyping; women's lack of confidence; the culture of organisations; a 'macho' style of politics; the gendering of roles within professions; the assumption of male career patterns; 'macho' management culture; and, last but not least, direct and indirect discrimination (Myers, 1999).

Turning to change in the political sphere, women in Scotland, as women elsewhere in the UK, were partially enfranchised in 1918, and fully enfranchised in 1928. Historically the representation of women in the UK Parliament has been very low, with the trend for an increase in women's representation only being evident in the last two general elections of 1992 and 1997. In Scotland, there were never more than five women MPs elected at a general election prior to 1997, when 12 were elected (Burness, 1998). Until the elections to the Scottish Parliament the total number of women who had served as MPs or MEPs for Scottish constituencies since women's enfranchisement in 1918 was 29.

Prior to the Scottish Parliament elections, women tended to

have a higher level of representation in local government than in Parliament, though the current level of representation of women, following the elections in May 1999, at 22.6 per cent is no different from the previous elections of 1995. This overall average conceals a wide range, with women comprising 36.7 per cent of councillors in South Ayrshire but only 8.6 per cent in North Lanarkshire (Scottish Local Government Information Unit, 1999).

The elections to the Scottish Parliament represented a significant achievement in terms of women's representation, even if it did not result in the 50:50 gender balance, for which many women actively campaigned. Women make up 37.2 per cent of MSPs. This figure puts Scotland near the top of the international league table in terms of women's representation.

Given the persisting inequalities between women and men, and the slow rate of progress towards equality, to students of gender relations in Scotland, misperceptions of the pace and extent of change can be a source of much frustration. There seems to be a popular orthodoxy that women have achieved equality or that we have reached a post-feminist state, where feminism is no longer needed.

However, sex equality legislation and equal opportunities initiatives, such as these supported by local government, are frequently poorly understood or misrepresented. For example, it is not uncommon to encounter the view that sex equality legislation in Britain consists of affirmative action, or positive discrimination, which in fact remains illegal in Britain. Generally when comments about this are made it is to say that women should not be given special treatment just because they are women. The reality is that they are not, and that legislation is designed to remove discrimination and bias. Thus an ill-informed view or perhaps almost deliberate misunderstanding of the legislation serves as a means of expressing resistance or opposition to women's equality. In comparative terms British equality legislation is less robust than that to be found elsewhere, for example, the USA, Canada, Australia, Norway, Sweden, and the Netherlands (see, for example, Bacchi, 1996).

Another view that is encountered is that the continuing

inequalities between men and women will disappear automatically as a result of women's educational achievements. This is a view frequently found in professional organisations, particularly those in which women now form about half of those graduating, for example law. The assumption here is that there is no longer any need to adopt special measures, or to scrutinise recruitment and promotion procedures for evidence of bias. Yet research carried out elsewhere in the UK, and more limited research in Scotland (see Brown, Breitenbach, and Myers, 1995; Myers and Brown, 1997) suggests that bias, discrimination, and resistance exist to prevent women reaching the top in their respective professions. Women are systematically under-represented at the top and underpaid in a wide range of professions. Within traditionally male dominated professions, the working environment for women may be one of persistent harassment. If this situation is to change an active commitment to women's equality, and measures designed to achieve this equality are necessary, including, for example, equal opportunities recruitment and promotion practices; family friendly working practices, such as flexible hours, job sharing, and career breaks; mentoring schemes; and specific training courses and support for women.

Gender Equality since 1997

Progress towards gender equality in Scotland in the twentieth century has been slow, and inequalities have persisted even if the degree of inequality has been eroded. The results of the Scottish Parliament elections were, however, a sign of change. To what extent is a process of transition going on, and to what extent do the new political institutions in Scotland create opportunities for further, and perhaps more rapid, progress towards gender equality?

Since the change of government in 1997 the profile of women's issues has been heightened. Ministers for Women were created and the Government made a commitment to prioritising issues such as childcare, family-friendly employment, and violence against women. Policy developments in these areas in Scotland are likely to be taken forward by the new Scottish Government. The commitment to open government and to consultation also marks a major change, and should provide a means by which women's organisations can influence policy making. In particular a Women in Scotland Consultative Forum has been set up to facilitate dialogue between women's organisations and the government.

Constitutional change has led not only to an increase in women's representation, it has also led to the creation of structures that will further promote equal opportunities. The recommendations of the Consultative Steering Group that there should be a standing Equal Opportunities Committee of the Parliament and that there should be an Equality Unit within the new Scottish Executive have been endorsed. At ministerial level the Minister for Communities and Deputy Minister for Communities have responsibility for equality issues included in their portfolios. The approach to policy development will be one of mainstreaming gender and other equality issues. This means that all areas of policy should be assessed for impacts on women, and other equality groups, such as minority ethnic communities, and people with disabilities. As a consequence policies should be modified where they are failing to address or are even reinforcing existing inequalities. In making progress towards gender equality, political and institutional processes will remain highly significant, because it is through these that power is exercised, and it is therefore crucial to keep under scrutiny the role that women and women's organisations play within them.

Increased women's representation and better access to decision-making will have an impact on policies, though it is not necessarily easy to predict how. Three priority issues for women in Scotland were identified through a consultation exercise carried out by the Women's Co-ordination Group in 1994. These priorities were: women's representation in political and public life, poverty and violence against women. Related to the issue of poverty are also such issues as childcare, and health. These continue to have immediate significance for women, and policies in these areas will have more immediate impact on women's lives, though they may also produce benefits for men. Indeed the powers of the Scottish

Parliament, covering major areas of social policy such as education, health, housing, family law, community care, and so on, are particularly crucial in having the potential to improve women's lives. However, a number of areas in which powers are reserved are also highly significant for women: social security, pensions, employment rights, and equality legislation itself.

It is important to make the point that such changes as have occurred in women's representation and the place of women's issues on the political agenda are a result of consistent campaigning and action of women themselves (see, for example, Breitenbach, 1996; Brown and Galligan, 1993; Brown, 1996 and between 1996 and 1998; Brown, McCrone and Paterson, 1998). It is certainly the case that since the late 1980s an increasingly coherent and cohesive women's movement has evolved in Scotland. Links between women in political parties, trade unions, local government, bodies such as the Equal Opportunities Commission, the voluntary sector, community groups and academics have been forged in such a way that communication systems and transmission of knowledge are now more effective. This experience of organisation is likely to continue to fuel the impetus for change, and will also serve as a body of knowledge and experience on which to draw in developing the new institutions and policies of the Parliament. There is therefore considerable scope for collaborative working for a range of agencies with government to carry out its commitment to the promotion of equal opportunities, though this does not mean that this process will necessarily be free of conflict or criticism.

A New Stage?

While the result of the first elections to the Scottish Parliament is one of which women in Scotland can rightly feel proud, it marks only a stage in the process and not the end. The goal of equal representation in political and public life has been clearly articulated, and it can be predicted that this will continue to be debated within political parties, not just in relation to parliamentary elections, but in relation to local government. Proposed reforms to the system of election to local government are likely to meet with women's support if they are seen to promise both better gender balance, and better representation of other groups in the population such as minority ethnic communities. In relation to public appointments made by the government, a commitment has already been made to improving representation of women. In addition, the increase in women's representation is not just seen as an end in itself, but it is widely believed that policies will change as a result of women's greater involvement in the political process (see Brown, 1998; Mackay, 1998).

If strategies for change are to be effective many sectors of society must participate in the process, and change and challenges will take place as much at the personal and social level as in the public sphere. Government and other public agencies will have a role in ensuring that their policies do not create, reinforce or exacerbate inequalities, and that the distribution of benefits and services for which they are responsible is equitable. But what takes place in the 'private' sphere is also of crucial importance. If McIvor is correct in his assessment of the characteristics of the Scottish family, then a great deal remains to be done.

While it would be wrong to generalise about all women in Scotland, many women have mobilised around the issue of representation in political and public life, many aspire to equality in decision-making, and in their working and professional lives. Many want to live in a country in which women are safe from violence and from poverty, and want to contribute actively to policy debates and to shape policies that are more sensitive to their needs. They want work to be organised in more family friendly ways and family responsibilities to be shared more.

There are, of course, men who support these aims politically, and personally in the way they organise work and family life. But the evidence is that so far the shift has been slight in terms of sharing childcare and domestic labour (see, for example, Jamieson, 1998), and that a re-evaluation of the 'norms' of masculine behaviour in Scotland remains as yet very tentative. Change in gender relations is ultimately about change in the balance of power, both within the sphere of family relationships and within the public sphere of work, civil society, and political life. We cannot therefore expect progress towards a fuller equality for women and men to be without controversy and conflict, but neither need we rule out negotiation and consensus.

Endnotes

1 For a statistical overview of and commentary on gender inequalities in Scotland, see the Gender Audits, published annually by Engender since 1993.

Section Four: Governance, Identities and Institutions

CHAPTER 23

THE
MODERNISER'S
GUIDE TO

GERRY STOKER

LOCAL

GOVERNMENT

What is the moderniser's perspective on local government? As in other areas there is a recognition of new 'realities'. The world has changed — and appears set to change still further. The modernisation project is about ensuring that our social, economic and political institutions provide an adequate and appropriate response to that changed world. This moderniser's guide to local government therefore starts with a look at the 'revolution' in society that is demanding a new response from local government.

Modernisers not only argue that the world has changed but also have a view on how government institutions, including those at local level, should adapt to new circumstances. The focus is less on specific measures that could be put in place and more on a number of reform directions. A key feature of the moderniser's perspective is its emphasis on evidence-based decision-making. Given the variety and diversity of Scottish local government it would be unwise to insist that one institutional device or mechanism should necessarily be applied to all cases. However what can be asserted is a number of reform challenges that should be met by all. These reform directions are outlined in the second part of this chapter.

The final concern to be addressed in this chapter is how a reform strategy should be devised. Evidence about how change takes place shows that there is a two-fold dynamic. First, external pressure, shock or a perceived sense of crisis appear to be key stimulants for reform. Second, for reform to be effective it requires local ownership, leaders and champions. In short a reform strategy must contain both top-down and bottom-up elements in order to be successful.

The Emergence of New Realities

The starting point in the moderniser's perspective is that old certainties have been challenged. The main changes are outlined below.

- People — or at least significant sections of them — are not so reliant on public services, except in core areas such as health and education.
- Changes in the form of production and consumption in the private sector — in particular the use of new information and communication technology — present a challenge to the public sector, if it is not to be left behind.
- Shifting technological capacity also provides new opportunities for the rapid exchange of information and expertise among the public. It offers new opportunities to express voice, to vote, or more broadly interact with government (see, for example, Castells, 1996).
- Globalisation provides an enormous challenge for national and local politics. If legitimate government relies on the consent of those affected by a decision, how in a more globalised, interconnected world can that consent be obtained within the traditional boundaries of political systems? What is the value of local politics in a globalised world?
- Changing employment patterns appear to extend the gap between achievers and non-achievers, which are in turn reflected in the operation of the political system. For the former group, the intensity of demands made at work may leave little scope for involvement in civic life and less interest given that capacity to opt out and to provide for themselves in the private sector. For the economically and socially excluded disenchantment, apathy and a sense of

hopelessness can keep them away from formal politics.

- Formal political institutions generally appear to have lost some of the confidence of the public. The capacity of political parties to mobilise public opinion and interest would appear to have declined.

- There is a drift towards a more direct, informal and episodic style of politics. People want to be involved but not on a sustained basis. Rather there is a shift towards issue-based, ad hoc, rapid mobilisation followed by disinterest and withdrawal, until the cycle begins again.

It should be noted that it is not the claim of modernisers that all these perceived changes impact to the same degree in every locality and in respect to all issues. Moreover the experience of change — both in its threats and opportunities — is experienced differently by various social and economic groups. Nevertheless the overall significance of the pattern of change cannot be ignored. The scale and depth of change demands a response from our local political and service delivery systems.

Directions of Change

There are at least five shifts in the ways of working in local government that are at the heart of the moderniser's agenda. Each is examined briefly below.

`there is a need to shift from a focus on inputs to a concern with outcomes.`

Boldly stated the ambition to focus on outcomes can appear glib. Yet as Mark Moore argues, the underlying philosophy of public managers (whether politicians or officials) should be to create public value (Moore, 1995). The issue that needs to be addressed is whether the public intervention which they are directing is achieving positive social and economic outcomes. The focus on generating public value brings in its wake some implications which carry considerable bite.

Public managers create public value. The problem is that they cannot know for sure what that is. Even if they could be sure to-day, they would have to doubt tomorrow, for by then the political aspirations and public needs that give point to their efforts might well have changed.

It is not enough, then, that managers simply maintain the continuity of their organisations, or even that the organisations become efficient in current tasks. It is also important that the enterprise be adaptable to new purposes and is innovative and experimental.

It is not enough to say that public managers create results that are valued; they must be able to show that the results obtained are worth the cost of private consumption and unrestrained liberty forgone in producing the desirable results. Only then can we be sure that some public value has been created.

Providing services is no longer a sufficient justification for state intervention funded by citizens — whether those services are provided directly or commissioned. The question that has to be answered is does the service advance valued social or economic outcomes. A constant readiness to think again about what is being achieved is also necessary. Modernisers do not expect public managers to assume that the solution to any problem is the input of more resources. There is a need to consider what more could be achieved with the resources and assets at your disposal. There is no prejudice against public spending but equally there is no automatic endorsement of it.

A commitment to in-house provision needs to give way to an open-minded approach to the procurement of services.

When the Conservatives insisted that services should be put out to tender on a compulsory basis, it was, perhaps, natural that for many in local government the commitment to in-house provision became an article of faith. Contracts were designed to put off the private sector and ensure that direct service organisations got the work. That might have been an understandable past politics, but has no future as far as modernisers are concerned. Effective procurement requires an open-minded approach to identify the best supplier, whether from the public, private or voluntary sector.

Consulting with users, benchmarking and open competition are among the mechanisms that will ensure a focus on end results. There is no ideological dimension to deciding who provides services and no particular moral virtue in people receiving their wages directly from government — especially when some of the lowest wages have been paid by the public sector. The assumption is that while in-house provision may be appropriate in some circumstances, in many others the advantages of private or voluntary sector provision will be greater. The private sector, for example, may be able to combine vitally needed investment with the responsibility for providing services. The voluntary sector may through their wider involvement be able to guarantee a more 'joined-up' or 'seamless' service for the public.

> *There is a need to give less emphasis to the legitimacy that stems from internal party input and give more recognition to the legitimacy of a wide range of stakeholders.*

Local politicians and officials have a particular legitimacy, given that local government is elected but there are valid claims to legitimacy from among others, business partners, neighbourhood leaders, those with knowledge about services as professionals or users, and those in a position of oversight as auditors or regulators. These diverse bases of legitimacy cannot be simply trumped by the playing of the political card, even that held by a majority group on a council. As well as a positive challenge to embrace stakeholders the recognition of multiple sources of legitimacy calls into question a narrow concept of party democracy. Parties should be outward-looking and not trapped in a private world of caucuses and meetings. Party politics will continue to have a role to play in organising candidates, elections and the practice of government but cannot undertake these roles in isolation divorced from a wider world of local and non-local stakeholders. There needs to be more sharing and communication between the formal world of party politics and that of other stakeholders, and councillors need to find ways of getting out of council buildings and into their communities.

There should be a shift from a culture that accepts public acquiescence in local decision-making to one that expects active citizen endorsement.
Although people rarely become wildly excited about the stuff of local politics, the system is unsustainable if we do not address the mounting evidence of public disinterest and apathy. Low turnout in some local elections, weak response to participation exercises and a general feeling that local government is run by 'them' rather than 'us' are symptoms of a wider malaise in our political system. The challenge is to find ways of engaging people on their own terms. Voting can be made easier and more meaningful. Consent beyond the ballot box can be obtained through various methods of public consultation and deliberation, such as citizens' juries. New information and communication technologies offer a range of further opportunities to encourage people's participation in a way that is flexible, attractive to them and not too time-consuming. The argument for finding new ways to engage with people is not just that government needs to listen and learn to design better policies and services, although that is important, but, effective channels of communication are essential to achieving many social and economic outcomes. For example, to launch a waste recycling scheme or change driving habits requires an intensive dialogue and high levels of trust between the public and authorities. More generally there is a need to rebuild public confidence in political institutions and the most powerful way to do that is to seek active citizen endorsement of the policies and practices of public bodies.

There needs to be a shift in emphasis away from service provision to a role of community leadership for elected local government.
Local government is about more than the services it provides. The future is about local government as a community leader working in partnership with others to provide vision and direction for the locality. Community planning will be a key instrument in developing this style of working providing that it does not become overly bureaucratic and cumbersome. Leadership is also crucial, and for Scotland's major cities the option of the directly elected mayor or

provost should be considered. Whatever form of leadership emerges should be accountable and visible, and checks and balances should ensure it is facilitative rather than commanding, or even dictatorial. But leadership is needed, and the issue of how best that leadership can emerge in a way that is capable of moving people and making them feel willing to join the process should not be ducked. Government needs to learn to steer with a light touch and the willingness, capacity and skills to act in such a way will have to be installed in our local government system. Such capacities do not automatically emerge and in many localities appear to be largely absent. The challenge is to find ways to develop shared vision, build partnerships and work across boundaries.

A Reform Strategy

Many of the directions of the reforms that are part of the moderniser's perspective have been initiated by, or experimented within local government. The agenda is not an alien one and draws much of its inspiration from the way in which innovators in local government have attempted to respond to the new challenges that they have faced. To a large extent the reforms go with the grain of the practical experience of people in the business of running local public organisations over the last decade or so.

Equally, there is a wide recognition among policy-makers and practitioners that considerable capacity for organisational inertia and a resistance to change exists in many institutions. The point to some extent is obvious: the word 'institutionalise' implies an attempt to make something sustainable, or even permanent, and we should therefore not be surprised if organisations do not all fully embrace change, or if they do it is on a rather ad hoc, or even half-hearted, manner.

Research, for example cited in McCalman and Paton (1992) and Thornhill et al. (2000), into managing change indicates two clear things. The first is that the immediate stimulus for change often comes from a sense of crisis, a challenge, a feeling of having to respond. The second is that for change to be successful and maintained, local ownership expressed through leadership, new mindsets and the capacity to gain new skills is required.

Modernisers in the light of these factors should favour a two-fold reform strategy. The first element is the hardest for ardent localist supporters of councils to accept: there is a need for central direction and intervention. Without the pressure for change and without disciplines imposed from the outside it is difficult to ensure that all organisations will change. No constitutional arguments about local autonomy should be allowed to cloud this judgement. The centre must create a dynamic for change to ensure that it has appropriate sticks and carrots to ensure that local authorities do modernise.

Modernisation, however, also demands a bottom-up development of ownership and commitment. There are a range of ways in which such a strategy might work:

- encouragement of benchmarking and peer review among councils;
- provision of support for experiments and initiatives by councils;
- reward schemes, including additional finance and powers for local authorities that modernise effectively;
- effective channels for networking and the dissemination of good practice;
- recognition that taking an initiative does not guarantee success and so a willingness to tolerate failure.

The task of modernising local government is complex and demanding. Yet there is no alternative, as somebody else once said in a different context. What has been suggested here are the directions and strategies that would inform a modernised local government. The policies that follow have to come from the policy-makers and politicians.

Chapter 24

RE-
ENERGISING
Matt Smith
THE PUBLIC
SECTOR

In his introduction to *The Red Paper on Scotland* editor Gordon Brown argues that 'Scotland desperately needs a widely articulated and sufficiently popular concept of welfare and need grounded in equality and reciprocity in forming social policies and social priorities' (Brown, 1975a: 10). He goes on to articulate the case for 'a regeneration of the public sector'. Much has changed in the past quarter century but the position of the public sector, far from having been regenerated, has continued to further erode. Now with a new Scottish Parliament we are in a position to react and initiate.

All previous attempts to create a Parliament for Scotland failed, so what made the difference this time? There are arguably two inter-linked causes: consensus and legacy. It can be argued that the legacy created the consensus and those of a nationalist disposition will argue that their case grew in popularity. But as electoral results made clear the nationalists never at any stage gained a majority, far less a consensus. The legacy of Thatcherism was far more influential, based on hostility towards the public services and a rejection of civic society, of untrammelled arrogance which could re-organise local government against all public opinion and of increasingly centralised government.

What was different here was the cause of public services and the bond that exists in Scotland to a greater extent than the rest of the UK as a whole. During the Thatcher-Major years many looked to the public services as a defence against the centralising state. The

Conservative Governments' constant hostility towards all parts of the public services was particularly rampant in Scotland. Nowhere was this more in evidence than in the case of the poll tax. Not only was it detested but imposed on Scotland. Above all, it made a statement that Scotland could be taken for granted and treated with contempt.

The experience of Conservative minority rule in Scotland produced not a negative reaction, but a positive reawakening. There was a growing realisation that we could do things better if we developed decision-making and policy closer to people and problems. Scotland could determine its own destiny in those areas that really matter in the nature and delivery of its public services. The matters for which responsibility now rests in Edinburgh are those that fall into the definition of public services: health, local government, education and much more besides.

The Anatomy of Scotland published in 1992 makes reference to this commitment to public provision in Scotland. In relation to the health service it states: 'Cultural differences between Scotland and England are reflected in the health service. Scotland is generally recognised to have a greater public service ethos, a greater sense of community, and this has produced marked differences from England.' (Christie, 1992: 59). It continues by quoting a former Secretary of the Scottish Health Service Planning Council writing in a similar vein: 'Scottish democratic humanism has produced a marked emphasis in the Scottish health service on collective, public sector provision as against individualistic or private provision. It has also led to a participatory planning ethos rather than a managerialist one' (p.59). On one of those public services, education, Peter Jones (1992: 98) has argued that:

> ...other features which make Scottish education different are the relatively small independent fee paying schools sector, a state sector which is more thoroughly comprehensive, a binary higher education divide which has been more complementary than competitive, and a more centralised administrative structure.

Throughout the difficult years of first Thatcher and then Major, when the occupancy of the Secretary of State's post was increasingly marginalised from Scottish public opinion, support for public services grew. Legislation to undermine this support was invariably imposed on an electorate that became increasingly hostile to Westminster and the agenda being pursued. When the allegedly populist concept of opt-out schools was introduced the uptake, in spite of bribes, was negligible. The introduction of the market to the National Health Service was roundly resisted across Scotland and created new alliances between local community campaigns and medical professionals. Strathclyde Regional Council met the removal of water from local government control, seen as a halfway house to eventual full-scale privatisation, with bitter opposition culminating in a referendum. The postal ballot resulted in an overwhelming rejection of the government's plans, yet the plans were implemented. And of course, having failed to persuade the Scots that the government knew best, the final insult was legislation to remove a tier of local government.

As the Scots clung to their traditions and rejected the Westminster agenda, a growing surge of support for devolved government emerged. Sometimes that seemed to favour outright separation, although at no time was this reflected in the ballot box; what did register was an increasing opposition to Westminster domination. A growing coalition emerged around an alternative and embraced many of those who, from different starting points, opposed the agenda being imposed upon them. There was a sense that there was a better way to govern — based on Scottish solutions and encouraging Scottish distinctiveness and difference.

A New Scotland: Reconnecting Public Sector Values
It is not without significance that the first piece of research to be published by the Central Research Unit of the new Scottish Executive confirms the view that Scots do have a close affinity with their public services. The first of its main findings states that 'Scottish residents are generally more satisfied with the public services they

receive than are their counterparts elsewhere in the UK' (Scottish Executive Central Research Unit, 1999: 1).

It identifies the five most important services to the public in order of importance as being:

GPs	46%
NHS Hospitals	38%
Refuse Collection	31%
Police and Fire	27%
Emergency Services	23%

The research stated that 'Scottish respondents found public services provision, significantly less faceless, less infuriating and more responsive than the UK panel generally' (p.2).

These findings raised few headlines, in contrast to the hype generated by negative stories about public services, even when they have little or no foundation. Yet they reflect something deeply significant about Scotland, our Parliament and our public services. It is a message that the new Parliament would do well to listen to and act upon.

There are many historic and cultural reasons why there is support in Scotland for public provision, particularly in the two key areas of education and health. Some argue that in educational terms the 'school in every Parish' policy set the pace. Whatever the historical reason there is little doubt that, barring a small percentage, Scots prefer public provision. It should be very clear that the reason we have a Parliament is to allow Scotland to determine its own destiny in those areas over which it has legislative control. There would be little point in the Parliament replicating the Westminster agenda: we need to take the full opportunity of developing Scottish solutions for Scottish problems, while not being ashamed (or lacking in confidence) of borrowing from the UK or elsewhere.

Values and Vision in Public Services

To take the argument forward we need to return to some core values. Scotland's public services are firmly rooted in equality, solidarity, social justice and democracy. They developed initially in response to appalling social conditions and have become a system of comprehensive public provision. They have contributed to economic growth, developed our infrastructure and collectively provided for many needs. Public services have been a civilising force during this century and must continue to be in the next.

We need to refound our public services with a new vision and values drawn from the commitment and enthusiasm of its workers, management and users. An appropriate starting point for benchmarking is the Consultative Steering Group's (1999: 3) principles:

- sharing of power between the people of Scotland, the legislators and the Scottish Executive;
- accountable to the public;
- accessible, open, responsive and developing procedures which allow a participative approach;
- recognising the need to promote equal opportunities.

The McIntosh Commission (Commission on Local Government and the Scottish Parliament, 1999: 12-13) on the future of local government and the Scottish Parliament drew on these principles to identify an agenda for local government, which is just as relevant to the public sector:

- delivering quality and cost-effective services;
- focusing on the customer;
- participation by the citizen;
- transparency.

Other key principles identified by McIntosh, relevant to a new public sector vision include:

- working in partnership with other agencies;
- developing effective partnerships with the business community;
- promoting active citizenship and social inclusion;
- good employment practice to aid innovation and motivation;
- promoting a positive public sector record of achievements.

Bringing this new vision to our public services has to involve recognising that they are currently in crisis. They have been re-organised, starved of funds, redefined, subjected to outsourcing, whether by compulsion or coercion and generally denigrated. Services are under-funded, and employees under-valued and demoralised.

As Tony Blair said when addressing the Charter Mark Awards Conference in January 1999:

> *We inherited an undervalued public sector. It is absurd that we ever got into the position under the previous administration where government seemed to devalue the very people it relied upon to deliver its programme. Where private was always best. Where the public sector was always demonised as inefficient. In the last twenty-one months I have met many people across the public sector who are as efficient and entrepreneurial as anyone in the private sector, but also have a sense of public duty that is awe inspiring. Most of them could be earning far more money in business. But they don't and you don't.*
>
> *Why not? Because of a commitment to public service. Because helping a five year old to read, coaxing a patient out of a coma, convicting a burglar is fulfilling in a way that money can't buy. This country needs its wealth creators, but it needs its social entrepreneurs as well. (Blair, 1999)*

In addressing this new agenda we need to take account of these core values, but we need to adapt them to present day conditions in a new Scotland. In tackling issues of equality and social justice we need to ensure that a level playing field is achieved and that all have equal access. In part that is a geographic argument and we already know, for example, that different parts of the country derive different benefits and results from the National Health Service, for example. We must also ensure that those from minority communities have equality of access and service.

Our schools have to deliver for all young people. We may not have many fee-paying schools but we do have a pecking order, largely derived from catchment areas and the socio-economic mix of the local population. Achieving equality and inclusiveness for all of Scotland's school students' must be the aim. And on higher and further education funding our Parliament has an opportunity to set out a distinctive approach

So too for solidarity and ensuring that all of our citizens are treated with dignity and respect. Tackling issues such as fuel poverty and inadequate housing are clearly priorities to ensure that everyone has an acceptable standard of living.

One area where the Parliament can act speedily is the area of democracy. There is little practical merit in electing a parliament for reasons of accountability and democracy if that principle only relates to the parliamentary level, while at service delivery level neither democracy nor accountability exist. One of the great curses of the last two decades has been when services have been torn out of local government: with the rise of the quangocracy reducing the degree of democratic scrutiny.

Why should it be the case that only services delivered by local government permit us to contact, to question, and ultimately to replace those who have responsibility? Councillors, like MSPs, are accountable, but many now in charge of our public services have no direct accountability. In the confused area of quangos where differing levels of remuneration are paid for no apparent reason appointments remain rooted to a system of patronage. As our Parliament removes the last vestiges of feudalism, this anomaly should be tackled. It is, of course, the case that some public appointments need to continue, but the system is far from open and the transfer of power and, more importantly spending power to the unaccountable, is unsustainable.

There are many other aspects of public provision that could be brought back within democratic accountability. And there is public support for this return. For example, when did you last hear anyone argue for a residential home for the elderly to be transferred to the private sector? Such transfers have almost always been done on the basis of a cost cutting exercise, one example of a trend that needs to be reversed. The recent McIntosh Commission in one of its recommendations, dealt with the issue of service delivery as follows:

...the option of transfer to local government should always be considered in any review of other bodies delivering public services; and likewise where new services are developed, prior consideration should always be given to whether local government should be their vehicle, subject to consideration of efficiency and cost effectiveness. (Commission on Local Government and the Scottish Parliament, 1999: 19)

Finance is the key to much of the required change. Within its fixed budget the Parliament will need to allocate and reallocate, distribute and redistribute, against a background of many conflicting demands. There are, of course, the tax varying powers that remain a future option, and rightly so. We must not forget that, in spite of the constant assurances the Scottish public received during the referendum campaign that varying provisions meant tax increases, they still returned a substantial majority. And perhaps politicians in Scotland need to be a bit more confident that the Scots are willing to pay for better services.

There are, of course, other methods by which funds can be raised beyond the tax powers and an early review of local government finance as recommended by the McIntosh Commission is required. The review could be undertaken by an independent commission or, indeed by Parliament itself.

Part of the argument we are beginning to hear from Westminster — allegedly the backlash — is that Scotland's share of the UK cake has contributed to better public services in Scotland. There is truth in that argument. Perhaps, if similar levels of expenditure were implemented in other parts of the UK there might be more support for public services, and a bit less cynicism.

Public services must provide best value and be open to frequent scrutiny, but best value must not become an alternative to compulsory competitive tendering and outsourcing. There is a case for a Quality Commission in Scotland that would have quite a different task from that exercised by the Accounts Commission. The latter's role was, and should remain, to deal with probity and not policy.

Then there is the Public Finance Initiative (PFI). The quick-fix arguments in support of such funding do not answer the best value questions (Coleshill, *et al.*, 1998). How is it that more expensive borrowing, paid over a lengthy period, is to the public's advantage? If, as it is suggested, deferred payments mean that we do not have to pay today — that should be a cause of concern, as future generations will themselves be unable to find capital as they will still be repaying our debts.

There is no good reason to continue with the current Public Sector Borrowing Requirement (PSBR) definition. Instead, there is much merit in the European model of General Government Financial Deficit (GGFD). This allows capital expenditure to be represented on the nation's balance sheet as the investment it is.

Opportunity Scotland

The changing worlds of work and society, of the debate about the knowledge economy and IT make the public sector's contribution more, not less vital as Charles Leadbetter (1999: 205) has pointed out:

> We trust the public sector to store great repositories of information about ourselves, the raw materials of the information economy. The Inland Revenue, the National Health Service and car-insurance agencies are the richest databases in the economy. Much of the public sector's work is processing information. The public sector is a significant investor in the knowledge economy, particularly through its investments in education.

We need a new agenda for the public sector, that is a challenge to all of us, not just public sector workers. We need a new vision of the public sector which recognises its talents, energies and commitment, and which uses that in new ways of developing services, consulting users and devising policy.

The political debate over the future of the public sector needs to recognise the different contributions people can make to economic and social wellbeing in society, and the role of public sector workers as civic and social entrepreneurs, and as providers of human and social capital. Together we can devise a new vision that embraces change and secures the place of the public sector centre stage in the new Scotland. There is much for us to do. We can provide relevant, reliable public services that bring in new models of practice and renew and re-energise our finest traditions. Some new thinking on old principles is required for the challenges ahead.

CHAPTER 25

A NEW VISION

JIM WALLACE

FOR LAW

REFORM

With the advent of the Scottish Parliament, law reform in Scotland is about to take on new impetus. Scottish law and law in Scotland illustrates the fact that Scotland is a nation, but not a state:

> It does have its own courts, but it shares with the rest of the United Kingdom a common highest court in non-criminal cases. Most of its tribunals are part of a United Kingdom organisation. It has its own legal profession. Some of its laws are peculiar to Scotland, some are common to the whole of Britain (i.e. England, Scotland and Wales), some are shared with the rest of the United Kingdom (i.e. with Northern Ireland as well). Some are separate in form, but almost identical in substance. (White and Willock, 1999: 7)

The Act of Union of the Parliaments preserved the separate Scottish legal system, and for nearly 300 years, new legislation for Scotland has been enacted by the UK Parliament. Thus, we have had a succession of Acts with the word '(Scotland)' in their title. We have had GB or UK Acts which became part of Scots law. We have also had UK Acts with 'extent' sections that specified that certain sections did or did not extend to Scotland.

Where a Bill was designed to cover Scotland primarily, the House of Commons would generally remit this Bill to a standing committee for Scottish legislation. In the closing years of the last Conservative Government, this process became somewhat absurd.

Committees have to represent the balance of the House and therefore the Scottish Standing Committee might have more English government backbenchers than Scots. This imbalance did not make for satisfactory debate. For Bills that applied to the whole of GB or the UK, including those with significant policy content for Scotland, the Standing Committee was unlikely to include many Scots at all.

To make matters worse, there was little time for Scottish legislation in the latter two decades. Despite an unprecedented volume of legislation reaching the statute book each year, there was rarely time for more than one or two Scottish programme Bills a session. At Westminster, the convention is that Bills that do not obtain Royal Assent in the session they are introduced lapse, and have to be introduced afresh after the next Queen's Speech. This meant very little flexibility to introduce Scottish Bills in the course of a year. Timing was of the essence.

Against that background, some significant law reform measures were achieved — the Family Law (Scotland) Act 1985 and the Children (Scotland) Act 1995, to name only two examples. But a queue of other badly needed reforms has built up. The Scottish Parliament now gives us the opportunity to deal with these reforms (St. J.N. Bates, 1997; O'Neill, 1999).

The Framework of Law Reform

There are three main sources of law reform projects. Firstly, there is the need for public law to regulate the conduct of public authorities in Scotland and to specify their powers and duties, including power to raise and spend money. There is a vast corpus of Scottish legislation on these matters. It covers almost all the powers and functions of the Scottish Executive, its Non-Departmental Public Bodies and local authorities. Every major policy change affecting these matters will require amendments to legislation. For example, primary legislation is required to set up new Non-Departmental Public Bodies or to wind up or reorganise those that already exist. Primary legislation is required to change the powers and duties of local authorities, or indeed the boundaries and structures of local government itself. The criminal law and the law relating to regulation of charities are other important devolved areas. The normal pattern is for the government of the day to consult widely on such changes, to publish proposals in White Papers and to introduce Bills.

Secondly, there are projects that affect Scots private law — that is to say the law governing the relationships of legal persons to each other. By legal persons I mean individuals or organisations with a legal personality, such as companies, local authorities, Non-Departmental Public Bodies or indeed the Crown. The field of Scots private law includes among other topics, legal capacity, family law, the law of obligations, property law, contract, damages, defamation, and succession. Many areas of private law have been developed more through case law than statute and there may be gaps in the law as well as areas that require modernisation. Such projects are often undertaken by the Scottish Law Commission, which under its founding statute, has responsibility for promoting reform of the law of Scotland.

Lastly, there are projects to consolidate, but not change, the law. Such consolidations have been carried out in the Education (Scotland) Act 1980, the Prisons (Scotland) Act 1989 and the Criminal Procedure (Scotland) Act 1995. There are other areas badly in need of this treatment.

The Scottish Parliament now gives us the opportunity to repatriate Scottish legislation to Scotland. The Parliament exercises devolved power. That means that the Westminster Parliament remains sovereign, but has delegated to the Scottish Parliament the power to make law for Scotland in any area which it has not reserved to itself under the Scotland Act 1998 (Bradley and Ewing, 1997).[1]

A wide range of subjects has been devolved. In practice, any subject previously covered by a Bill with '(Scotland)' in its title will probably be suitable for the Scottish Parliament. The practice of attaching Scottish provisions to GB or UK legislation for the convenience of finding a suitable legislative vehicle will also largely be ended. Instead the Scottish Parliament will consider and enact such proposals. This practice should lead to a better quality of legislation more suited to Scotland's needs.

Legislative competence will, however, become an issue in relation to each measure. It will be necessary for the Scottish Executive to certify that any Bill introduced is within its legislative competence and for the Presiding Officer of the Parliament to certify likewise. Legislation which is outwith competence would be open to challenge and could be struck down. The final court to rule on this issue will be the Judicial Committee of the Privy Council.[2]

The Scottish Parliament provides the opportunity to make faster progress with law reform. Instead of one or two Bills a year, our legislative programme for the first year of the Parliament includes eight. We have already shown our ability to react quickly by introducing emergency legislation to ensure that public safety is the primary test in considering the discharge from hospital of restricted patients under the Mental Health (Scotland) Act 1984.

Another advantage is that Bills will not lapse after a year. The Parliamentary session will last from one election to the next and Bills can be carried forward. Thus there can be a rolling programme of legislation to last the four years of the Parliament and there will not be the unseemly dash sometimes seen at Westminster for a Bill to complete all its stages before the next Queen's Speech.

Our programme includes several important reforms of the law. In the public law area, we will have an Education Bill and a Bill to set up National Parks. There will be a Bill on ethics in public bodies, and a Bill that will enable local communities to buy rural land that could otherwise be sold to an absentee landlord. We will also introduce a Transport Bill to deal with congestion on our roads.

We have already introduced a Bill setting out rules under which the Scottish Executive and other bodies can undertake expenditure and for the production of accounts and for auditing accounts and conduction value for money examinations. The Bill also provides for the accountability of officials in the Executive and public bodies. This will be followed up early next year, and in future years, with a Bill proposing annual expenditure allocations.

There will also be significant private law reforms resulting from reports of the Scottish Law Commission. We are introducing a Bill to abolish the feudal system of land tenure, which has been in place in Scotland for around 800 years but has now outlived its usefulness. We will also be reforming the law on adults with mental incapacity or who are unable to communicate because of a disability. We shall ensure that, where necessary, decisions about their finances and welfare can be made by others with proper protection against abuse.

New Ways of Making Law

The procedures whereby Bills will be enacted will make history in this country. Firstly, there will be more emphasis than ever before on pre-legislative scrutiny and consultation. This will start with extensive consultation by the Executive on their legislative proposals before they are even introduced in the Parliament. In some cases, as with our Education Bill, consultation will be based on a draft Bill.

Before any Bill receives its consideration in principle from the Parliament (equivalent to 'Second Reading' in Westminster parlance) it will be referred to a suitable subject committee of the Parliament. The Bill will have to be accompanied by an explanatory memorandum that explains the policy that the Bill is designed to achieve, how it achieves that policy and what other options were considered. It will have to set out what consultation has been carried out and how the responses have been taken into account. The memorandum will have to cover the financial and manpower effects of the Bill. It will also have to cover an appraisal of the Bill's impact on various key matters, such as equal opportunities, rural and island communities, the voluntary sector and human rights. The subject Committee will scrutinise the Bill and the memorandum very carefully. The Committee may decide that it requires to take evidence and to carry out its own consultation. These steps, whether taken by the Executive in advance of introduction or by the Parliament itself, will ensure the very fullest involvement of relevant organisations and individuals in the pre-legislative scrutiny process. Only after the subject Committee reports back to the Parliament that it is satisfied with the principle of the Bill, will it formally be debated by the Parliament. As I have indicated, this will be equivalent to Westminster's Second Reading debate.

Thereafter the Bill will be committed to the subject Committee again for line by line consideration. This will be the first opportunity for MSPs to table amendments. I have no doubt that, as at Westminster, the various organisations who have an interest in the subject matter of a Bill will inspire amendments and brief committee members. The difference is that Parliament will be much more accessible to them than before. Instead of the long trip to London by plane or sleeper, they will only have to come to Edinburgh. Information technology should, indeed, make it possible for much of the work to be done from their own home base.

When the Committee has finished its work, it will report back to the full Parliament that will again debate the Bill and take further amendments where appropriate. After that process is complete - and it may be interrupted by a second remit to the Committee - the Bill will have to lie for a month during which further competence issues may be raised. Only then will it receive Royal Assent.

This process may seem drawn out but is not when compared to the double scrutiny at Westminster of Commons and Lords. That process allows the government of the day to introduce legislation which is less than perfect, knowing that there will be no fewer than six opportunities for amendments — Committee stage, report and third reading in each House. The Scottish Executive will have no such luxury. It will have to get the Bill right on introduction, since the Committee will immediately be examining the principle of the Bill and will already be receiving representations from anyone who is dissatisfied with the outcome of consultation held by the Executive. This process will be a challenge for the Executive but should lead to better prepared legislation at the outset of the process and less need for radical amendment on the way.

Looking Ahead

I will conclude by looking ahead to the possible shape of future legislative programmes. Our Bills on land reform and on abolition of feudal tenure are part of a wider package of legislation on land and property law reform, and two or three pieces of such legislation are expected to be introduced in the Parliament in each year of its current four year term. The Bill abolishing feudal tenure will be followed by a Bill reforming the law on real burdens (the conditions that are attached to title deeds about how land or property can be used). The Scottish Law Commission is currently working up its report on real burdens and a draft Bill, following consultation. This package will also include Bills abolishing leasehold casualties, and reforming tenement law. These much needed social measures will implement existing Scottish Law Commission reports.

Secondly, I would expect a future legislative programme to feature a Bill on Family Law, implementing the proposals on which my predecessor Henry McLeish consulted in Improving Scottish Family Law. Among other things, this initiative would implement the remaining proposals of the Commission in their 1993 report on Family Law, which were not covered in the Children (Scotland) Act 1995.

There are many other outstanding Scottish Law Commission reports, too many to list here. I do not expect that the Parliament will have time to address them all in the first four years and in the meantime the Commission will continue to publish further reports and Bills. There will also be the need for action in other public law areas, such as the regulation of charities in Scotland.

Our new Parliament will therefore be kept very busy. Amongst all of this bustle, however, I hope that it will be possible to take a longer view and to ensure that there are coherent threads running through our law reform programme. We have a concentration of excellent judges and academic lawyers in Scotland, as well as the Faculty of Advocates and the Law Society of Scotland, and the Scottish Law Commission itself. I hope that these experts will guide and advise the Executive and the Parliament on what the priorities for law reform should be. We also look to them to guide us on what fundamental principles of Scots law require to be preserved and how to avoid a piecemeal approach. Above all, a Scottish Parliament should give us the opportunity for systematic and coherent development of the law of Scotland and we must strive to achieve this.

Endnotes

1 See Sections 28–30 and Schedules 4 and 5 Scotland Act 1998. It should be noted that there is a genuine prohibition on the Scottish Parliament enacting legislation which is incompatible either with the European Convention on Human Rights (as incorporated into UK law by the Human Rights Act 1998, or with European Community law (Section 29 (2) (d) Scotland Act 1998).

2 See Sections 31–33 Scotland Act 1998. The Secretary of State for Scotland (and in theory, any other UK Secretary of State) can also in certain circumstances prevent a Bill passed by the Scottish Parliament becoming law (Section 35, Scotland Act 1998). Challenges to the competence of legislation made by the Scottish Parliament or Scottish Ministers can also be raised in court proceedings after the legislation has been passed (Schedule 6, Scotland Act 1998).

Chapter 26

Modernising

the Scottish

Peter Mackay

Civil

Service

Four years after leaving the Scottish Office I am perhaps better aware of its faults. But I am also more conscious of its strengths and its achievements. It has shown adaptability, versatility and determination in seizing the initiative from Whitehall for driving forward the devolution proposals to a successful conclusion, unlike the abortive Whitehall-led 1974-79 exercise. And that was done with the largely home grown talent which over the last 30 years has acquired, and successfully absorbed, a steady stream of new functions, transferred by administrative devolution from Whitehall by governments of both main parties.

We are at the end of the beginning of the devolution project and the Parliament is in its first full session. The question is whether the former Scottish Office staff now in the Scottish Executive and the Scotland Office, brought up on the Westminster conventions and the ground rules of a majority government, can satisfy the appetite for change and policy innovation evident in Scottish society, and serve the coalition ministers and the Parliament in a creative and cost efficient way. I think they can and will, but changes of emphases will be necessary, whilst sticking to the traditional virtues of political impartiality, and selection and promotion on merit free of political influence, which will be guaranteed by remaining part of the UK civil service, as provided in the Scotland Act.

There is no doubt that key staff are willing to contemplate

change, but the issue to be considered must be whether the service as now constituted is appropriately staffed and organised to meet the demands made of it.

What is meant by 'the Scottish Civil Service'?

First, we must define what we mean by 'the Scottish Civil Service'. There are many more civil servants in Scotland working for non-devolved UK departments, such as in the Departments of Social Security and Defence, the Employment Service and Benefits Agency, Customs and Excise and the Inland Revenue, than are employed by the Scottish Executive and its agencies. This chapter is primarily about those civil servants (excluding the Scottish Prison Service) who work for the Scottish Executive and its agencies, although the staff of the UK departments in Scotland are a resource which should be drawn on to strengthen the range of skills available to the Executive.

Changes Now in Progress in the UK Civil Service as a Whole

As part of the UK civil service, the staff of the Executive are subject to the pressures for civil service reform and modernisation imposed across the UK and reflected in the government's White Paper *Modernising Government* published in March 1999 (Cabinet Office, 1999). This sets out an agenda reflecting the seven challenges which the Prime Minister posed the civil service in 1998 to reform in ways which would allow it to:

- implement constitutional change in a way which would preserve the UK civil service and close working between the UK and devolved administrations;
- integrate the EU dimension into policy thinking;
- improve the quality of public services in a joined up way;
- create a more innovative and less risk averse culture;
- improve collaborative working across organisational boundaries;
- better manage the civil service to meet these challenges;
- think ahead strategically.

In pursuit of these challenges, radical moves are afoot to reform the civil service as a whole. All of this agenda is as relevant to the Scottish Executive as to the rest of the civil service. The issue, then, is what more needs to be done in Scotland to cater for particular Scottish needs. And, in addition, there is a need to assess what weaknesses of the old Scottish Office should be redressed and which strengths must be retained.

The Strengths of the Scottish Office

The greatest single strength of the Scottish Office over the years has been the commitment of its staff to Scotland. That commitment was as true of those who joined from Whitehall or elsewhere in the UK, as of those born and educated in Scotland. While staff from time to time move south for career development to work in the Treasury or the Cabinet Office, the ambition of most staff is to continue to work in and for Scotland. This sense of commitment is far less common in Whitehall — except perhaps amongst the masochistic zealots in the Treasury — where most staff are assigned initially almost casually to one department and, unless they are very senior, may expect to remain in that one for the rest of their career. The second major strength was that all policy staff at middle management level and above had experience across a number of the constituent parts of the Scottish Office, and so could bring experience in, say education and housing, when dealing with issues such as health or social work. That experience also meant that they were less likely to be 'departmental' in policy debates within the office as they could better understand their colleagues problems.

The Weaknesses of the Scottish Office

Most Scottish Office weaknesses exist to a greater or lesser extent in other departments. The first major weakness is that it is too inbred and too homogeneous. Too many staff have spent all, or most of their, careers in the Scottish Office and while a corporate memory is useful, and indeed essential, it can be a discouragement to innovators to be told that an idea was tried twenty years ago and failed. Moreover, an individual's past mistakes were not readily forgotten, even if they were faults of enthusiasm rather than inaction. While the imminence of devolution prompted recruitment of a number of fast stream staff from Whitehall and outside, the majority of senior staff are Scottish Office born and bred and proud of it, although they may have got to the top by a variety of professional routes, having entered as administrators, economists, statisticians, research officers or planners.

The second major weakness is that the number of people with genuine innovative policy-making ability is small in relation to the overall number of staff. The quality of many staff at junior and middle management level aged 35 and above is mediocre. This is a hangover from the days when, like the clearing banks, the bulk of recruitment was at age 16 or 18 (other than the handful coming in each year by the fast-stream graduate entry route) and promotion was entirely from within.

The Scottish Office was slow to adapt to the change in the market place from the 1960s onwards when most other departments were actively recruiting junior managers at graduate level. As a result the clerical entry route did not, as it used to, provide a rich enough stock to supply the need for imaginative policy-makers with a blend of experience and ideas.

The third main weakness is that because the Scottish Office was largely a headquarters department with a very small field organisation (other than the agriculture and fisheries local offices), there is, outside the Prison Service, a relative absence of solid management experience amongst most middle and senior managers. This deficiency differs from the major UK-wide departments, where staff will often have run major organisations with hundreds, if not thousands of staff, dealing directly with the public. In the Scottish Office it was perfectly possible, and indeed common, to rise to a very senior level without ever managing more than a handful of people and never having to deal directly with the public.

The Challenge Now

The major challenge now facing the Scottish Executive is to ensure that a broad and deep pool of talent exists within the Executive civil service, with the experience and the brains to devise the new distinctively Scottish and 'joined up' policies which the rhetoric of the devolution campaigners and Scottish Ministers have led the public to expect (Leicester and Mackay, 1998).

The policies will have to be deliverable in practice — by local government, public agencies and the private sector — so practical experience will be as important as bright ideas. And the political reality is that the size of the Executive's budget is unlikely to increase, and resources available for increased staff can only be found at the expense of frontline services and at some political cost. So the assumption must be that new policy staff will be funded by efficiency savings - reducing staff elsewhere, particularly in clerical and support areas where savings from IT and contracting-out beckon.

Scotland is a small country and the pool of talent available in the public sector is a scarce resource. There is no point in denuding local government, the NHS, Non-Departmental Public Bodies (better known as quangos) and the voluntary sector to increase the firepower of the Executive civil service, when the former remain the main deliverers of the public services. The question then is what can be done to help good staff broaden their experience and develop their careers through a variety of public and voluntary bodies, and how can the Executive tap the talents in these bodies? For those who have reached their ceiling in one part of the public sector, there may still be rewarding and fulfilling opportunities in others. Some middle grade civil servants may find more job satisfaction elsewhere, and we must move away from the feeling that a civil service job must be for life.

The Vision

I look forward to the day when a majority of the most senior people in the Executive's civil service will have spent at least one third of their career working in local government, the health service, the voluntary sector, the arts, other government departments and the private sector. I look forward too to the time when it is expected that the Executive's internal team dealing with, say new housing legislation, will include people who have worked in a housing association, local authority housing department or Scottish Homes. I also look forward to the day when a local authority chief executive comes from the Executive civil service or a local authority chief executive becomes head of a Scottish Executive department (though the differential between senior civil service and local government salaries will inhibit the latter move). This world of more permeable, flexible organisations in the public, private and voluntary sectors with a higher degree of mobility between them is a prerequisite to developing 'joined up' and holistic government (Perri 6, 1997b).

Achieving these Objectives

There are six key areas for action.

— The Executive should widen the range of posts advertised for external recruitment normally on five year renewable contracts so new entrants are coming in at every level. Such recruitment, of course, implies that others must leave either voluntarily or compulsorily, and at a cost that will be a charge on the Scottish Block.

— Agreement should be sought with key local government and voluntary sector players on a systematic and reciprocal programme of secondments in and out of the Executive service.

— The work of the Centre for Scottish Public Policy, Scottish Council Foundation and other independent public policy agencies should be encouraged, by allowing staff to contribute in a personal capacity to 'think tank' policy debates, without assuming that they are committing their ministers or department. Such discussions stimulate creative policy discussion, and help develop informal networks and better understanding.

— Arrangements should be made with other government departments in Scotland for permanent and temporary interchange. Many staff in such departments want to stay in Scotland and do not seek promotion their merits justify because that would mean leaving Scotland. I know, from my own experience as Director of the Manpower Services Commission in Scotland in the 1980s, how much practical talent exists. Younger Scottish Executive staff could benefit by taking on managerial roles in local benefit and employment offices. Indeed many of these local offices could also act as information points (supported by IT) for the Scottish Executive and Parliament giving it local outlets accessible to the Scottish public.

— The Scottish Executive should review the role of the major Scottish Non-Departmental Public Bodies (NDPBs), such as Scottish Homes, Scottish Natural Heritage, the Scottish Environmental Protection Agency, the Scottish Arts Council, Scottish Enterprise and the Scottish Tourist Board, to see whether their nominally independent status under an appointed board makes sense in the post devolution world. There would be considerable efficiency savings if these bodies became agencies of the Executive, like Historic Scotland and the Scottish Prison Service, and their boards became advisory rather than nominally executive. This would eliminate the need for duplication and second guessing by the relevant 'sponsor division' in the Executive (as at present) and would more accurately reflect the fact that in practice in all NDPBs the tune is called by the provider of funds — that is, the responsible minister. Most importantly it would more closely engage the expert and talented specialist and experienced staff of the NDPBs in policy formation within the Executive and help to fill the talent gap.

— The various public and voluntary sector employers should establish joint programmes for staff training and career development, which would help create shared appreciation of common problems, develop networking, encourage partnership and facilitate the kind of interchange envisaged above.

These action points will take time to produce results. Some will be driven by the UK-wide civil service reforms now under way, or the separate initiatives already begun by the impressive new management team now in charge at St Andrews House. They will demand some major changes in individual career expectations, but the public sector cannot be (and ought not to be) insulated from what is happening in the wider world. If the end result is policies better fitted to Scottish needs, within a UK and EU environment, delivered more efficiently effectively and accountably, then the changes will be worthwhile. Without them there is a real danger of a 'Scottish civil service' crippled by budgetary restrictions, no longer able to depend on Whitehall for policy development and unable to import new talent. But the Scottish Office has successfully coped with major change throughout the last century or so, and I am sure its successors will rise to the new challenges.

CHAPTER 27

MODERNISING

ANDREW WILSON | # THE SCOTTISH

PARLIAMENT

Having been up and running for only a matter of months, it may seem an odd assertion to some that such a new institution needs modernising. In part this assertion is in recognition of the fact that, despite the detailed legislation that set it up and the high quality work of the Consultative Steering Group, the Parliament in many ways is still feeling its way. It is up to us all to define exactly what it will do and how it will operate. In the wider UK government context, renowned for institutional inertia and conservatism, it is therefore a rare opportunity to get reforms in first.

It is a unique feature of the Scottish psyche that having waited long and worked hard to secure our Parliament, it immediately became the subject of a knocking campaign. The Parliament's first weeks have been ignominious, with PR disaster following PR disaster. Topics such as holidays, pay and the bizarre story of the medals were seized upon by an unfriendly media. The fact that relative costs and holiday times are dwarfed by the comparatively profligate and 'workshy' Westminster level of government has been ignored. It is pointless to suggest that all this hoo-ha was needless, and conspiracy theorists could argue that it was a deliberate attempt to downplay the Parliament's status. What is important is that in Scotland — probably more than any other country in the world — the 'People's Parliament' has yet to prove itself to an expectant, but cynical, public.

In this chapter I argue that the Parliament must take the lead in constantly improving itself — to grow in status, stature and effectiveness. Such a process will also allow the Parliament to restore and build public faith — in our democratic process and in the value of government and public service itself. The aim must be to take the lead in making Scotland the most modern democratic governance system in the world. There are various aspects to this aim, but I will concentrate on the immediate opportunities the Parliament has for taking the lead in securing closer ties between citizens and government in delivering public services. This is the best way to begin the process of rebuilding public faith in the Parliament, in democratic processes and in public service itself.

Firstly, by examining the context in which the Parliament operates, I will argue that it is a constantly changing and evolving one, and if the Parliament is to succeed it must move quickly in line with, and ahead of, the times and European trends. Looking then at the main roles of the Parliament, I will touch briefly on its function as a legislature and check on the Executive. Most importantly, I will then examine the opportunities to pioneer new ways of allowing contact between citizens, their representatives and public services. The Parliament's opportunity to become the exemplar of conduct in public service and more widely will then be discussed. My overall theme is of a constantly evolving process, where the Parliament responds to changes in its democratic context and is not afraid to operate at the cutting edge of new ways of working.

An Evolving Parliament

It is important to recognise that any parliament operates within the limits to its powers — practically and legally. However in examining the Scottish Parliament it is critical to note that the context it operates within is, and should be, subject to constant change. In the modern world the role of government and nation-states is constantly evolving. In a European Union of growing power, the Scottish Parliament will have to keep one eye on the sharing sovereignty process at a supra-national level, and the other on delivering its own domestic commitments.

The anomaly of Westminster as the extra layer of government in the middle will be the subject of ongoing interest as the Parliament continues the process of working. The Concordats of 'understandings' between the Scottish and Westminster Parliament are a — somewhat uneven and one-sided — attempt to rationalise the relationship, but it is difficult to see how the current settlement can withstand more than a temporary test of time. At the same time there is no formal structure for changes and improvements other than through Westminster (Mitchell, 1999). How this resolves itself remains to be seen.

The logic of devolution is that, in the areas not reserved to Westminster, the most appropriate level of governance is at a Scottish level. As Europe grows it is clear that the appropriate level of governance in other areas, such as monetary policy, will be at that level (Burrows, 1999). As policy-making power evolves from Westminster to Europe there is every reason to expect that a similar process will see the logic for more powers to flow to the Scottish level. The common factor in both processes is that it will be Westminster that cedes sovereignty. For example it is difficult to see how a coherent anti-poverty (or social inclusion) strategy can work unless fully dovetailed with an integrated tax and benefit system. However, at present, these policy competencies lie at different levels in the UK. Put simply we need to ensure that ideological opposition to independence or an emotional attachment to the 'British' system and to Westminster are not allowed to obstruct clear thinking about the most appropriate way to govern ourselves. Perhaps the most important aspect of 'modernising the Parliament' will be in increasing its powers to the same level as that of other countries.

However, that process will be far easier to manage and sustain if the Parliament has demonstrated an ability to evolve, reform and modernise its own way of working and in how it fulfils its current roles. The Parliament has three key roles in Scottish public life — as legislature; as the interface with the people; and underpinning all its activities, a role as exemplar in the work of public service in the government, community and in public life.

The Legislature

Here the Parliament's job is to scrutinise and improve the work of the Executive, acting as a check on its power. This role has yet to be fully tested, but there are some early lessons. There is some scope for the Parliament to bring its own legislative programme to bear but in reality, with the Partnership Agreement having secured old fashioned 'Elective Dictatorship' the Executive has overarching control. In the context of a minority administration, or of a more equal coalition partnership, the Parliament's standing would be improved. However this outcome is a function of election results and parties, not parliamentary structure. What can be attended to immediately is the Parliament's role in examining the work of the Executive. The pre-legislative committee structure is a massive step forward on the Westminster model, but how it will work in practise remains to be seen. The legislature is uni-cameral, so the committee stage needs to work extremely well.

Two key structural points are worth making at this early stage. The first is resource based — the balance of knowledge is overwhelmingly with the Executive. The resources of the civil service and the controversial policy advisers massively outweigh the research capabilities of the legislature. The Parliament research unit is minute compared to its House of Commons counterpart, and while staffed by an able and conscientious team, it cannot compete. Without its poor resources being improved, it is difficult to see it being able to employ the cutting edge research methods that most modern businesses now enjoy. Added to this problem, the Committee Clerks who serve the Parliament are similarly pressured in terms of resources — although not in terms of staff ability, coming from among the best of the new generation of Scottish Office administrators and others.

This situation is mirrored by the 'Short-Money' and allowances dispute in the early days of the Parliament, the outcome of which sees the non-Executive parties grossly under-resourced compared to their Westminster counterparts. The office of the leader of the UK opposition, as one individual, receives more public resources than the entire SNP group of 35 MSPs in the Scottish Parliament. In addition, the SNP leader is the only oppostion leader at any level of government in the UK whose office is not subject to allocated funding for that purpose. Properly resourcing a modern legislature is critical but politically difficult in a context when the public standing of the Parliament is low. This makes it all the more important for the Parliament to perform well with what it has.

Committee structures follow the departmental and ministerial structure of the Executive. This pattern constrains Parliament's ability to follow cross-departmental policy subjects on the basis of policy implementation and delivery, rather than the traditional accounting for the flow of resources through the departmental chain. The Parliament needs to remain alive to how it rationalises this question. However, perhaps the most important issue is for the Committees to retain an interest in the impact of legislation after it has gone through the Parliament, to ensure an assessment of its implementation by the administration, as well as its effectiveness and efficiency.

The Parliament as Pioneer

As well as performing the role of the legislature, the Parliament must both represent the people and ensure a close interface between citizens, representatives and government. The Parliament must find new ways to perform this role. Clearly the need to travel the country and be of the people, not above them, is well rehearsed. The scope for bypassing the traditional party route to accessing the legislature through civic institutions is also an area, which has attracted a great deal of debate and interest. However, the Parliament has to capture innovation as its main ally and pioneer new ways of empowering the citizen-representative-government interface.

The way in which people perceive and communicate with their government at all levels is always changing, and at present is probably approaching a low point in recent history. Electoral turnout is plummeting — witness the growth across the Western world of the 'non-party of non-voters' (Beck, 1994) — and perceptions of public services and public servants are poor (Archibugi *et al.* 1998; Dunn, 1992; Huntington, 1991). The Parliament must take the lead in dealing with these issues, and seize the opportunities that modern methods of communication offer. Communication is changing rapidly, and it is easy to envisage a Scotland soon where citizens have as easy access to the Internet as they now do to the phone or television, and where the majority of business is carried out by electronic means. There seems to have been little or no appreciation, in this country at least, of the opportunities which this provides for democracy — both in terms of delivering actual services in a quick and efficient way, but also by allowing people previously unprecedented access to democracy and the parliamentary process.

In the US, the citizen to government communication is as likely to take place via the internet as by any other medium. Tax returns are filed electronically and public sector job vacancies advertised and applied for over the Net. Most colleges encourage electronic rather than written applications. There also exists an extremely well used labour exchange — the US Electronic Job Bank. Several publicly funded sites give voters a chance to enter into real-time discussions with policy experts and elected representatives on pertinent local and national issues. These genuinely useful, simple and interactive facilities give some idea of how the government and democracy of the future can operate. Compare and contrast this approach with the few faltering steps taken by Westminster to embrace the electronic revolution. Internet access in the UK is lower than the EU average, and four years after Tony Blair promised a PC in every classroom, a substantial proportion of secondary and primary schools throughout Scotland are still not hooked up to the Net.

The one large-scale IT project that Westminster has undertaken, (to enable all major benefits to be paid via smart card) has proved an unmitigated disaster. In reality, the size of UK government administration leads to scale inefficiencies that are much less of an issue at the more manageable Scottish level, where good governance is easier to achieve. Inevitably this means that in the UK most citizens' interactions with government are not generally pleasant, with most transactions clerically based and bureaucratic. Scotland with its new democratically elected Parliament is not, and should not be, shackled by the same outmoded thought processes. As the twentieth century draws to a close, we are uniquely placed to take advantage of building new technology into the framework of the new Scottish Government.

The first challenge is increasing access to technology — a necessary pre-requisite to any broad-based campaign to harnessing new technology to increase awareness and efficiency of government. Giving everyone in Scotland his or her own email address and means of accessing it should be a priority. Email addresses are easily transportable in the same way that phone numbers will become, and it should be easy for the individual to access email from any terminal. There is no reason why email addresses cannot be issued with National Insurance numbers, or at least based on them, and with appropriate technology this would enable easy communication, more secure than traditional mail. It is easy to see how public access terminals could be sited within public facilities.

'The Scottish Parliament Helpline' and 'The Scottish Parliament On-line Advice Service':
Modern Public Service Solutions to Everyday Problems

It is remarkable that in a world dominated by easy access telephone services that no all-encompassing public service equivalent exists. The Scottish Parliament can fill the gap by developing a one-stop low-cost helpline allowing anyone access to advice on public services and how to reach them. Dovetailed with properly financed Citizens' Advice Bureaux, this would ensure a user-friendly service of immediate public benefit. The Parliament could also develop an internet based information service, installed in public access points, such as libraries, schools and colleges, along with stand alone kiosks — like the tourist information points — located in public facilities such as supermarkets. These could be called Scottish Parliament Public Services Access Points. The process of putting such facilities together would bring together public agencies, departments and different levels of government, facilitating a more 'holistic' or 'joined-up' approach. The Scottish Executive should also pioneer projects that encourage highly connected groups, such as students and businesses, to interact with Government by electronic means.

These opportunities are immense and the Scottish Parliament is in a perfect position to facilitate, and lead this debate between government and the wider public. The days of public services being viewed as backward bureaucratic dinosaurs can come to an end, and in leading the process the Parliament could provide firm evidence of its success in its major role as the leader, or exemplar, of how to conduct public service relationships in the twenty first century.

The Parliament as Exemplar

With this type of refocusing, it is easy to see how the Parliament can bury the early days of poor PR. There is no question that the prospects for delivering a modern good governance system in Scotland are far greater than those within the old and dated structures of Westminster and Whitehall. In leading this process, both within the wider government community and in Scotland overall, the Parliament needs to stick to a clear set of structured principles applicable to all levels of public service.

New research from leading international governance advisers coincided with the appointment of the new European Commission in September 1999. It researched the guiding values of public service across Europe and identified nine key principles of good governance and public administration. These provide a useful framework against which to measure the Scottish Parliament's ability in leading the process of good governance across the Scottish Government Community (Andersen Consulting, 1999). The nine principles are:

— Accountability: for actions and decisions taken, and for public resources expended. This is a principle ever more important, and is about more than accounting for the allocation of public resources — it is now about accounting for policy outcomes against social and economic objectives.

— Accessibility: to services, to officials, and to the processes and records that affect citizens. This access goes hand-in-hand with accountability and transparency and should also reinforce co-ordination. One-stop shop access is key.

— Transparency: of the connection between processes and decision making and the public interest. Vital in the democratic process, it is important that it is not allowed to act as a disincentive for innovation. However involving the public at the start of an innovation process makes it easier to carry stakeholders along through a policy development process.

— Integrity: of word and act with colleagues, with politicians and with the public. Ethical conduct is critical in gaining and preserving public trust. The recent Standards Committee investigations into the 'Lobbygate' affair were critical, and will be a key measure of the Parliament's ability to respond quickly and to secure integrity.

— Flexibility: of processes and mindsets to respond to circumstances. The Parliament must respond to changes in its macro-context but also to other changing demands. The need for continuous change is paramount.

— Quality: of policy outcomes achieved, and of citizens' experience of receiving a public service. There is no universal benchmark for measuring the quality of public services but the Parliament can take the lead in ensuring that every part of the Scottish government community performs to the level of the best in its field both domestically and increasingly important — internationally.

— Innovation: in approaches to solving problems and in methods of service provision. This is intrinsically linked with the need to learn new lessons and, as with quality, it means structures that allow the adoption of best practises from home and abroad.

— Fairness: in dispensing public resources and in weighing the interests of the citizens. This principle hits directly at the question of equal access to representatives and governing institutions and, once again, the Parliament must take the lead in this process.

— Co-ordination: of objectives, priorities, decisions and actions within the public services. This is probably the key issue currently exercising the minds of public service deliverers across Europe. The Parliament provides an excellent hub to interface with the various spokes of the wheel, and can lead the co-ordination process.

With these principles underpinning its work, the Scottish Parliament is in a perfect position to take the lead in modernising both the new democracy and the delivery of public services across Scotland. The opportunity to restore public faith in both our democracy and in public services is there.

Conclusion: Keeping the Process Alive

There is undoubtedly a temptation in some quarters to regard the Scottish Parliament as a finish to John Smith's 'unfinished business'. This position tends to come from those who either never wanted the Parliament in the first place, or who regard it as a regrettable but necessary step to contain the advance of the SNP.

The attempt to tag the SNP as 'wreckers' comes from such quarters and motivations. Enthusiasts and cynics exist in all parties but one thing is certain, if there is any party with a vested interest in ensuring the Parliament is a success it is the SNP. This calculation is based on the judgement that Scots do not tend to build on failure. Those of us who wish to see the Parliament grow believe it will only do so on the basis of success. If partial devolution is a good thing, its success makes a powerful case for more of a good thing. The Parliament is both the subject and the catalyst for the process. It must continually prove its own worth as an institution, as a legislature and as an exemplar and leader of change. In so doing, it will be making a continuous case for normal powers and status, just like any other modern nation-state.

It is with that motivation in mind that this chapter has been written. Modern Scottish Nationalism is about driving Scotland forward and growing faith in our ability to govern ourselves. Everyone who is interested in the good government of Scotland has the opportunity to be part of that process, where they choose to jump off is then up to them.

CHAPTER 28

BRITISHNESS

JOYCE McMILLAN | AFTER

DEVOLUTION

In autumn 1999, at a British Council seminar in Germany, I find myself listening as a man from the British Embassy tries to explain Britain's recent attempts to 'rebrand' itself to an audience of senior German regional officials. It is a matter, he says, of trying to correct false images of Britain as a place of pin-stripes and royal palaces, tradition and history; of projecting a new sense of the country as a modern, dynamic, successful multi-cultural society. But they are not slow on the uptake, the top public servants of the region of Hesse; and almost as soon as the Embassy man sits down, they ask the obvious question. We all know, they say, that it is difficult to sell an image successfully unless there is some substance behind it. So is this updating of the idea of Britain just a cosmetic thing, aimed at foreigners? Or does it, they continue, reflect a real change in the way the British see themselves?

And of course, neither the Embassy man nor I really know the answer to these questions; in all the debate about the shifting identities of Scotland, Wales and both parts of Ireland that has swept across these islands in the last twenty years, the core identities of the United Kingdom, Englishness and Britishness, have remained largely silent. But now, it looks as though that is about to change; because here in Scotland, as the new politics of devolution takes shape, the question of British identity — whether we still have it, what it means, whether it is capable of renewal — is emerging as

285

one of the main sites of tension and dispute. For twenty years now, under the grip of the Thatcher and Major governments, many Scots have been working to develop a sense of Scottish identity strong, real and contemporary enough to support the claim for self-government; and the result has been the widespread acceptance, at least in theory, of an idea of Scottishness that is pluralistic and post-modern, outward-looking, inclusive, non-sectarian, and, by historic standards, fairly secure in itself. But as that debate reaches a temporary resting-place in the Parliament on the Mound, the spotlight inevitably switches to the other side of the devolution equation, to Scotland's residual Britishness, and what kind of future it has.

Rebranding Britain

Post-devolution, political Scotland is behaving like a newly-formed volcanic island, its topography still heaving and shifting so rapidly that only a fool would attempt to map it. But it is clear enough that the idea of Britishness is entering some kind of crisis, not only in Scotland but across the UK. It is one of the paradoxes of British history that despite the brief 1960s flowering of a more modern and inclusive 'swinging' identity, the image that has generally represented Britain to the world — the typical British gentleman, stiff upper lip, country house parties, aristocracy, fair play and village cricket matches — has always been a hopelessly exclusive one, in terms of class, culture and geography. And despite John Major's doomed final attempt to appeal to that kind of national imagery in the early 1990s, phenomena such as the 'rebranding Britain' exercise suggest that it is now understood, even at the heart of British government, that this old imagery needs to be actively challenged and replaced.

Of course, new Labour's early attempts at rising to this task, through campaigns such as the 'Cool Britannia' initiative, have been inept and shallow to the point of counter-productiveness, and hopelessly London-centred. For most of its history, the Labour Party has been a kind of silent junior partner in the business of Union, always loyal in public, but privately given to cracking rude jokes about Tory jingoism and hanging around with Irish nationalists; it has no tradition of articulating positive images of Britain, and is adjusting with difficulty to its new post-1997 role as the leading party of Union. But the fact that Cool Britannia existed at all is an acknowledgment that change is needed; the question is whether it will go deep enough.

For meanwhile, out in society, there are changes afoot that make the idea of Cool Britannia seem like a laughably late and inadequate response to shifting self-perceptions across Britain. Most Scots under 35 now say that they do not feel British at all, not even as a subsidiary or second identity. The English, too, have suddenly taken to sporting St. George's flag at football matches, rather than the Union Jack. There is the nervous flight from the old, militaristic imagery of traditional British state events that has characterised recent major royal occasions in Britain, from the heady post-Protestant exoticism of Diana's funeral, through Prince Edward's kitsch-medieval-heritage wedding, to the official opening of the Scottish Parliament, with its careful combination of British royal ceremonial and Scottish civic tradition; as if even the Royal family, in its modernising mode, now finds the traditional trappings of Britishness too alienating and old-fashioned. Most importantly of all, perhaps, there is the effective collapse of the old Conservative and Unionist Party, for the last two hundred years the guardians par excellence of the UK political settlement. Of course the Tories are not defunct, either north or south of the border. But David McLetchie's group of Tories in the Scottish Parliament — instinctively a modern centre-right party, business-friendly, Europe-friendly and happy to work with new Scottish institutions — seem increasingly to inhabit a different political planet, and certainly a different country, from William Hague's southern Tories.

There is a body of Scottish nationalist thought that has a straightforward explanation for this growing sense of cultural confusion. For some theorists of nationalism, for example, the British identity has always been a forged and 'artificial' one, imposed by an elite for its own commercial and military ends, and bound eventually to be brought down by the forces of popular democracy (see Colley,

1992; Grant and Stringer, 1995). At its most extreme, this argument dismisses British identity as a corrupt and damaging delusion. But even the most moderate nationalists of this school see the UK much as UK Independence supporters see the European Union, as a pragmatic project which always lacked emotional and cultural substance. If the UK project was essentially bound together by the triple forces of Protestantism, Empire, and war against continental powers, they argue, then its day is obviously done. The wars are a thing of the past; the Empire has gone; and as for Protestantism, there must be few cases in history when a tradition and the word that describes it have lost so much status in so short a time.

Beyond the Break-up of Britain

One of the interesting features of the current Scottish scene is the emergence of an increasingly robust series of counter-arguments against this persuasive 'break-up of Britain' position (see Nairn, 1981). First, there is a growing feeling that for all its elegance, this argument is based on a set of negative assumptions about the Union — that it has been problematic for the majority of Scots, and that the UK has proved intrinsically unreformable — which are difficult to square with the facts.

The enthusiastic participation and high profile of Scots both in the institutions of the British state at home, and in the building of the Empire overseas; the fact that until the 1980s, the Union had been broadly successful in providing most Scots with levels of economic prosperity and social welfare which, although far from perfect, could stand comparison with conditions anywhere else in the world; the political freedoms enshrined in a system which, for all its flaws, has nonetheless been admired across the world, particularly in the nineteenth century and in the aftermath of the Second World War, for its capacity to combine gradual democratic reform with civil peace: none of these are obvious characteristics of an unreformable or reactionary state in which Scots exist as an suppressed minority.

Secondly, there is the sense that social democrats, as people whose first concern lies with democratic and humanitarian values, are bound to reject essentialist arguments that assign superior qualities of morality or authenticity to particular national identities; indeed twentieth century history is littered with cases, from Russia to Serbia, in which the British left has run into serious trouble over its inability to grasp that a particular national identity is not a fixed moral quantity, but a force that can be used for both positive and negative purposes.

At the moment, Scottish and Irish nationalism are routinely seen as fashionable, positive and authentic, whereas 'being British' — in the years after 1945 a general byword for all that was brave and admirable — is currently dead in the water both as a moral value and as a style item. In the end, we are obliged to recognise that all national identities are 'forged' or constructed at some stage in history, and that all of them acquire, with time, accretions of affection and loyalty on one hand, and enmity on the other. The British state, as the case in point, has certainly forfeited the loyalty and affection of many Scots through its imperialist arrogance, its elitism, its frequent ruthless defence of mercantile capitalism, and its trashing of the welfare state ideal under Margaret Thatcher. However, it has also won and consolidated loyalty and affection through its long tradition of parliamentary democracy and radical activism, particularly in the labour movement; through the courage and idealism — now largely discredited, but real enough at the time — that underpinned many of its imperial adventures; through its occasional stands against fascism and dictatorship in Europe; and through the construction of the welfare state in the postwar years.

That means, thirdly, that there can be no clear-cut distinction between 'real' national allegiances with strong emotional content, and 'artificial' loyalties which are purely pragmatic; indeed after almost 300 years of full incorporating Union, during which Scots have been heavily complicit in every adventure the British state has undertaken, it would probably be much easier to take Scotland out of Britain, in a strictly political sense, than to take the emotional strand of Britishness out of Scotland. It takes only a short walk around smaller Scottish cities such as Perth and Inverness, with their colossal war memorials, to understand the fierce complexity and conflicting passions that mark our continuing close relationship with the British armed forces. Conversely, it does not take much time around the British trade union movement to recognise that there can, on occasions, be a straightforwardly reactionary dimension to the current tendency to equate radicalism with Scottish self-determination.

At its best, a feeling for issues of national identity and self-expression is a powerful adjunct to a sophisticated understanding of how economic and political power works. In an age when socialism has become the analysis that dare not speak it name, and when there has been a systematic dumbing-down in popular understanding of how economic power shapes lives, the politics of national identity can too easily become a dim-witted substitute for the politics of real solidarity with people facing exactly the same economic pressures and problems, whether in the regions of England or elsewhere.

Fourthly, the 'break-up of Britain' thesis depends on a series of assumptions about the unreformability of Britain, and its likely reversion to the four original national identities, that can seem rigid, reactionary, and downright unhelpful in confronting some of the most complex issues facing the peoples of Britain and Ireland now, notably the impasse in Northern Ireland, and the question of democratic renewal in England itself. So far as England is concerned, proponents of the breakup theory often seem to be predicting and anticipating the 'English backlash' against Scottish home rule, and the 'rise of English nationalism', in exactly the same terms as the leader-writers of the *Daily Telegraph* and *The Spectator*.

Despite the noise created by a few Westminster Tories with their strident demands for an English Parliament, and by their cheerleaders in the right-wing press, the main substantial political development in England, in response to the Scottish Parliament, has been the setting up of regional Constitution Conventions, on the Scottish model, in the north-east and north-west of England, and in Yorkshire and Humberside. But because the growing democratic movement for decentralisation in England does not fit the neat theory of reversion to old national loyalties, it tends to be ignored; and the jingoistic ranting of a few neurotic reactionaries around Westminster misread as representing the mood of the whole nation.

As for Northern Ireland, it goes without saying that any theory which suggests a reversion to four basic national identities — English, Scottish, Irish, Welsh — is unlikely to contribute constructively to a peace process which demands respectful recognition of both the Catholic-Irish and British-Unionist identities in the province; indeed it comes perilously close to the traditional, patronising and (for Unionists) insulting nationalist view that the British identity of Ulster Unionists is a kind of delusion, from which they will recover on the day they bring themselves to admit that they have really been Irishmen all along. Add to all this the misgivings of many of Britain's black citizens, who find themselves reasonably comfortable with the broad idea of British citizenship, but not at all comfortable with the idea of themselves as English, and you have a theory which seems increasingly out of touch with the complex reality of identity in these islands at the end of the century (see Kerevan and Marr, 1998).

Finally, there is the question of whether the current low profile of British identity, particularly among younger people in Scotland, is not exaggerated by the fact that Scottish identity has seemed under threat over the last twenty-five years, and has therefore been endlessly debated, fought for, modernised and redefined; whereas it has, until now, been possible to take Scotland's British identity entirely for granted, or to let it exist somewhere below the horizon of consciousness. The current generation of Scottish under-30s hardly seems aware of the mass of British-based institutions — the NHS, social security system, London-based broadcasting networks — that still form part of the bedrock of their lives. But that passive attitude to the 'British dimension' of Scottish life might undergo a rapid change if its continuation seemed threatened; and it is perhaps because of a growing post-devolution awareness of this unspoken British element in Scottish life that some young modernisers in the SNP — notably their Finance spokesman Andrew Wilson — have recently begun to develop a 'third way' position on the issue of Britishness in Scotland, suggesting that in an age of multiple identities, the SNP can afford to be relaxed about the British strand in Scotland's history, and need no longer regard it as a canker to be rooted out and rejected (Wilson, 1999). After independence, runs this argument, Scotland would still be British in a historical and cultural sense; but without a clean break from the old structures of the British state, it will never be possible to rebuild the institutional relationships among the nations of Britain on the right basis of equality, mutual respect and genuine pluralism.

A New Convergence?

This is the point, of course, at which Scottish nationalism almost finesses itself out of existence, and begins to merge with the wilder shores of old-fashioned Liberal federalism. If Britishness remains meaningful at the cultural and socio-economic level, then the case for rejecting political institutions at that level becomes increasingly fragile; and the constitutional aims of the new Labour and SNP projects — both apparently interested in creating a new web of relationships among the nations and regions of the archipelago, based on decentralised governments that work closer to the people and can therefore achieve higher levels of consent, responsiveness and accountability — become ever more difficult to distinguish.

No doubt all of this will seem several bridges too far for most SNP activists, in a party where many still feel that although other plural identities may be acceptable, Britishness remains the psychological enemy, to be shunned at all costs. Some will dismiss the new Labour reform programme as a cosmetic exercise and an elaborate con-trick, the shadow of home rule without the substance; others will point to the torrent of self-hating derision and contempt showered on the Scottish Parliament during its first weeks of life, and argue that whatever the economic and political numbers suggest, the Union has damaged Scotland's psyche in ways that can only be healed with the coming of full independence.

In the end, the gradual convergence of visions on both sides of the constitutional debate tends to support the conclusion that the precise institutional arrangements agreed among the nations of these islands will finally be less important than the capacity we show, within those institutions, for genuinely respecting and embracing the complexity of our cultural inheritance, and for advancing the cause of deep participative democracy in the twenty first century. There is still a tendency, in matters of national belonging, to regard pluralism or dualism of identity as an untidiness to be suppressed, rather than a positive quality to be celebrated. 'You've got a problem, then, haven't you', one senior Scottish nationalist once said to me, when I told him that I definitely felt both Scottish and British; and in the same way, old-fashioned British nationalists persist in dismissing devolution as a 'mess', rather than as a way of representing a diversity that really exists.

Yet only a glance across the Irish Sea suggests that to understand that so far from posing a problem, the capacity to recognise and respect the presence of different strands of belonging and affinity, both within the individual and within the community, may often be the only effective key to a society at peace with itself. The question of how that sense of pluralism is best achieved in Britain and Ireland - whether by a steady evolution of British institutions, or by a 'clean break' with the British past and a new set of relationships — increasingly looks like a matter of strategy rather than principle; what is clear is the importance of resisting all theories of identity, British or Scottish, Unionist or separatist, that make that pluralism more difficult to sustain.

Governments in Britain and elsewhere will have to face the truth that strong though national and regional loyalties may be, for most people they come a poor second, third or tenth to practical concerns about the quality of their day-to-day lives. Where a nation or community is threatened from outside, people will of course rally around the flag. In normal times, governments have traditionally won the positive allegiance of their people by delivering on social-democratic tasks such as the provision of good public education and healthcare, the development of infrastructure, the relief of poverty, and the offer of genuine social security, particularly to children, and to the old and sick. It is a commonplace of Scottish politics to recognise that the British state lost the loyalty of many Scots during the 1980s because it elected a government which deliberately chose not only to withdraw from some of those tasks, but to renege noisily on the idea that government should carry them out at all. However, few seem willing to draw the obvious conclusion; that wherever governments embrace policies and rhetoric of this kind — and they often feel, in post-modern global conditions, that they have little choice — they risk setting up a cycle of disaffection and decay in the political structures and identities they represent.

Behind the present process of constitutional change in Britain, in other words, there lies not only a story of cultural evolution in these islands, but also a series of deeper questions about the changing role of governments in the twenty first century, and how they are to retain the loyalty, respect and involvement of their people in an age when they can no longer perform many of the tasks that have traditionally expected of them. For in the end, it is the failure of imagination, intelligence and compassion in government, at any level, that transforms quiet cultural identities into political fields of dreams; and sets us yearning for smaller, kinder countries, that remember the meaning of words such as liberty, equality and fraternity, and will not let us down.

| NOREEN BURROWS | # A NEW UNIONISM?
SCOTLAND'S PLACE IN
THE NEW EUROPE |

There are a number of key questions concerning Scotland and Europe. Firstly, what is Scotland's place in the new Europe? Secondly, what is the new Union of Europe? And, finally, has Scotland's position changed because of the arrival of a Scottish Parliament, or due to changes at European level? These and other questions and their associated debates need to be set within discussions of identity and citizenship. If Europe is a contested notion then so also are these questions. Furthermore, no clear definition exists of ideas such as multi-layered governance.

This chapter is set against the geographical context of the European Union post the Treaty of Amsterdam of May 1999. In one sense this immediately narrows the debate down to a Union of Europe consisting of Western democracies with a developing tradition of co-operation, based on ideas of democracy, pluralism and a commitment to a market-oriented society operating in a global context. However, the New Union of Europe could be defined in much wider terms to include the aspirant members of Central and Eastern Europe — those countries that Milan Kundera described as being accidentally cut off in the post-Second World War settlement.

Characterising the New Europe

What is interesting about the new Union of Europe is its potential for flexibility. This term has acquired a specific legal meaning in the Treaty of Amsterdam, allowing some countries to go at a different pace of integration than others in some policy areas (Treaty of Amsterdam, Articles 43–45). However the Union is flexible in many other ways. It has been described by many writers as a multi-layered organisation meaning that within the Union there are several different communities (Curtin and Dekker, 1999). There is an economic community, a foreign policy community, a home affairs community, a defence community and so on. These communities overlap, so not only is the New Union multi-layered, it is also multi-textured. There are differences in scale and depth between and within these policy areas. For example, agricultural policy, as is well known, is excessively detailed and interventionist, whereas foreign policy matters are scarcely co-ordinated.

The New Union is also flexible in its external relations, and is continually negotiating and renegotiating its position vis-à-vis third states. This might be on specific issues such as trade disputes, where matters may appear to be superficial and irrelevant but are neither, as they form part of a wider regulation of world trade. The recent banana dispute between the European Union and United States is a good example. However, negotiations are ongoing on a much wider conceptual basis, going to the heart of the Union's relations with its neighbours. Scores of agreements exist that set up continuing and, on the whole, friendly relations with countries on the southern and eastern flanks of the EU. The neglected dimension — the northern flank — is currently being championed by the Finnish Presidency in an attempt to balance out what the Finns perceive as an over emphasis on the southern dimension of the Union's external relations.

The EU is therefore a complex structure or set of structures, characterised by flexibility and fluidity. It is concerned both with relations between members, and relations with non-members. Some non-members may become members — the process of enlargement is itself never static. The Union sometimes moves at great speed developing policy in great bursts of energy and other times it characterised by inertia. The term 'lourdeur' has been applied to these periods of seeming inactivity. Some members want the Union to integrate more deeply to forge a single European state with its own constitution and political institutions, but others balk at this prospect. The New Europe is characterised by a lack of homogeneity, and is multi-lingual and multi-ethnic. Its political formation changes as frequently as there are general elections in the member states. Some parts of the Union are more deeply entrenched than others. In these circumstances, how can we ever begin to consider questions of a European identity?

Identity, Ethnicity and the European Union

There are at least four overlapping terms that need to be discussed. The first is nationality. This term has both a legal and non-legal meaning. Closely related is the term citizenship, which again can have a legal and a non-legal meaning. Nationality and citizenship in the context of EU law are, as we will see below, conflated. Ethnicity implies 'a sense of kinship, group solidarity and common culture' (Hutchison and Smith, 1996: 3). Identity is a somewhat looser term implying group solidarity and a sense of community but without the bonds of kinship. Individuals may have several, or multiple, identities.

In law, those who are nationals of one of the member states of the EU are European citizens. This legal status was conferred by the Maastricht Treaty in 1992. However European citizenship 'complements' rather than 'replaces' national citizenship (Article 17) and confers only one additional right not already available under European law to nationals of the member states. That is the right to avail oneself of the consular and diplomatic protection of the other member states. Nationals of the member states of the EU have a wide variety of economic and social rights and certain limited political rights such as the right to vote in local and European elections in the states in which they happen to be residing. These rights arise not from the idea of citizenship of the Union, a legal concept introduced only lately, but from the principle of non-discrimination on the grounds of nationality that was enshrined in the Treaty of Rome establishing the original European Economic Community of the six in 1957. Non-nationals of the member states, except in certain specifically defined circumstances, do not derive these rights. There is, as yet, no universal principle of racial or ethnic equality in European law.

However, it can be argued that 'nationality is a state of mind corresponding to a political fact' (Kohn, 1994: 162) and not only a legal status conferred by an accident of birth in terms of where and to whom one is born. The political facts and the legal facts are not always congruent. As Lyle Lovett reminds us 'I'm a long tall Texan' and not a long tall national of the United States of America. The political and legal fact is that the EU exists, but there are also other overlapping legal and political facts. The existence of the member states is also a political and legal fact, and within some of the member states there exists an 'ethno-regionalism'. All of this makes the link between the state of mind and nationality more problematic as it introduces concepts of identity and ethnicity.

I would argue that not only could there not be an 'ethno-Europeanism' but that we should not strive to create one. Instead citizenship of the EU should be seen as just another facet of our multiple identities. However it must become an important facet, because without the link between our state of mind and the political fact we are in danger of creating and maintaining institutions that are anti-democratic and 'alegitimate'. Failing to engage as Europeans — complex, fluid and flexible as that process is — creates a democratic black hole over policy areas that have a direct bearing on the welfare and human rights of ourselves and those who wish to be in contact with us.

To take the argument first that an ethno-Europeanism cannot be created. In this I would reverse the argument put forward by Hechter and Levi (1994: 188) on how a sense of ethno-regionalism is created. Taking Scottish ethnicity as an example, they argue that the basis of this sense of ethnicity and its protection results from anchoring institutional autonomy in the Acts of Union. In doing so important occupational niches were created for the middle classes which then had a material incentive in upholding a distinct and different Scottish culture (see Paterson, 1994). As the mass of the population comes into contact with these institutions they become 'likely to identify' with the culture. The Acts of Union therefore did not assimilate Scottishness into Englishness but preserved it.

In the same way the Treaty on European Union, most recently amended by the Treaty of Amsterdam in 1999, does not assimilate the member states but specifically preserves key institutions. It does not touch on religious issues, and leaves intact constitutional structures of member states. Its policy on culture is largely to support national and regional variety. It creates the principles of subsidiarity and flexibility that allow considerable scope for member states to call into question each and every policy development, and even allows for some to opt out — the most recent example being the UK opt-out on several aspects of justice and home affairs policies. The EU gives a material incentive to a limited section of the professional classes across Europe to develop a European sense of themselves — Professors of European Law for example. But the majority of the population, who do not come (except indirectly) into contact with the EU, do not identify with it — the state of mind and the political fact do not coincide. It is therefore not surprising that the most recent elections for the European Parliament produced such a tidal wave of apathy.

Arguably, it is impossible to create a sense of ethnicity at the European level based on any tie of kinship, since kinship is dependent on the existence of a framework to enforce the rules of the community mediated by an elite class. This simply does not accord with the operation of the EU. In that sense we will never consider ourselves either as a community or as individuals to be first European, then something else. The fact of being European, in the sense of being connected in some way with the EU, does not lead to a sense of kinship at the level of the region or of some of the member states. A transcendent European ethnicity is an impossibility; it is a contradiction in terms.

It is also undesirable to try to create such an ethno-Europeanism. Flexibility (in the general rather, than the legal sense of the word) and fluidity are useful attributes of a system of government that is multi-textured, multi-layered and multi-ethnic. The problems of ethno-regionalism as manifested in Scotland, mediated over the years by institutions controlled by the professional classes, have led to a certain dominance of culture in terms of language(s), religion, conservative social values (for example on the place of women in society) and the lack of a sense of diversity. An ethno-Europeanism would equally tend to entrench a dominant view within Europe. Countless writers have identified Europe with, for example Christianity, thereby defining Europe in terms of a dominant religious form and one that begins to exclude a re-definition of what it is to be European (Davies, 1997). In this respect is Russia European or Asian? Is Turkey European?

However, there are dangers in not developing any sense of European identity as compared to ethnicity. Citizens of the EU who by definition are nationals of the member states and not nationals of the Union need to identify with the political fact of the existence of the EU, as part of their potential multiple identities, for very sound reasons. If the EU is seen to be too far removed from the 'peoples of Europe' that it is intended to serve then it becomes 'alegitimate', meaning it cannot acquire such support and therefore cannot acquire legitimacy. It would not be a form of unelected or unaccountable dictatorship in any traditional sense of the word but, it would become a system of government incapable of being legitimated. If there is such a word, the new Union of Europe would not be legitimatisable, it would be alegitimate. At the same time the Union would become anti-democratic. Its demos, we the peoples of Europe, would be too far removed from the Union.

The Europeanisation of Scottish Policies

What are the implications of these debates and issues for the new Scotland? In particular, is it possible to set out an agenda for Scottish European policy based on ideas of flexible and fluid identities?

The first and most obvious point is the need for the Scottish Parliament and Executive to set their own European agendas and priorities. This agenda and these priorities need not reflect those adopted for other parts of the UK. Flexibility might mean Scotland moving in some areas at its own pace, which makes sense since some European policies have a far greater impact in Scotland than others. This is because of the structure of the Scottish economy and society but also because of the devolution settlement. Given the reservation of international affairs and defence to the UK, the Scottish Parliament (perhaps more explicitly the European Committee of the Scottish Parliament) might only want to keep a watching brief on developments within the Common Foreign and Security Policy.

There are however, key policy areas where a pro-active approach to European policy might enable Scotland to follow its distinct European line. The devolved institutions are obliged to implement European obligations. These obligations exist in many of the areas devolved to Scotland. One obvious example is environmental policy. Here, Scotland has the opportunity to forge a distinct approach to the implementation of environmental regulations to suit the needs of both urban and rural communities within the context of a wider environmental strategy. As long as Scottish institutions respect European obligations, nothing would preclude Scotland from developing this Scottish dimension. The Scottish Executive and Parliament would need to develop a pro-active approach to Europe and an inter-active relationship with officials within the European Commission and Members of the European Parliament. This is a question of targeting the relevant networks through such organisations as Scotland Europa and Scotland House. The effect of the Europeanisation of Scottish policies in key areas would bring Europe to the regional level, thereby engaging Scotland in a political dialogue with Europe directly rather than through the mediation of London. Scotland in Europe then begins to have a real meaning, and enables citizens to identify with both levels of governance as part of their multiple identities.

The Scottish Executive and Parliament must determine priorities for its broader European agenda. However, European matters are genuinely cross-cutting. This means that there is substantial cross-cutting across the work of certain of the subject committees of the Scottish Parliament. The Justice and Home Affairs Committee, the Committee on Enterprise and Life-long Learning, the Committee on Transport and Environment and the Committee on Rural Affairs all deal with issues where there is a substantial European component. It would seem sensible for close collaboration to develop between members of these committees and members of the European Committee. It would also seem sensible to encourage individual members or sub-committees of the European Committee to develop expertise in the European dimension of one or more of the subject committees. This would allow subject committees to become pro-active in determining how to react to proposed or existing European legislation and policies.

Full use should also be made of the opportunities that devolution brings to engage in meaningful discussions at the level of the UK. One key set of relationships are those between the European Committee and the European scrutiny committees of the Westminster Parliament. Apart from the fact that these committees will cover much of the same ground, albeit with different priorities, the Westminster scrutiny committees benefit from the so-called 'scrutiny reserve' that commits the UK government not to agree to any course of action within the Council of Ministers until parliamentary scrutiny has been completed. The European Committee of the Scottish Parliament does not benefit from such a reserve but close co-operation between the Scottish and Westminster committees will allow parliamentarians in Scotland to raise fears and worries. Inter-parliamentary European Committee consultations, or at least an exchange of agendas and minutes, would strengthen parliamentary control on European matters. This aspect has received less consideration than other more obvious but equally useful levels of co-operation at inter-ministerial meetings and at the level of government departments by way of concordats.

The European Committee of the Scottish Parliament is pivotal in creating the necessary link between levels of governance (the political and legal facts) and the state of mind that can be summed up in the phrase Scotland in Europe. However the Committee must act within the parameters of a clearly defined set of European priorities. These priorities have not been articulated by the Scottish Executive or by the Parliament as a whole. The European Committee could take the lead and set out its view of Scottish European priorities to form the basis of a wider debate. In a sense these priorities are determined by the nature of the devolution settlement. Rural affairs and agriculture, the environment, enterprise and aid to the Scottish economy by way of structural funds or other supports, and aspects of justice and home affairs, are some of the obvious areas where there is overlap between devolution and Europe. By definition these must be priorities. Macro-economic policies, defence issues and so on undoubtedly impact on Scotland, but a distinct Scottish voice cannot be forged in these areas given the limitations of the Scotland Act. Concentrating on the achievable in terms of Scottish European policy may forge a true sense of a Scottish European identity.

CHAPTER 30

THE WORK AND PLAY ETHIC IN THE NEW SCOTLAND

PAT KANE

We all think we know what the work ethic is, the 'play ethic', however, might require some explanation. When Max Weber (1930) first defined the work ethic at the end of the nineteenth century, the full title of his book was *The Protestant Work Ethic and the Spirit of Capitalism*. Weber described how the unruly pleasures of the European labouring classes — their Happy Mondays and seasonal festivals, their public carousing and regular celebrations — were clamped down from the late eighteenth century onwards by a powerful alliance of evangelicalism and capitalism.

Whether with a Methodist, Presbyterian or Calvinist accent, the cry went out to the new, shiftless proletariat of the factories and enclosures, hammering home the new ethic: work is good, play is bad. In Weber's words, the moral climate 'turned with all its force against one thing: the spontaneous enjoyment of life and all it had to offer' (quoted in Abrams, 1997: 65). As an eighteenth century sermoniser put it: 'the soul's play-day is always the devil's working-day'. Or, as another more famously put it: 'the devil makes work for idle hands'. By such a combination of cultural propaganda and economic coercion, the rich textures of pre-industrial society were neatly, some would say brutally, divided into two realms: work and non-work. And particularly in the Victorian era, by which time the regime of industrial capitalism ruled supreme over the world of work, political attention turned to the realm of non-work.

How might society deprive the devil of his labour? By the great nineteenth century the answer lay in the programmes of municipal creation; swimming baths, sports grounds, concert halls, and public parks, libraries, museums and galleries. In fact, the whole infrastructure of modern 'leisure services' is unchanged, in its outline and essence, from the great Victorian projects of public amenity.

The Leisure Society and the Age of Informationalism

There is a pertinent (or impertinent) question to ask here. In thinking about leisure policy — leisure still defined as the realm of non-work — how much do contemporary politicians and administrators still fear that 'the soul's play-day is always the devil's working day' and that 'the devil makes work for idle hands'? In my opinion, the fear is still very much there. But, one might concede, the stakes today are very much higher. If Weber wanted to revisit his thesis at the cusp of the twenty first century, he might call his book *The Protestant Work Ethic and the Spirit of Informationalism*. I think, however, he would find that a very difficult book to write indeed.

For the difference between 'capitalism' and 'informationalism' (coined by the great Catalan sociologist Manuel Castells) is the difference between one modern revolution and another (Castells, 1996: 195-200). I would argue that an information age requires an entirely new 'ethic' of human activity than its predecessor - an ethic that can enlist us to its demands and challenges, just as effectively as evangelical self-discipline did for the Age of Industry. If the work ethic was the very spirit of capitalism, what kind of ethic will embody the spirit of informationalism?

I would argue that we need a play ethic to help legitimate the new economies and societies of the West in the coming century. I would be as militant, indeed as evangelistic, about its virtues as the Presbyterians and Methodists of the eighteenth and nineteenth centuries were about the work ethic. For we only need to look around us, open our eyes and ears to the tumult of the moment, to see how redundant, indeed how destructive, the Protestant work ethic is in the age of information.

Contrary to earlier presumptions in this century about the inevitability of technological progress creating a 'leisure society', the information age (if it maintains its present course) will actually intensify and increase the pervasiveness of the work ethic, enabling it to penetrate every area of our lives. At a basic level, a knowledge economy is simply more competitive. Businesses use IT to streamline their practices and increase efficiency; digital networks of money and ideas subject companies to the rigours of the global marketplace. And workers within all industries feel the demands of this increased competition.

The New Evangelism of the New Economy

These demands are many and proliferating. 'Getting up to speed with the new economy' means accepting that its pace is irremediable, not to be checked in any way. In this climate, the work ethic mutates and bloats into a life ethic. Everything that one does — including those activities we do in what we call our leisure time — exists under an increasingly stern injunction: make it useful to the new knowledge economy.

Sometimes I suspect that when this government (and other modernising regimes in Europe and beyond) repeats its mantra 'education, education, education', what it actually means is 'no leisure, no leisure, no leisure'. Certainly in the UK, a massive new social infrastructure is being constructed, whose aim is to colonise our non-work time with 'useful toils and labours'. Whether it is homework compulsions, shorter school holidays and longer school days, or nightly curfews on children, the University of Industry, the panoply of life-long learning schemes, the BBC's new Knowledge channel, the New Deal — applying its take-it-or-leave-it menu of workfare options to the unemployed — Blairism seems to be on a relentless search to identify 'idle hands', and rescue them from the devils of inefficiency, non-improvement, and lack of commitment to the maximisation of national prosperity.

The only difference between this evangelism, and that of the industrial heyday, is that it has much better means of transmitting its values — an informational network of computers, phones and microwaves that increasingly weaves together home and work, public and private realms. When digital culture becomes a majority reality, in about five years time, then there will be no excuse for children and adults not to take their knowledge-work back to the hearth; not to programme their evenings, and their weekends, as periods of educational self-improvement to the greater social and economic good.

They could, of course, use the same digital technology to watch the next Old Firm game from about seven different possible camera angles, or surf the net for sites about Buffy the Vampire Slayer, or e-shop for cargo pants in a Seattle on-line store. If the attempt to create a new work ethic faces any obvious challenge in the information age, it is from the thrills and spills, the hedonistic pleasures of consumer culture. If you are in the affluent majority, and fully geared up, you are only one click away from the pleasure of your choice in the digital universe.

It is obvious that if any value predominates in the mediascape of Ally McBeal, Lara Croft and the Phantom Menace, it is that of play, rather than work. From the perspective of some future government, eager to use its informational infrastructures to maximise the people's efficiency, one can imagine that screen-time spent in front of these diversions — rather than the latest regime of upskilling or course-work — could easily be regarded as play of a thoroughly unethical kind. The devil makes work for idle keyboards, perhaps.

Redefining the Play Ethic

The classic definitions of play do not really clarify the central issue: whether the very idea of a play ethic — a vision of the good and just life centred on innovation, creativity and self-satisfaction — is workable. The best definition of play in the twentieth century comes from the Dutch historian Johan Huizinga, in his book *Homo Ludens* (Man the Player). Huizinga defines play as 'a voluntary activity or occupation executed within certain fixed limits of time and place, according to rules freely accepted but absolutely binding, having its aim in itself, and accompanied by a feeling of tension, joy and the consciousness that it is 'different' from 'ordinary life" (Huizinga, 1949: 146). As a description of what we're doing when we're watching The Sopranos, building Sim City 3000 or dodging paintballs, it is not bad at all.

In fact, one could quite easily imagine a cynical play ethic in an information age. Michael Wolf's new book *The Entertainment Economy* tells how most large companies, whether they like it or not, are in show-business - or at least, in the business of show (Wolf, 1999). Even if they are selling widgets and grommets, they have to sell them with much better service and marketing, with much more concern taken about branding and design, in order to compete in markets that mature with incredible speed. But most of contemporary economic life centres on service and communication anyway — the searching out of ever-more particular tastes and niche products.

In order to keep the whole shebang of late capitalism going, we may need at least a hedonist's ethic — forever dissatisfied with what we are offered, forever willing to try something new: eager both to work in ways that exploit our creative and emotional resources, and to consume services from people who work that way too. A play ethic accepts that the endless cultural variations generated by the interplay of human desire, and the human imagination, is a positive and dynamic element in our lives. It seems impossible to imagine this without the marketplace as one crucial way of registering the necessary creative chaos of being human in the twenty first century.

Yet all marketplaces have to have their limits — even one as powerful as the marketplace of contemporary capitalism, with its seemingly unstoppable complex of innovative technology, consumer desire and global reach. Sociologists such as Daniel Bell saw this as capitalism's inescapable cultural contradiction — to function properly, it needs both docile producers and avid consumers, and the second identity tends to subvert the values of the first (Bell, 1979).

But the hope that the play ethic expresses is that informationalism, capitalism's latest turn, can allow us to be both active producers and avid consumers. Because what makes informationalism work is knowledge — and knowledge only comes alive in the heads and hearts of the people who both originate it, and put it into practice. And the more valuable their sensibilities become to their organisations, the more they will realise their own value as human beings.

Holding to a play ethic — whose prime value is that one's own creativity and sense of purpose has to be given full respect — will make informational workers place new demands on their businesses and organisations. It is a work ethic which encourages people to subject themselves to workplace presenteeism. It is a play ethic which gives people the strength to demand that networked technologies enhance the quality of life, by allowing work to be done outwith the surveillance of managers and overseers, closer to home, family, and community.

And one should always be clear about the gendered nature of the play ethic (Abrams, 1997). There could almost be no more radical info-worker's demand at the moment than the father who opposes a culture of over-work because he wants to spend more time with his children; this is, almost literally, an ethic of play as valuable and life-enhancing, rather than as distraction from utilitarianism and productivism. The play ethic means challenging and reconceptualising the gendered division of time which results in the most over-worked and over-stressed male workers enjoying more free time than most women who are subjected to the triple burden of childcare, housework and paid work.

Whether through a heightened appreciation of the environment, an intensification of one's relations with kin and friends, a greater sense of cultivating the self and the interior world, a philosophical and spiritual stance towards worldly activities: the new reformist politics of an informational world must be anchored in what I call 'lifestyle militancy'. The educated, potentialised info-worker should be in the vanguard of that growing movement towards popular autonomy — deciding their life-priorities as strong, self-determined characters, and fitting their working and organisational duties around that self-determination.

There is a popular and democratic struggle to deploy the productivity and efficiency gains of the second industrial revolution to better, more humane ends - in fact, as the original (and much misunderstood) Luddites had, in order that it may 'benefit the commonality'. But where we get the resources for that struggle should be an open question. Evolving a play ethic addresses the essential question of meaningful human activity in an informational age - that is, the question of poiesis, to use the Greek word. How might I make a mark on my world - a mark that might add value to that world?

The expressive nature of information technologies - the way the same digital systems can be used to administer and control large groups of people or to liberate those individuals into new worlds of creativity and collaboration — is the radical moment of this new age. We must look amongst the writers, artists, film-makers, musicians, loving parents, civic entrepreneurs who are trying to realise this radical potential: we must recognise their unalienated pleasure in their activities and use that as the measure against which we find our workplaces and organisations wanting.

In so far as Scotland exists under the conditions of informationalism, Scots will strive to forge their own play ethic. The question of how much our cultural specificity feeds into that struggle is for another occasion.

NOTES ON THE
CONTRIBUTORS

Wendy Alexander is MSP for Paisley North and Minister for Communities in the Scottish Executive. Before being elected to the Scottish Parliament, she was special adviser at the Scottish Office. Prior to that appointment, she was a management consultant and a researcher for the Labour Party. She is a graduate of INSEAD, Warwick and Glasgow Universities. In the past she has made contributions to a number of edited collections, including *The World is Ill-Divided* (Edinburgh University Press, 1990) and *The State and the Nations* (IPPR, 1996).

Rowena Arshad is the Director of the Centre for Education for Racial Equality in Scotland. She is also an active trade unionist, convenor of the EIS Anti-Racist Committee and STUC General Council member representing the Black Workers Committee. She has worked in race equality in the UK for almost 15 years as an educator and community worker.

Esther Breitenbach has been active in the women's movement since the early 1970s, and has written numerous articles on women in Scotland. She has worked in adult and community education, in the voluntary sector, and in academic research and teaching. She is currently on secondment to the Scottish Executive, from the Department of Social Policy, University of Edinburgh.

Noreen Burrows is Jean Monnet Professor of European Law at the University of Glasgow. Her research interests include European

Social Law, particularly sex discrimination, and she has many publications in this field. She is currently researching devolution in Scotland, Wales and Northern Ireland in the context of membership of the EU, and a book on this subject is to be published in 2000 by Sweet and Maxwell.

Sara Carter is Senior Research Fellow in the Department of Marketing at the University of Strathclyde, Glasgow. She has undertaken a number of research studies on the issue of women in business, including projects financed by the Department of Employment and Shell (UK) Ltd, the Economic and Social Research Council, the European Union, Scottish Enterprise and Glasgow Development Agency. Her publications on this topic include a book *Women as Entrepreneurs* (Academic Press, 1992) and several articles in academic and practitioner journals.

Patricia Findlay is Senior Lecturer in Organisation Studies at the Department of Business Studies and Management School at the University of Edinburgh. Her wide range of publications focus on industrial relations. She is currently involved in researching union recruitment campaigns prior to the implementation of the Employment Relations Act 1999. She is also a panel member of Employment Tribunals (Scotland). She has previously researched in the areas of organisational change and innovation, performance appraisal, responses to plant closure, and labour utilisation strategy in the electronics industry.

Robina Goodlad is Professor of Housing and Urban Studies in the Department of Urban Studies at the University of Glasgow. Previously she established the Tenant Participation Advisory Service. She has carried out research into a range of housing and urban issues and has published numerous articles, reports and books.

Russel Griggs is Executive Director of Scotland the Brand. Over the years, he has held a number of senior posts in the private sector throughout the UK. He first joined the Scottish Development Agency in the early 1980s. In 1990 be became Head of Company Development in Scottish Enterprise. In 1993 he was appointed Director of Business Development at Scottish Enterprise and was responsible for The

Business BirthRate Program. He was also responsible for Scottish Enterprise's venture capital arm Scottish Development Finance. In 1996 he became responsible for Overseas Business Development in the USA for Scottish Enterprise. Since returning, he has been appointed Director of the Scottish Science Trust and is a Non Executive Director of a number of companies and organisations. He is a Visiting Professor at the University of Glasgow and Glasgow Caledonian University as well as a Fellow of the Royal Society of Arts.

Gerry Hassan is a political consultant and former Director of the Centre for Scottish Public Policy. He is author of *The New Scotland* and *Scotland's Parliament: Lessons for Northern Ireland*, and has contributed to *The Blair Agenda*, *The Moderniser's Dilemma: Radical Politics in the Age of Blair* and *Now's the Hour: New Thinking for Holyrood*. He edited the recent *A Guide to the Scottish Parliament: The Shape of Things to Come* and is co-author of the forthcoming *Post-Nationalist Scotland* and co-editor of *The Scottish Labour Party: Histories, Ideas and Institutions*.

Rosie Ilett works in public health, promoting accessible and equitable models for women. Bringing this work together with an earlier career in librarianship, she has written widely on gender, health information and medical librarianship in a range of academic and popular journals in the UK and Australia. She is currently researching the impact of feminism on British librarianship.

Sue Innes is a writer and researcher, and an Honorary Research Fellow at the University of Edinburgh. She edited *Children, Families and Learning: A new agenda for education* (Scottish Council Foundation, 1999) and is author of *Putting Gender on the Agenda: Opportunities for participative democracy and gender equality in the Scottish Parliament* (Engender, 1999) and *Making it Work: Women, Change and Challenge in the 1990s* (Chatto and Windus, 1995). As a journalist she wrote extensively on social policy, education and gender. She is currently working on a book on the history of social feminism in Britain 1900-1939, and works part-time for the Official Report of the Scottish Parliament. She has children at school and university.

Pat Kane is Associate Editor of the *Sunday Herald* and lead singer of the neo-jazzers Hue and Cry. He is a widely respected broadcaster working across a range of media: TV, radio, print and internet. He is author of *Tinsel Show: Pop, Politics, Scotland* (Polygon, 1992) and has contributed to the collections *Fatherhood* (Victor Gollancz, 1997) and *The Politics of Risk Society* (Polity, 1998).

George Kerevan teaches economics at Napier University, Edinburgh. He has been convenor of Edinburgh District Council's economic development committee, chair of the Edinburgh Tourist Board and a member of Lothian and Edinburgh Enterprise. He has served on the boards of the Traverse, 7:84, and the Edinburgh Festival and Film Festival. During 1997-98 he was SNP environment spokesperson.

Sue Laughlin has worked in public health for a number of years focusing on poverty, unemployment and health and developing a social model of women's health. As a founder member of the Scottish Politics of Health Group, she co-authored *Glasgow: Health of a City*. Recently she co-wrote *Poverty and Health: Tools for Change* (Public Health Alliance) and chairs the Health and Low Income project of the UK Public Health Association.

Janet Lowe is Principal of Lauder College in Dunfermline. She was a member of the Garrick Committee and is currently a member of the Board of Scottish Enterprise, the Board of the Scottish Further Education Unit and the Scottish Consultative Council on the Curriculum. She chairs the Scottish Wider Access Programme (East) Consortium and Fair Play. Her personal commitment to lifelong learning includes part-time research for a doctorate in education at Stirling University.

Peter Mackay spent more than 30 years in the Scottish Office and was seconded for three years to the Department of Employment group in Scotland and then Whitehall. He finished his career with five years as head of the then Scottish Office Industry Department. He is now a visiting professor at Strathclyde Graduate Business School. He is also a member of the Competition Commission, on the board of a Scottish quango, and a director of the Business Banking Division of the Bank of Scotland.

Jack McConnell is MSP for Motherwell and Wishaw, and Minister for Finance in the Scottish Executive. He is 39, originally from the Isle of Arran and was a mathematics teacher in Alloa before becoming General Secretary of the Scottish Labour Party from 1992 to 1998. Between 1984 and 1993 he was a councillor in Stirling, serving as Council leader from 1990 to 1992.

Gavin McCrone is now Visiting Professor at the University of Edinburgh. Before this appointment he was Professor at the University of Glasgow. From 1970-1992, he was Chief Economic Adviser to successive Secretaries of State for Scotland and, additionally, was head of the Industry and Environments Departments. He has made a number of contributions to publications examining Scotland's finances, most recently *An Illustrated Guide to the Scottish Economy* (Duckworth, 1999).

Joyce McMillan is chief theatre critic of *The Scotsman*, and writes a political/social column for the paper. She is involved in Scottish and European campaigns for democracy and human rights, and was a member of the government's 1998 Consultative Steering Group on the procedures of the Scottish Parliament.

James Mitchell is Professor of Politics at the University of Sheffield. He is author of *Conservatives and the Union* (Edinburgh University Press, 1990) and *Strategies for Self-Government* (Polygon, 1996). He is co-author of *Politics and Public Policy in Scotland* (Macmillan, 1991) and *How Scotland Votes: Scottish Parties and Elections* (Manchester University Press, 1997). He is author of the forthcoming *Devolution in the United Kingdom* (Manchester University Press) and co-author of *Scotland Decides: The Devolution Issue and the 1997 Referendum* (Frank Cass).

Tom Nairn is a journalist, author and teacher. He is based at Edinburgh University Graduate School and his home is the Republic of Ireland. He is author of *The Left Against Europe* (Penguin, 1973), *The Break-Up of Britain* (New Left Books, 1977; Verso 2nd edition, 1981), *The Enchanted Glass* (Radius, 1988) and *Faces of Nationalism* (Verso, 1997). His forthcoming book *After Britain* will be published by Granta Books in January 2000.

Lindsay Paterson is Professor of Educational Policy in the Faculty of Education, University of Edinburgh. He has written on many aspects of the sociology of education — in particular on the effects of social disadvantage and on the expansion of higher education and he has written widely on Scottish politics and culture. His publications include *Education, Democracy and the Scottish Parliament* (Scottish Local Government Information Unit, 1997), *The Autonomy of Modern Scotland* (Edinburgh University Press, 1994) and *A Diverse Assembly: The Debate on a Scottish Parliament* (Edinburgh University Press, 1998).

John Pearce has worked with the community business sector since 1992. He is currently Company Secretary and a Director of Community Business Solutions Network. He is a leading practitioner in the field of social accounting and audit, and an associate member of the Institute of Social and Ethical Accounting. He manages CBS Network's support for community enterprise and a micro-credit initiative in South India. His research has focused on children's museums and their relevance to the UK, LETS and home maintenance for low-income owner-occupiers, and the nature and extent of the social economy in the UK. His publications include *The Social Audit Workbook* and *Measuring Social Wealth* (both New Economics Foundation, 1996), *At the Heart of the Community* and *Centres of Curiosity and Imagination* (both Calouste Gulbenkian Foundation 1993 and 1998).

Courtney Peyton is Business Director of the sustainability consultancy thirdwave Scotland Ltd., which provides advice and practical, commercially-sound solutions to both the public and private sectors at the strategic level. She is a Principal of the Edinburgh Sustainable Architecture Unit, University of Edinburgh, where she has taught part-time. Prior to founding thirdwave, she was an architectural conservation consultant to UK architects and developers domestically and abroad for many years. She is the Sustainability Advisor to the National Technical Committee for the Architectural Heritage Society of Scotland.

Eleanor Shaw is a Lecturer in Marketing at the University of Strathclyde. Eleanor's doctoral research explored the impact which social networks have on the development of small, professional service firms. Her research and teaching interests are in the areas of: small firms, entrepreneurship, industrial networks and relationships. She has published in the area of small firm networks and presented at both European and American marketing and small firm conferences. She is a founder member of the Academy of Marketing's Special Interest Group in the Marketing/Entrepreneurship Interface of which she is presently Academic Co-ordinator.

Matt Smith is the Scottish Secretary of UNISON and President of the STUC. He serves on the Scottish Council Development and Industry, the Church of Scotland Church and Nation Committee, the Scottish Local Government Information Unit, the Centre for Scottish Public Policy Board of Directors and the Broadcasting Council for Scotland. He was a member of the recent McIntosh Commission on Local Government and the Scottish Parliament.

Gerry Stoker is Professor of Political Science in the Department of Government, University of Strathclyde in Glasgow. His main research interests are in local government, urban politics, and cross-national policy transfer. Between 1992 and 1997 he was Director of the ESRC Local Governance Research Programme. He has authored or edited over a dozen books. He is also a member of the Academic Panel of Advisers to the Department of the Environment, Transport and the Regions and Chair of the Local Government Network.

Paul Thompson is Professor of Organisational Analysis at the University of Strathclyde, Glasgow. He is currently editor of a number of academic series as well as of *Renewal: A Journal of New Labour Politics*. He is the author of *The Nature of Work*, and, with others, *Working the System, Work Organisations, Workplaces of the Future* and the recently published *Organisational Misbehaviour*. Current research focuses on workplace innovation in the Scottish spirits industry and employment practices in call centres.

Ian Thomson, an Associate of thirdwave (Scotland) Ltd., is a lecturer in the Department of Accounting and Finance, University of Strathclyde, where he specialises in social and environmental accounting and management courses. Research conducted since 1990 includes examining the role of environmental accounting in organisational change, business concepts of sustainability, cleaner technology implementation, waste minimisation, industrial ecology, sustainability and the financial sector, sustainable tourism. He has also taught at the Universities of Aberdeen, Brunel and Heriot-Watt. He has served as a director of Friends of the Earth Scotland and International Research Associate at the Centre for Social and Environmental Accounting Research.

Jim Wallace QC is Deputy First Minister and Minister for Justice in the Scottish Parliament. He has been leader of the Scottish Liberal Democrats since 1992. He was elected as MP for Orkney and Shetland in 1983. When Orkney and Shetland were separated into two constituencies for the Scottish parliamentary elections, he was elected as the MSP for Orkney. Prior to 1983 he practised as an advocate at the Scottish Bar. He was appointed in Queens Council in 1997. He lives on Orkney, and is married with two daughters.

Chris Warhurst lectures at the University of Strathclyde, Glasgow. His teaching, research and publications focus on work, management and labour issues. Publications have appeared in various languages in the US, the Middle East, and West and East Europe. Current research analyses employment in the 'New' Glasgow, and new forms of organisation - especially those associated with knowledge work. A comparative project researching the transfer of soft technologies to Scotland through MNC foreign direct investment is in development. He is author of *Between Market, State and Kibbutz* (Mansell, 1999) and co-edited *Workplaces of the Future* (Macmillan, 1998) and *The Management and Organisation of Firms in the Global Context* (Hungarian Academy of Sciences, 1999).

Andy Wightman is a writer specialising in land reform and the author of *Who Owns Scotland?* (Canongate, 1996) and *Scotland: Land and Power. The Agenda for Land Reform* (Luath, 1999). He is an Honorary Research Fellow at Aberdeen University, a member of the Scottish Executive Consultative Panel on Land Reform and Programme Director of the Caledonia Centre for Social Development's Land Programme.

Andrew Wilson MSP is the Shadow Finance Minister for the SNP in the Scottish Parliament. He studied at the Universities of St Andrews and Strathclyde in Glasgow. He then entered the Government Economic Service as an Economist and worked in the UK Forestry Commission. He then joined the Scottish Office as an economist in the Education and Industry Department. In 1996 he joined the headquarters staff of the SNP, working as party economist. In 1997 he joined the Economics Office of the Royal Bank of Scotland as a business economist. His political interests are public finance, the economy, housing and freedom of information.

Alf Young is an award-winning journalist and has been the Deputy Editor of *The Herald* since 1997. Before this time he was economics editor for the same newspaper. He has also worked for *The Scotsman*, *The Sunday Standard* and Radio Clyde. His other appointments include being a member of the Scottish Office group advising the Conservative Steering Group on financial aspects of Home Rule and Special Adviser to the Scottish Affairs Committee Inquiry into inward and outward investment. When not working, he enjoys gardening, the arts, walking and cooking. He lives in Strathblane with his partner and their two sons.

REFERENCES

Abrams, R. (1997) The Playful Self: Why Women Need Play in their Lives, London: Fourth Estate.

Aldrich, H. (1989) 'Networking among women entrepreneurs' in O. Hagen, C. Rivchum and D. Sexton (eds.) Women owned businesses, New York: Praeger.

Alexander, M. (1998) Finding Home, Edinburgh: Ecological Planning and Design Services.

Andersen Consulting (1999) Reinventing the Wheel, London: Andersen Consulting.

Applebaum, E. and Batt, R. (1994) The New American Workplace, Ithaca, NY: ILP Press.

Archibugi, D., Held, D. and Kohler, M. (eds.) (1998) Re-Imagining Political Community, Cambridge: Polity Press.

Ashworth, J. (1999) 'Time is running out for the clocking-in mentality', The Times, 18 September.

Bacchi, C. (1996) The Politics of Affirmative Action: Women, Equality and Category Politics, London: Sage.

Ball, M. (1998) School Inclusion: The school, the family and the community, York: Joseph Rowntree Foundation.

Barley, S. (1996) The New World of Work, London: British-North American Committee.

Barnett, A. (1997) This Time: Our Constitutional Revolution, London: Vintage.

Bauman, Z. (1999) In Search of Politics, Cambridge: Polity Press.

Beck, U. (1992) Risk Society: Towards a New Modernity, London: Sage.

Beck, U. (1994) 'The Reinvention of Politics' in U. Beck, A. Giddens and S. Lash (eds.) Reflexive Modernisation, Cambridge: Polity Press.

Bell, D. (1979) The Cultural Contradictions of Capitalism, London: Heinemann, 2nd edition.

Bentley, T. (1998) Learning Beyond the Classroom: Education for a changing world, London: Routledge.

Beveridge, C. and Turnbull, R. (1989) The Eclipse of Scottish Culture, Edinburgh: Polygon.

Beveridge, C. and Turnbull, R. (1997) Scotland After Enlightenment, Edinburgh: Polygon.

Blair, T. (1996) New Britain: My Vision of a Young Country, London: Fourth Estate.

Blair, T. (1998) The Third Way, London: Fabian Society.

Blair, T. (1999) Speech to Charter Mark Awards on Modernising Public Services, 26 January.

Bonnett, A. (1999) 'Constructions of Whiteness in European and American Anti-Racism' in R. Torress and L. Mirdon (eds.) Race, Identity and Citizenship: A Reader, Oxford: Blackwell.

Booth, J. (1999) 'Scotland has highest racism rates in the UK', Scotsman, 10 May.

Bradley, A.W. and Ewing, K.D. (1997) Constitutional and Administrative Law, London: Longman, 12th edition.

Brand, J. (1978) The National Movement in Scotland, London: Routledge & Kegan Paul.

Breitenbach, E. (1996) 'The Women's Movement in Scotland in the 1990s', Waverley Papers, Department of Politics, University of Edinburgh.

Breitenbach, E., Brown, A. and Myers, F. (1998) 'Understanding Women in Scotland', Feminist Review, 58.

Brewer, J.D. (1989) 'Conjectural History, Sociology and Social Change in Eighteenth Century Scotland: Adam Ferguson and the Division of Labour' in D. McCrone, S. Kendrick and P. Straw (eds.) The Making of Scotland: Nation, Culture and Social Change, Edinburgh: Edinburgh University Press.

Brown, A. (1996) 'Plans for a Scottish Parliament: Did Women Make a Difference?' Waverley Papers, Department of Politics, University of Edinburgh.

Brown, A. (1998) 'Women and Political Culture in Scotland II', Gender and Scottish Society, Unit For The Study Of Government In Scotland, University of Edinburgh.

Brown, A, Breitenbach, E , Myers, F (1995) Equality Issues in Scotland: A Research Review. Manchester: Equal Opportunities Commission.

Brown, A. and Galligan, Y. (1993) 'Changing the Political Agenda for Women in the Republic of Ireland and in Scotland', West European Politics, 2.

Brown, A., McCrone, D. and Paterson, L. (1998) Politics and Society in Scotland, London: Macmillan, 2nd edition.

Brown, A., Myers, F., Breitenbach, E. (1994) 'Researching Women in Scotland: Problems and Opportunities', Scottish Affairs, 8.

Brown, G. (1975a) 'Introduction: The Socialist Challenge' in G. Brown (ed.) The Red Paper on Scotland, Edinburgh: Edinburgh University Student Publications Board.

Brown, G. (ed.) (1975b) The Red Paper on Scotland, Edinburgh: Edinburgh University Student Publications Board.

Brown, G. and Alexander, D. (1999a) New Scotland, New Britain, London: Smith Institute.

Brown, G. and Alexander, D. (1999b) 'Overwhelming rejection of nationalist vision', The Scotsman, 8 May.

Brush, C. G. (1997) Proceedings of the Conference on Women Entrepreneurs in Small and Medium Enterprises, Paris: OECD.

Bryce, T.G.K. and Humes, W. (1999) Policy Development in Scottish Education, Glasgow: Universities of Glasgow and Strathclyde.

Burness, C. (1998) 'Women and Political Culture in Scotland I', Gender and Scottish Society, Unit For The Study Of Government In Scotland, University of Edinburgh.

Burrows, N. (1999) 'Relations with the European Union' in G. Hassan (ed.) A Guide to the Scottish Parliament, Edinburgh: Centre for Scottish Public Policy/The Stationery Office.

Buttner, E.H. and Rosen, B. (1989) 'Funding new business ventures: are decision makers biased against women entrepreneurs?', Journal of Business Venturing, 4:4.

Byers, S. (1999) 'People and knowledge: towards an industrial policy for the 21st century' in G. Kelly (ed.) Is new Labour working?, London: Fabian Society.

Byrne, L. (1997) Information Age Government: Delivering the Blair Revolution, London: Fabian Society.

Cabinet Office (1999) Modernising Government, London: The Stationery Office.

Callander, R.F. (1986) 'The Law of the Land' in J. Hulbert (ed.) Land: Ownership and Use, Dundee: Andrew Fletcher Society.

Callander, R.F. (1998) How Scotland is Owned, Edinburgh: Canongate.

Capra, F. (1996) The Web of Life, London: HarperCollins.

Carter, I. (1975) 'A Socialist Strategy for the Highlands' in G. Brown (ed.) The Red Paper on Scotland, Edinburgh: Edinburgh University Student Publications Board.

Carter, N.M. and Allen, K.R. (1997) 'Size determinants of women-owned businesses: choice or barriers to resources?', Entrepreneurship and Regional Development, 9:3.

Carter, S. and Cannon, T. (1992) Women as Entrepreneurs, London: Academic Press.

Carter, S. and Hamilton, D. (1996) 'Gender as a determinant of small business performance: insights from a British study', Small Business Economics, 8.

Carter, S. and Rosa, P. (1998) 'The financing of male- and female-owned businesses', Entrepreneurship and Regional Development, 10:3.

Castells, M. (1996) The Information Age: Economy, Society and Culture: Volume One: The Rise of the Network Society, Oxford: Blackwell.

Caulkin, S. (1997) 'So, a little knowledge is not quite so dangerous', Observer, Business Supplement, 28 September.

Centre for Education for Racial Equality (CERES) (1999) Bilingualism, Community Languages and Scottish Education: A Challenge for Policy-makers and Practitioners in a Devolved Scotland, Edinburgh: Centre for Education for Racial Equality (CERES), University of Edinburgh.

Children in Scotland (1999) A Manifesto for Scotland's Children, Young People and Families, Edinburgh: Children in Scotland.

Christie, B. (1992) 'Doctors, Medicine and Health' in M. Linklater and R. Denniston (eds.) Anatomy of Scotland: How Scotland Works, Edinburgh: Chambers.

Clark, R. (1999) The Importance of Having a Scottish Identity, Glasgow: Scotland the Brand.

Clark, S. and McGregor, A. (1997) Community Business Works: Community Business and the Intermediate Labour Market - the West of Scotland Experience, University of Glasgow, Training and Employment Research Unit Research Paper.

Clayton, A.C., Williams, R. And Spinardi, G. (eds.) (1999) Policies for Cleaner Production, London: Earthscan.

Coffield, F. (1997) Introduction and Overview: Attempts to Reclaim the Concept of the Learning Society, Journal of Educational Policy, 12:6.

Coleshill, P. N., Gibson, A., Jaconelli, A. and Sheffield, J. (1998) 'The Private Sector Initiative: Private Opportunity at the Public's Cost?', Scottish Affairs, 24.

Colley, L. (1992) Britons: Forging the Nation 1707-1837, Newhaven: Yale University Press.

Commission for Racial Equality Scotland (1999) Racial Equality Matters: An Agenda for the Scottish Parliament, Edinburgh: Commission for Racial Equality Scotland.

Commission on Local Government and The Scottish Parliament (1999) Moving Forward: Local Government and The Scottish Parliament, Edinburgh: The Stationery Office.

Community Business Scotland (1998) unpublished survey, West Calder: Community Business Scotland.

Consultative Steering Group (1999) Shaping Scotland's Parliament: Report of the Consultative Steering Group, Edinburgh: The Stationery Office.

Convention of Scottish Local Authorities (1998) Housing into the Millennium: A New Agenda for Councils, Edinburgh: COSLA.

Crick, B. and Millar, D. (1995) To Make the Parliament of Scotland a Model for Democracy, Edinburgh: John Wheatley Centre.

Crouch, C. (1999) 'The Skills Creation Triangle Out of Balance', Renewal, 7: 4.

Crouch, C., Finegold, D. and Sako, M. (1999) Are Skills the Answer?, Oxford: Oxford University Press.

Cully, M., O'Reilly, A., Millward, N., Forth, J., Woodland, S., Dix, G. and Bryson, A. (1998) Workplace Employee Relations Survey, London: HMSO.

Cunningham, J. (1999) 'Racism is Alive and Kicking in Scotland', The Herald, 21 June.

Curtin, D. and Dekker, I. (1999) 'The EU as a multi-layered international organisation' in P. Craig and G. de Burca (eds.) The Evolution of European Union Law, Oxford: Oxford University Press.

Danson, M. and Whittam, G. (1999) 'The Scotch Whisky Industry: Issues for Trade Unionists', proceedings of the 1st Scottish Trade Union Research Network Conference, University of Paisley.

Davies, N. (1997) Europe: A History, London: Pimlico.

Davis, S. and Davidson, B. (1991), 2020 Vision, New York: Simon and Schuster.

Denver, D., Mitchell, J., Pattie, C. and Bochel, H. (2000) Scotland Decides: The Devolution Issue and the Referendum of 1997, London: Frank Cass (forthcoming).

Department for Education and Employment (1998) The Learning Age: A Renaissance for a New Britain, London: The Stationery Office.

Department for Education and Employment (1999) Learning to Succeed; A new framework for post-16 learning, London The Stationery Office.

Department of Trade and Industry (1998a) Fairness at Work White Paper, London: HMSO.

Department of Trade and Industry (1998b) Our Competitive Future: Building the Knowledge Driven Economy, London: The Stationery Office.

Devine, T. (1999) The Scottish Nation 1700-2000, London: Allen Lane.

Dewar, D. (1998) Hansard Written Answers, 20 January, col. 488.

Dewar, D. (1998-99) 'Foreword', Corporate Scotland 1998-99, Glasgow, Johnston Media.

Dewar, D. (1999) First Minister's Reply to the Queen, 1 July.

Dewar, D. and Wallace, J. (1999) Partnership for Scotland, Edinburgh: Scottish Labour Party and Scottish Liberal Democrats (internet edition).

Dicken, P. (1992) Global Shift, London: Paul Chapman Publishing.

Doyal, L. (ed.) (1995) What Makes Women Sick: Gender and the Political Economy of Health, London: Macmillan.

Drucker, P. (1986) 'The changed world economy', Foreign Affairs, 64:4.

Dunlop, A. (1993) 'An United Front?: Anti-racist mobilisation in Scotland', Scottish Affairs, 3.

Dunn, J. (1992) Democracy: An Unfinished Journey, Cambridge: Cambridge University Press.

Economist (1996) 'The nation state is dead. Long live the nation state', 23 December.

Economist (1997) 'The visible hand', 20 September.

Educational Institute of Scotland, (1999) Anti-Racism and Education: Breaking Down the Barriers, Edinburgh: Educational Institute of Scotland.

Edwards, P., Armstrong, P., Marginson, P. and Purcell, J. (1996) 'Towards the Transnational Company?' in R. Crompton, D. Gallie, and K. Purcell (eds.) Corporate Restructuring and Labour Markets, London: Routledge.

Elkington, J. (1997) Cannibals with Forks, London: Capstone.

Engender (1993-1999) Gender Audit, Edinburgh: Engender.

European Network for Economic Self-help and Local Development (1997) Key Values and Structures of Social Enterprises in the European Union: Concepts and Principles for a New Economy; Berlin: Technologie-Netzwerk Berlin in co-operation with the European Network for Economic Self-help and Local Development.

Fay, M. and Williams, L. (1993) 'Sex of applicant and the availability of business "start-up" finance', Australian Journal of Management, 16:1.

Feinstein, L. (1998) Pre-school Educational Inequality? Discussion paper 404, London: Centre for Economic Performance.

Findlay, P. (1992) 'Electronics: A 'Culture' of Participation?' in M. Beirne and H. Ramsay (eds.) Information Technology and Workplace Democracy, London: Routledge.

Findlay, P. (1993) 'Union Recognition and Non-unionism: Shifting Fortunes in the Electronics Industry in Scotland', Industrial Relations Journal, 22:3.

Findlay, P., Marks, A., McKinlay, A. and Thompson, P. (1999) Reluctant partners? employee attitudes to company-union partnership agreements, mimeo, University of Edinburgh.

Findlayson, A. (1999) 'Revisioning the economic: New Labour, democracy and markets', Renewal, 7:2.

Finlay, R. (1994) Independent And Free: Scottish Politics and the Origins of the Scottish National Party 1918-1945, Edinburgh: John Donald.

Fry, M. (1987) Patronage and Principle: A Political History of Modern Scotland, Aberdeen: Aberdeen University Press.

Gardner H. (1985) The Mind's New Science, New York: Basic Books.

Gardner H. (1999) The Disciplined Mind: What all students should understand, New York: Simon and Schuster.

Gibson, H. and Botham, R. (1999) 'Sticking together - industrial clusters and solidarity', Proceedings of the 1st Scottish Trade Union Research Network Conference, University of Paisley.

Giddens, A. (1990) The Consequences of Modernity, Cambridge: Polity Press.

Girardet, H. (1992) The Gaia Atlas of Cities: New Directions for Sustainable Urban Living, London: Gaia Books.

Glasgow Development Agency (1997) New Start, Glasgow: Glasgow Development Agency.

Glasgow Development Agency (1999) Glasgow Economic Monitor, Spring, Glasgow: Glasgow Development Agency.

Glendinning, M. and Page, D. (1999) Clone City: Crisis and Renewal in Scottish Architecture, Edinburgh: Polygon.

Goffee, R. and Scase, R. (1985) Women in charge: the experience of female entrepreneurs, London: Allen and Unwin.

Goodlad, R. (1999) A Housing Vision for Scotland, London: Labour Housing Group.

Gould, P. (1998) The Unfinished Revolution: How the Modernisers Saved the Labour Party, London: Little Brown.

Grant, A. and Stringer, K.J. (eds.) (1995) Uniting the Kingdom: The Making of British History, London: Routledge.

Gray, J. (1998) False Dawn: The Delusions of Global Capitalism, London: Granta.

Gray, R.H., with Bebbington K.J., and Walters, D. (1993) Accounting for the Environment, London: ACCA, PCP.

Grove, A.S. (1997) Only the Paranoid Survive, London: Harper Collins.

Hampton, K. (1998) Youth and Racism: Perceptions and Experiences of Young People in Glasgow, Glasgow: Scottish Ethnic Minorities Research Unit.

Handy, C. (1994) The Empty Raincoat, London: Hutchison.

Hassan, G. (1996) 'New Labour and the Politics of New Scotland' in M. Perryman (ed.) The Blair Agenda, London: Lawrence and Wishart.

Hassan, G. (1998a) 'Caledonian Dreaming: The Challenge to Scottish Labour' in A. Coddington and M. Perryman (eds.) The Moderniser's Dilemma: Radical Politics in the Age of Blair, London: Lawrence & Wishart.

Hassan, G. (1998b) The New Scotland, London: Fabian Society.

Hawken, P. (1994) The Ecology Of Commerce, London: Harper Business.

Hechter, M. and Levi, M. (1994) 'Ethno-regional movements in the West' in J. Hutchison and A. Smith (eds.) Nationalism, Oxford: Oxford University Press.

Henwood, D. (1996) 'Work and its future', Left Business Observer, 72, Internet edition.

Hesketh, A. (1998) 'Reward in this life', Guardian, Higher supplement, 24 February.

Hillman, J. (1998) 'The Labour Government and Lifelong Learning', Renewal, 6:2.

Hisrich, R. and Brush, C.G. (1986) The woman entrepreneur: starting, financing and managing a successful new business, Lexington, Mass.: Lexington Books.

HM Treasury (1979) Needs Assessment Study, London: HMSO

HM Treasury (1988-1998) Public Expenditure Statistical Analyses, London: HMSO.

HM Treasury (1999) The Modernisation of Britain's Tax and Benefit System, no 4: Tackling Poverty and Extending Opportunity, London: The Stationery Office.

Holstein, W., Reed, S., Kapstein, H. Vogel, T. and Weber, J. (1990) 'The stateless corporation - forget multinationals today's giants are really leaping boundaries', Business Week, 14 May.

Howson, A. (1992) 'No gods and precious few women: gender and cultural identity in Scotland', Scottish Affairs, 2.

Hulizinga, J. (1949) Homo Ludens: A Study of the Play Element in Culture, London: Routledge and Kegan Paul.

Humes, W. (1986) The Leadership Class in Scottish Education, Edinburgh: John Donald.

Hunter, J. (1998) 'The Defining Issue: Land Reform and Rural Betterment in the Highlands and Islands' in R.F. Callander and A. Wightman (eds.) Understanding Land Reform in Scotland, Edinburgh: Unit for the Study of Government in Scotland, University of Edinburgh.

Huntington, S. (1991) The Third Wave: Democratisation in the Late Twentieth Century, London: University of Oklahoma Press.

Hutchison, J. and Smith, A. (1996) Ethnicity, Oxford: Oxford University Press.

Independent Inquiry into Inequalities in Health (chaired by Donald Acheson) (1998), London: The Stationery Office.

Ingersoll Engineers (1996) The Way We Work, London.

Innes, S. (ed.)(1999) Children, Families and Learning: A new agenda for education, Edinburgh: Scottish Council Foundation.

Jamieson, L. (1998) Intimacy, Cambridge: Polity Press.

Johnson, S. and Storey, D. (1993) 'Male and female entrepreneurs and their businesses' in S. Allen and C. Truman (eds.) Women in business: perspectives on women entrepreneurs, London: Routledge.

Johnston, P. (1993) 'Feminism and the Enlightenment', Radical Philosophy, 63.

Johnston, T. (1909) Our Scots Noble Families, Glasgow: Forward Publishing Company.

Johnston, T. (1920) A History of the Working Classes in Scotland, Glasgow: Forward Publishing Company.

Johnstone, A. (1997) 'An Engaging New Line in Sales Talk', Herald, 14 August.

Jones, P. (1992) 'Education' in M. Linklater and R. Denniston (eds.) Anatomy of Scotland: How Scotland Works, Edinburgh: Chambers.

Jones, P. (1999) 'The 1999 Scottish Parliament Elections: From Anti-Tory to Anti-Nationalist Politics', Scottish Affairs, 28.

Kavanagh, D. and Morris, P. (1994) Consensus Politics: From Attlee to Major, Oxford: Blackwell.

Keating, M. and Bleiman, D. (1979) Labour and Scottish Nationalism, London: Macmillan.

Keep, E (1997) 'There's no such thing as society...some problems with an individual approach to creating a learning society', Journal of Education Policy, 12:6.

Keep, E. and Mayhew, K. (1997) Vocational education and training and economic performance' in T. Buxton, P. Chapman and P. Temple (eds.) Britain's Economic Performance, London: Routledge.

Keep, E. and Mayhew, K. (1999) 'Towards the Knowledge Driven Economy - Some Policy Issues', Renewal, 7:4.

Kelly, E. and Maan, B. (1999) 'Muslims in Scotland: Challenging Islamophobia' in J. Crowther, I. Martin and M. Shaw (eds.) Popular Education and Social Movements in Scotland Today, Leicester: National Institute of Adult and Continuing Education (NIACE).

Kemp, A. and Stephen, L. (1998) Expenditures in and Revenues From the UKCS: Estimating the Hypothetical Scottish Shares 1970-2000, North Sea Oil Occasional Paper No. 70, University of Aberdeen.

Kennedy, H. (1997) Learning Works, Coventry: Further Education Funding Council.

Kenny, M. (1995) The First New Left: British Intellectuals after Stalin, London: Lawrence and Wishart.

Kerevan, G. (1981) 'The Origins of Scottish Nationhood', Bulletin of Scottish Politics, 2.

Kerevan, G. (1999a) 'Architecture and Politics in 20th Century Scotland', Arca, 2.

Kerevan, G. (1999b) 'The great proletarian myth', The Scotsman, 12 July.

Kerevan, G. and Marr, A. (1998) 'Is Home Rule Enough?', Prospect, August-September.

Kohn, H. (1994) 'Western and European Nationalisms' in J. Hutchison and A. Smith (eds.) Nationalism, Oxford: Oxford University Press.

Koper, G. (1993) 'Women entrepreneurs and the granting of business credit.' in S. Allen and C. Truman (eds.) Women in business: perspectives on women entrepreneurs, London: Routledge.

Labour Force Survey Quarterly Bulletin (1990-1999), London: Department of Employment.

Land Reform Policy Group (1999) Recommendations for Action, Edinburgh: Scottish Office.

Latour, B. (1999) 'Ein Ding ist ein Thing - A Philosophical Platform for a Left (European) Party', Soundings, 12.

Leadbetter, C. (1999) Living in Thin Air: The New Economy, London: Viking.

Leicester, G. and Mackay, P. (1998) Holistic Government: Options for a Devolved Scotland, Edinburgh, Scottish Council Foundation.

Leidner, R. (1993) Fast Food, Fast Talk, Berkeley: UCP.

Levitas, R. (1998) The Inclusive Society?: Social Exclusion and New Labour, Basingstoke: Macmillan.

Levitt, T. (1983) 'The Globalization of Markets', Harvard Business Review, May-June.

Lindsay, I. (1997) 'The Uses and Abuses of National Stereotypes', Scottish Affairs, 20.

Lister, R. (1998) From Equality to Social Inclusion: New Labour and the Welfare State, Critical Social Policy, 18:2.

Littlewood, B. (1998) 'He can't be wounded, because he's got no heart', Gender and Scottish Society, Unit For The Study Of Government In Scotland, University of Edinburgh.

Macbeath, J. (1999) Schools must speak for themselves: The case for self-evaluation, London: Routledge.

MacInnes, J. (1998) The End of Masculinity, Milton Keynes: Open University Press.

Mackay, F. (1998) 'Women Politicians and the Ethic of Care', Gender and Scottish Society, Unit For The Study Of Government In Scotland, University of Edinburgh.

MacLeod, M. (ed.) (1999) Centre for Scottish Public Policy: Health Commission, Edinburgh: Centre for Scottish Public Policy.

MacWhirter, I. (1999) 'Think big - and get the better of the bitching press', Sunday Herald, 5 September.

Managing Director (1998) World Directors Forum, Oriana.

Mandelson, P. and Liddle, R. (1997) The Blair Revolution: Can New Labour Deliver?, London: Faber and Faber.

Marks, A., Findlay, P., Hine, J., McKinlay, A. and Thompson, P. (1998) 'The Politics of Partnership? Innovative Employee Relations in the Scottish Spirits Industry', British Journal of Industrial Relations, 36:2.

Marquand, D. (1999) The Progressive Dilemma: From Lloyd George to Blair, London: Weidenfeld and Nicolson, 2nd edition.

Mazower, M. (1998) Dark Continent: Europe's Twentieth Century, London: Allen Lane.

McCalman, J. and Paton, R. (1992) Change Management, London Paul Chapman Publishing.

McCrone, D. (1992) Understanding Scotland: the Sociology of a Stateless Nation, London: Routledge.

McCrone, D. (1998) The Sociology of Nationalism: Tomorrow's Ancestors, London: Routledge.

McCrone, G. (1999) Scotland's Public Finances From Goschen to Barnett, Fraser of Allander Quarterly Economic Commentary, Glasgow: University of Strathclyde, March.

McGregor, A., Clark, S., Ferguson, Z. and Scullion, J. (1997) Valuing the Social Economy: The Social Economy and Economic Inclusion in Lowland Scotland, University of Glasgow, Training and Employment Research Unit with Community Enterprise in Strathclyde and Simon Clark Associates.

McIvor, A. (1996) 'Gender Apartheid? Women in Scottish Society' in T.M. Devine and R.J. Finlay (eds.) Scotland in the Twentieth Century, Edinburgh: Edinburgh University Press.

McLean, R. (1990) Scottish Labour and Home Rule: Part One: Mid-Lanark to Majority Government: 1888-1945, Broxburn: Scottish Labour Action.

McLean, R. (1991) Scottish Labour and Home Rule: Part Two: Unionist Complacency to Crisis Management: 1945-1988, Broxburn: Scottish Labour Action.

Meadows, D.H. (1997) 'Places to Intervene in a System', The Whole Earth Magazine, internet edition, http://www.WholeEarthMag.com.

Merkinch Community Enterprise and Alana Albee Consultants and Associates (1997) Community Enterprises Survey in the Highlands and Islands of Scotland, Inverness: Highlands and Islands Enterprise.

Miles, R. and Dunlop, A. (1986) 'The Racialization of Politics in Britain: Why Scotland is Different', Patterns of Prejudice, 20:1.

Milkman, R. (1998) 'The New American Workplace: High Road or Low Road?' in P. Thompson and C. Warhurst (eds.) Workplaces of the Future, London: Macmillan.

Millar, J. and Donaldson, H. (1999) 'Setting the Agenda for Human Resource Management', Proceedings of the 1st Scottish Trade Union Research Network Conference, University of Paisley.

Mitchell, J. (1996) Strategies for Self-Government: The Campaigns for a Scottish Parliament, Edinburgh: Polygon.

Mitchell, J. (1998) 'Contemporary Unionism' C.M.M. Macdonald (ed.) Unionist Scotland 1900-1997, Edinburgh: John Donald.

Mitchell, M. (1999) 'Relations with Westminster' in G. Hassan (ed.) A Guide to the Scottish Parliament: The Shape of Things to Come, Edinburgh; Centre for Scottish Public Policy/The Stationery Office.

Moore, M.H. (1995) Creating Public Value: Strategic Management in Government, Cambridge, Mass.: Harvard University Press.

Morton, G. (1999) Unionist Nationalism: Governing Urban Scotland 1830 - 1860, East Linton: Tuckwell.

Mulgan, G. (1998) 'Whinge and a Prayer', Marxism Today, November/December.

Myers, F. (1999) 'Women in Decision-Making in Scotland: a Review of Research', Women's Issues Research Findings No 2, Edinburgh: Scottish Office Central Research Unit.

Myers, F. and Brown, A. (1997) Gender Equality in Scotland: a Research Review Update, Manchester: Equal Opportunities Commission.

Nairn, T. (1975) 'Old Nationalism and New Nationalism' in G. Brown (ed.) The Red Paper on Scotland, Edinburgh: Edinburgh University Student Publications Board.

Nairn, T. (1981) The Break-up of Britain: Crisis and Neo-nationalism, London: Verso, 2nd edition.

Nairn, T. (1989) 'The Timeless Grin' in O. Dudley Edwards (ed.) A Claim of Right for Scotland, Edinburgh: Polygon.

Nairn, T. (1997) Faces of Nationalism: Janus Revisited, London: Verso.

Nairn, T. (2000) After Britain: The Return of Scotland, London: Granta Books (forthcoming).

National Advisory Group for Continuing Education and Lifelong Learning (chaired by R. Fryer) (1997) Learning for the twenty-first century, London: Department for Education and Employment.

National Committee of Inquiry into Higher Education (chaired by Sir Ron Dearing) (1997a) Higher Education in a Learning Society, London: HMSO.

National Committee of Inquiry into Higher Education (chaired by Sir Ron Garrick) (1997b) Higher Education in a Learning Society: Report of the Scottish Committee, London: HMSO.

Network East (1999) 'Bhangra and Bravehearts', BBC2, 25 August.

New Economics Foundation (1998) Social Economy Briefing, London: UK Social Investment Forum.

Newton, T. (1996) 'Postmodernism and Action', Organization, 31:1.

O'Neill, S. (1999) 'The Scottish Legal System' G. Hassan (ed.) A Guide to the Scottish Parliament: The Shape of Things to Come, Edinburgh: Centre for Scottish Public Policy/The Stationery Office.

OECD (1994) Jobs Study: Evidence and Explanations Pts 1 & 2, Paris: OECD.

Ohmae, K. (1995) The End of the Nation State, London: HarperCollins.

Olm, K., Carsrud, A.L. and Alvey, L. (1988) 'The role of networks in new venture funding of female entrepreneurs: a continuing analysis.' in B.A. Kirchoff, W.A. Long, E. McMullan, K.H. Vesper and W.E. Wetzel, Jr. (eds.) Frontiers of Entrepreneurship Research, Wellesley, Mass.: Babson College.

Osler, D. (1999) New Community Schools Conference, Glasgow, 19 April.

Parry, R. (1997) 'The Scottish Parliament and Social Policy', Scottish Affairs, 20.

Parry, R. (1998) 'The View from Scotland' in H. Jones and S. MacGregor (eds.) Social Issues and Party Politics, London: Routledge.

Pateman, C. (1988) The Sexual Contract, Cambridge: Polity Press.

Paterson, L. (1994) The Autonomy of Modern Scotland, Edinburgh: Edinburgh University Press.

Paterson, L. (1998a) A Diverse Assembly: The Debate on a Scottish Parliament, Edinburgh: Edinburgh University Press.

Paterson, L. (1998b) 'Education, local government and the Scottish Parliament', Scottish Educational Review, 30:1.

Paterson, L. (1998c) 'Where now for Scottish Autonomy?', Renewal, 6:4.

Patrick S. (1999) 'Glasgow's Renewed Prosperity: A Joint Economic Strategy for Glasgow', special article in Glasgow Economic Monitor, Spring, Glasgow: Glasgow Development Agency.

Pearce, J. (1993) At the Heart of the Community Economy; London: Calouste Gulbenkian Foundation.

Peat, J. and Boyle, S. (1999) An Illustrated Guide to the Scottish Economy, London: Duckworth.

Peck, J. (1999) 'Getting Real With Welfare-to-Work: (Hard) Lessons from America', Renewal, 7:4.

Penn, H. and Moss, P. (1996) Transforming Nursery Education, London: Paul Chapman Publishing.

Perkins, D. (1981) The Mind's Best Work, Cambridge, Mass.: Harvard University Press.

Perri 6 (1997a) Escaping Poverty: From Safety Nets to Networks of Opportunity, London: Demos.

Perri 6 (1997b) Holistic Government, London: Demos.

Peters, T. And Waterman, R. (1982) In Search of Excellence, New York: Harper and Row.

Peyton, C.H. (1996) Architectural Conservation and Sustainable Architecture: From Conflict to Collaboration, Edinburgh: Heriot-Watt University.

Porter, M. (1990) The Competitive Advantage of Nations, London: Macmillan.

Powell, C. (1999) 'UK's stuffy image costs business dear', Sunday Times, Business section, 26 September.

Reich, R. (1993) The Work of Nations: Preparing Ourselves for 21st Century Capitalism, London: Simon & Schuster.

Riding, A.L. and Swift, C.S. (1990) 'Women business owners and terms of credit: some empirical findings of the Canadian experience', Journal of Business Venturing, 5:5.

Rogers, R. (1999) 'Ties between Scots unions and bosses still distant', Herald, 10 September.

Rosa, P. and Hamilton, D. (1994) 'Gender and Ownership in UK small firms', Entrepreneurship Theory and Practice, 18:3.

Rowntree, J. (1999) We Can't All Be White, London, Joseph Rowntree Trust.

Rudduck, C. (1986) 'A Strategy for Handling Controversial Issues in the Secondary School' in J.J. Wellington (ed.) Controversial Issues in the Curriculum, Oxford: Basil Blackwell.

Russell, M. (1999) 'Lessons that must be learned by the SNP', Scotland on Sunday, 19 September.

Sassoon, D. (1996) One Hundred Years of Socialism: The Western European Left in the Twentieth Century, London: IB Tauris.

Sassoon, D. (1999) 'European Social Democracy and New Labour: Unity in Diversity?' in A. Gamble and T. Wright (eds.) The New Social Democracy, Political Quarterly, Special Issue.

Saville, R. (1996) Bank of Scotland: A History 1695-1995, Edinburgh: Edinburgh University Press.

Schuller, T (1998) 'Three Steps Towards a Learning Society', Studies in the Education of Adults, 30:1.

Scottish Constitutional Convention (1995) Scotland's Parliament. Scotland's Right, Edinburgh: Scottish Constitutional Convention.

Scottish Council for Voluntary Organisations (1997) Head and Heart: the Report of the Commission on the Future of the Voluntary Sector in Scotland, Edinburgh: Scottish Council for Voluntary Organisations.

Scottish Enterprise (1996) The Business Birth-rate Strategy Update, Glasgow: Scottish Enterprise.

Scottish Enterprise (1997) Scottish Labour Market and Skill Trends, Glasgow: Scottish Enterprise.

Scottish Enterprise (1998) 1998 Strategic Review Consultation Document, Glasgow: Scottish Enterprise.

Scottish Enterprise Network (1999) The Network Strategy, Glasgow: Scottish Enterprise.

Scottish Executive (1999a) Fair Shares for All : Report of the National Review of Resource Allocation for the NHS in Scotland, Edinburgh: The Stationery Office.

Scottish Executive (1999b) Improving our schools: Consultation on the Improvement in Scottish Education Bill, Edinburgh: The Stationery Office.

Scottish Executive (1999c) Land Reform: Proposals for Legislation, Edinburgh: The Stationery Office.

Scottish Executive (1999d) Making it work together: A programme for government, Edinburgh: The Stationery Office.

Scottish Executive Central Research Unit (1999) General Research Findings No. 1: The People's Panel in Scotland Wave One (June-September 1998), Edinburgh: Scottish Executive.

Scottish Funding Councils for Further and Higher Education Study (1999) Gender and Lifelong Learning Strategy, Edinburgh: Scottish Higher Education Funding Council.

Scottish Homes (1997) Scottish House Condition Survey 1996, Edinburgh: Scottish Homes.

Scottish Local Government Information Unit (1999) The 1999 Scottish Elections, SLGIU Bulletin, 113.

Scottish Office (1988-1998) Government Expenditure and Revenue in Scotland, Edinburgh: HMSO.

Scottish Office (1997) Scotland's Parliament, Edinburgh: HMSO.

Scottish Office (1998a) New Community Schools Prospectus, Edinburgh: HMSO.

Scottish Office (1998b) Opportunity Scotland: A Paper on Lifelong Learning, Edinburgh: The Stationery Office.

Scottish Office (1998c) Partners in Participation: Consultation on a National Strategy for Tenant Participation, Edinburgh: Scottish Office.

Scottish Office (1999a) Investing in Modernisation: An Agenda for Scotland's Housing, Edinburgh: The Stationery Office.

Scottish Office (1999b) Skills for Scotland, Edinburgh, The Stationery Office.

Scottish Office Department of Health (1999c) Towards a Healthier Scotland, Edinburgh: The Stationery Office.

Scottish Office, Welsh Office and Department of Education for Northern Ireland (1998) Higher Education for the 21st Century: Response to the Dearing Report, Sudbury: DfEE Publications.

Shaw, E. (1997) 'The Real Networks of Small Firms' in D. Deakins, P. Jennings and C. Masson (eds.) Small Firms: Entrepreneurship in the 1990s, London: Paul Chapman.

Siann, G., Wilson, F. and Rowan, M. (1998) 'Gender differences and similarities in attitudes to work and the family', Gender and Scottish Society, Unit For The Study Of Government In Scotland, University of Edinburgh.

Sillars, J. (1975) 'Land Ownership and Land Nationalisation' in G. Brown (ed.) The Red Paper on Scotland, Edinburgh: Edinburgh University Student Publications Board.

St. J.N. Bates, T. (ed.) (1997) Devolution to Scotland: The Legal Aspects: Contemplating the Imponderable, Edinburgh: T & T Clark.

Stephens, M. and Goodlad, R. (1999) 'Review of International Models of Housing Governance: a report to Scottish Homes', Research and Information Report 69, Edinburgh: Scottish Homes.

Stewart, S. (ed.) (1998) The Possible Scot: Making healthy public policy, Edinburgh: Scottish Council Foundation.

Stoker, G. (1998) 'Governance as Theory: Five Propositions', International Social Science Journal, 155:1.

Stoker, G. and Perri 6 (1997) Bringing It All Together: A New Model for London Governance: Essays on the New Government for London, London: Association of London Government.

Swann J. and Brown S. (1997) 'The implementation of a national curriculum and teachers' classroom thinking', Research Papers in Education, 12:1.

Talbot, R. (1998) Community Building Toolkit, Edinburgh: thirdwave (Scotland) Ltd..

Taylor, M. (1999) 'They have to toe the Labour line', Guardian, 11 May .

Taylor, S. (1998) 'Emotional Labour and the New Workplace' in P. Thompson and C. Warhurst (eds.) Workplaces of the Future, London: Macmillan.

Thatcher, M. (1993) The Downing Street Years, London: Harper Collins.

thirdwave (1999) Building Sustainably Toolkit, Edinburgh: thirdwave (Scotland) Ltd..

Thompson, P. (1993) 'Postmodernism: Fatal Distraction' in J. Hassard and M. Parker (eds.) Postmodernism and Organisations, London: Sage.

Thompson, P. and Lucas, B. (1998) The Forward March of Modernisation: A History of the LCC 1978-1998, London: Labour Co-ordinating Committee.

Thompson, P. and Warhurst, C. (1999) 'Ignorant Theory and Knowledgeable Workers: Myths and Realities of Workplace Change', in D. Robertson (ed.) The Knowledge Economy, London: Macmillan (forthcoming).

Thompson, P., Warhurst, C. and Callaghan, G. (2000) 'Human Capital or Capitalising on Humanity? Knowledge, Skills and Competencies in Interactive Service Work' in H. Willmott, M. Chumer, R. Hull and C. Pritchard (eds.) Managing Knowledge: Critical Discussion of Work and Learning, London: Macmillan (forthcoming).

Thomson, I. with Talbot, R. (1998) New Business, New Scotland: Foundations for a Sustainable Scottish Economy, Edinburgh: thirdwave (Scotland) Ltd..

Thornhill, A., Lewis, P., Millmore, M. and Saunders, M. (2000) Managing Change, London: Prentice-Hall.

Tight, M. (1996) Key Concepts in Adult Education and Training, London: Routledge.

Townsend, P., Whitehead, M. and Davidson, N. (eds.) (1992) Inequalities in Health: The Black Report and the Health Divide, Harmondsworth: Penguin.

Undy, R. (1999) 'New Labour's 'Industrial Relations Settlement: The Third Way?', British Journal of Industrial Relations, 37:2.

Van Auken, H.E., Gaskill, L.R. and Kao, S. (1993) 'Acquisition of capital by women entrepreneurs: patterns of initial and refinancing capitalisation', Journal of Small Business and Entrepreneurship, 10:4.

Vickery, G. (1999) 'Business and industry policies for knowledge-based economies', OECD Observer, 215.

Von Weizasäcker, E., Lovins, A. and Lovins, L.H. (1997) Factor Four: Doubling Wealth, Halving Resource Use, London: Earthscan.

Walker, A. and Walker, C. (eds.) (1997) Britain Divided: The Growth of Social Exclusion in the 1980s and 1990s, London: Child Poverty Action Group.

Warhurst, C. and Thompson, P. (1998) 'Hands, Hearts and Minds: Changing Work and Workers at the End of the Century' in P. Thompson and C. Warhurst (eds.) Workplaces of the Future, London: Macmillan.

Warhurst, C., Nickson, D. and Shaw, E. (1998) 'A Future for Globalisation?' in T. Scandura and M. Serapio (eds.) Research in International Business and International Relations, vol.7, Stamford, Conn.: JAI Press.

Warhurst, C., Nickson, D., Witz, A. ansCullen, A.M. (2001) 'Aesthetic Labour in Interactive Service Work: Some Case Study Evidence From the 'New Glasgow', Services Industries Journal, 21: 3 (forthcoming).

Waters, M. (1995) Globalization, London: Routledge.

Watkins, J. and Watkins, D. (1984) 'The female entrepreneur: background and determinants of business choice - some British data', International Small Business Journal, 2:4.

Weber, M. (1930) The Protestant Work Ethic and the Spirit of Capitalism, London: Unwin.

White, R. (1995) 'Preface' in T.E. Graedel and B.R. Allenby, Industrial Ecology, Englewood Cliffs, Prentice Hall.

White, R.M. and Willock, I.D. (1999) The Scottish Legal System, Edinburgh: Butterworths, 2nd edition.

White, S. (1998) 'Interpreting the Third Way: not one road but many', Renewal, 6:2.

Whitehead, M. (1987) The Health Divide, London: Health Educational Council.

Whitehead, M. (1997) Bridging the Gap: working towards equity in health and health care, unpublished Ph.D. thesis, Stockholm: Karolinska Institutet.

Wightman, A. (1996) Who Owns Scotland?, Edinburgh: Canongate.

Wightman, A. (1999) Land and Power: The Agenda for Land Reform, Edinburgh: Luath Press.

Wilkinson R.G. (1996) Unhealthy Societies: the afflictions of inequality, London: Routledge.

Wilkinson R.G. (1999) 'Health, hierarchy and social anxiety', paper to the New York Academy of Sciences Conference on Socio-economic Status and Health in Industrial Nations, New York.

Wilkinson, H. (1994) No Turning Back: Generations and the Genderquake, London: Demos.

Willetts, D. and Forsdyke, R. (1999) After the Landslide: Learning the Lessons from 1906 and 1945, London: Centre for Policy Studies.

Wilson, A. (1999) 'Finding the Fast Track to Independence', Sunday Times Lecture, 1999 Scottish National Party Conference, Inverness, 23 September.

Wolf, M. (1999) The Entertainment Economy: The Mega-media Forces that are Re-shaping Our Lives, London: Penguin.

World Commission on Environment and Development (1987) 'Our Common Future' (The Bruntland Report), Oxford: Oxford University Press.